Who was to blame?

Was it Richard Herrin, for whom love turned into an obsession that drove him beyond all restraint when it was threatened?

Was it Bonnie Garland, for giving herself to this young man so completely, and then beginning to doubt her decision when new horizons beckoned?

Was it Bonnie's parents, who rejected their daughter's lover and tried to destroy their affair?

Or was it the law, that had to decide what the punishment would be?

This book does not take sides. It does tell the whole intensely moving, piercingly revealing story of the fatal romance of Richard Herrin and Bonnie Garland.

THE YALE MURDER

"A love story, a murder, and a question of justice . . . a riveting tale" —*Newsday*

Berkley Books by Peter Meyer

DARK OBSESSION
DEATH OF INNOCENCE
THE YALE MURDER

THE YALE MURDER

PETER MEYER

BERKLEY BOOKS, NEW YORK

The names of some of the persons in this book
have been changed.

This Berkley book contains the complete
text of the original hardcover edition.
It has been completely reset in a typeface
designed for easy reading and was printed
from new film.

THE YALE MURDER

A Berkley Book / published by arrangement with
Empire Books

PRINTING HISTORY
Empire Books edition published 1982
Berkley edition / June 1983

ISBN: 0-425-07278-9

A BERKLEY BOOK ® TM 757,375
Berkley Books are published by The Berkley Publishing Group,
200 Madison Avenue, New York, New York 10016.
The name "BERKLEY" and the "B" logo
are trademarks belonging to Berkley Publishing Corporation.

PRINTED IN THE UNITED STATES OF AMERICA

10 9 8 7 6 5 4 3

Acknowledgments

The author wishes to acknowledge the aid of the two opposing attorneys in this case, Jack Litman, who defended Richard Herrin, and William Fredreck, then an Assistant District Attorney of Westchester County and the prosecutor at Herrin's trial.

The thirty hours spent speaking with Richard Herrin at the Eastern Correctional Facility in Napanoch, New York, were invaluable in reconstructing the background and motivation of the man who had killed the woman he had hoped to marry.

I would also like to acknowledge the cooperation of the scores of friends and classmates of Bonnie Garland and Richard Herrin who made it possible to retell the story of their lives, including their days at Yale and their tragic love.

More than one hundred other persons who had some particular knowledge of the story—high school and college teachers, policemen and detectives, priests and brothers, court officials, newspaper reporters and journalists, psychiatrists—gave freely of their time in the hope of adding to the accuracy of this book.

PETER MEYER
New York City, March 1982

To my father
Henry Meyer
Philosopher and Builder

Contents

CHAPTER ONE

The Confession

IT WAS A serene July evening in the affluent New York suburb of Scarsdale. The temperature had fallen twenty degrees from the daytime heat and a cool breeze now moved through the trees that branched protectively over the deserted streets. A light rain grazed across the roofs of the community's stately homes.

A few hundred feet from one of Scarsdale's main streets, Fenimore Road, the three-story stucco and brick Tudor home of Mr. and Mrs. Paul Garland stood relatively isolated on a half-acre corner lot. Like other houses in this community of corporate managers and professionals seeking a retreat from Manhattan twenty miles away, the Garland home was washed with a sense of calm, almost of invincibility. The house was dark now except for a light burning in the window at the top of the impressive structure.

A half-mile down Fenimore at the small colonial brick headquarters of the Scarsdale Police, Desk Officer Craven had just finished his four-to-midnight shift. It had been an uneventful Wednesday evening. Craven's first entry into the police log was a note that "THE TELETYPE IS NOT PRINTING THE LETTER 'L'." His second, at 6:07 P.M., was a complaint that a dog on Ferncliff Road was off the leash, harassing its neighbor.

The town was sensitive to any intrusion on its peace, whether from obstreperous animals or unwanted strangers. That year, the police had received reports of 142 prowlers, and were taking every precaution. Even "dark houses" were duly noted by patrolling police cars. At 11:23 P.M., Officer Craven made his final entry for July 6, 1977: The Scarsdale Volunteer Ambulance Corps would be in their quarters all night, and could be reached by phone in an emergency. At midnight, Craven was replaced by Officer Loeber. There would be no more entries until seven o'clock the next morning. As far as the police were concerned, Scarsdale was sleeping peacefully.

At a few minutes past midnight, a car pulled up at the side of the Garland home, almost directly below the lighted bedroom. Eighteen-year-old Patrick, the Garland's eldest son, thanked his friend for the lift and walked up the driveway. As he passed the family's brown Impala on his way toward the back door, Patrick glanced up momentarily at the light atop the darkened house. He gave it little thought. The room belonged to his older sister, Bonnie, who often stayed up late when she was home from college.

Patrick entered the breakfast room, and after closing the back door, locked it from the inside with the key that hung on the doorjamb. The house was protected: No one could get in. Even those who wanted to leave had to find the key in order to open the door. Patrick dawdled about in the kitchen, making himself a late-night snack, careful not to rouse the family.

Upstairs his parents, Joan and Paul Garland, had been in bed since eleven. Mr. Garland, a prominent New York attorney, usually rose early to make the commuter train to his law offices in Manhattan. Patrick's younger brother was asleep in his room along the same second-floor hallway. His grandfather, who was staying at the house while he recovered from a stroke, was in bed in the television room just below Bonnie. The twenty-year old Yale senior slept in her apartment-sized room on the third floor, a few steps above the family bedrooms on the second floor.

Only the light which shone dimly across the driveway outside the breakfast room indicated that his older sister and her houseguest, Richard Herrin, were probably still up. Patrick had seen them just a few hours before in Bonnie's bedroom, when he had asked if they wanted to go out for dinner. Bonnie had been sitting on the couch and Richard had been on the bed, leaning against the wall. They had both seemed sullen, as if they had been interrupted while talking about something important. They had declined Patrick's dinner offer, explaining that they had already eaten.

Bonnie and Richard had long been inseparable, their names pronounced as virtually a single word by friends at Yale University. They had met almost three years before on the Ivy League campus when Richard was a senior and Bonnie a new arrival at the New Haven school. They were not an incongruous-looking couple. Both were tall, almost indifferent in their dress, and somewhat overweight, although friends had recently commented on Bonnie's slender new figure.

Neither was obsessed by accomplishment, though Richard had started his Yale career on a scholarship fresh from being valedictorian of his Los Angeles *barrio* high school, and Bonnie had become a dedicated singer at Yale. Bonnie and Richard were considered uncomplicated, easy-going youngsters, perhaps more concerned with "love" and sharing good times than others at Yale.

Despite similarities in build and personality, Richard and Bonnie came from backgrounds that were profoundly different. Bonnie's vibrant red hair and lightly freckled face were outward signs of the energy that had taken her through Madeira, the prestigious Virginia girl's school, and carried her on to Yale, her father's

alma mater. She had just returned to Scarsdale elated
after a six-week tour of Europe with the Yale Glee Club,
where her clear soprano had made her an outstanding
soloist of the group.

Herrin, who had stayed overnight three times in the
large Garland house, had come to Bonnie's home across
worlds, socially and geographically. For him, the
Garland home represented an opulence he had never
known. Bonnie's bedroom alone was almost as large as
the entire house in which he had spent part of his early
years, cramped into two tiny rooms with his Mexican-
American mother and stepfather, the head of his bed
butting up against the refrigerator, boxes of flea-market
merchandise at his feet.

Richard's visits to Scarsdale had been memorable for
the couple, who often stayed up late in Bonnie's bedroom, talking, watching television from her bed, and
making love. The Garland house was spacious and solid
enough to protect the privacy of their trysts. Though
Richard was given the ground floor study as his
bedroom, he and Bonnie usually ignored the subtle obstacle and would sleep together in her room until
wakened by an early morning alarm. Richard would
then steal down the back stairs to the study to maintain
the appearance, if not the substance, of propriety.

This time was apparently no different. Richard had
arrived at the house the day before from Texas
Christian University, where he was a graduate student in
geology, and the couple had slept together in Bonnie's
room that night. The light in Bonnie's room this Wednesday evening seemed to signify that the young lovers
were once more preparing for bed.

In these moments after midnight, the large house was
silent. Patrick Garland had shut off the light downstairs
and started up the back stairs to his second floor room.
Closing the door behind him, Patrick turned on the air
conditioner, adjusted the stereo so that the music would
not disturb Bonnie and Richard or the rest of the
family, and began to study for his summer school class.

By two o'clock in the morning, with the light and the

stereo still on and the air conditioner still softly humming, Patrick was asleep in bed. He could not hear the footsteps or the labored breathing of the young man padding barefoot down the stairs right outside his door.

RICHARD HERRIN moved quickly, if awkwardly, down the darkened stairway, his six-foot, two-hundred-pound frame colliding against the wall just as he reached the landing below Patrick's bedroom. As he hurriedly descended the final steps to the kitchen, he panicked as his body again made contact with the wall, stumbling about in places that should have been familiar to him.

He found the back door, but it was locked. Herrin knew the family kept a spare key hanging near the back door, but he had forgotten its position. In the dark he groped futilely about for a light switch, fearful that he would be trapped by someone awakening before he found a way out of the house. What if there were a burglar alarm? He had never asked, but he knew that if there were one, the entire family would soon be up.

Herrin remembered the small bathroom off an adjacent hallway and threw its switch. With the sliver of light that now angled into the breakfast room, he could see the key dangling to the left of the back door where Patrick had left it two hours before. As he opened the door and stepped out of the house, he had only one thought: He had to kill himself.

The pavement was still damp from the light rain, but the wetness did not register in Herrin's mind as he ran barefoot down the outside stairs, and onto the asphalt driveway. In his haste he had left behind his shoes, socks, and shirt, and dressed only in a pair of beige corduroy pants, he rushed half-naked into the night.

The Impala was parked exactly where he and Bonnie had left it earlier that day after a trip to Columbia University to enroll Bonnie in summer classes. With the keys he had grabbed off the nightstand in Bonnie's bedroom, Herrin headed for the door on the driver's side. The car would be his escape; that much he knew as he threw himself onto the front seat. Herrin fumbled with the keys in the ignition, but the car refused to start. He remembered that the seat belt had to be fastened, a movement he accomplished as if in a dream.

Even in the dark he could see the blood. It spotted his pants, his feet, his chest and arms and hands. Something he had never noticed before struck him: Blood had an odor. In the enclosed space of the car he could smell it all over him.

If he were stopped by a policeman, Herrin knew that the blood would arouse suspicion and destroy his hope of a swift suicide. With a red bandana pulled from his back pocket, he tried desperately to wipe the blood away, but as he brushed forcefully at the dark splotches, he saw that they were already fast.

Herrin reached for the ignition key again. He feared that the noise of the engine firing would wake the Garlands and block his escape. As the silence was broken by the first turning of the car's motor, Herrin looked anxiously about him for a response to his intrusion into the early morning stillness, but the Garlands did not seem to have awakened and there was no one in sight.

He backed the car out of the driveway and onto the street, shadowed only by the giant broadleaved trees, then drove away. He did not know where he was going, only that he wanted to find a hill, speed down it, crash and end his life.

HERRIN STEERED the Impala onto Fenimore Road, then drove in chaotic circles through the night, fearful that the police would prevent his suicide. There seemed to be police cars all about him in the maze of near-deserted streets. Careful not to attract attention, Herrin kept the Impala at a cautious speed, stopping at all red lights even though no other cars contested his right of way. He drove through Scarsdale, then White Plains, passing a business district and a large industrial complex, but the terrain was flat, useless to his death wish.

He drove until he spotted a sign pointing to the Taconic Parkway. The name jogged Herrin's memory back to his geology courses at Yale, where he had learned that "taconic orogeny" was a term for the mountain-building caused by the collision of massive belts of the earth's crust. Somehow, he thought as he turned the car onto the parkway, this road would lead him to the mountains from which he would plunge to his death.

The Taconic Parkway was a novelty when it opened in the early 1930's at Kensico Dam, near the place where Herrin entered, twelve miles north of the Garland home. Designed to follow the contours of the area, it plied its way steadily northward, wandering through the forested Taconics, one of the oldest mountain ranges in North America.

Herrin decided not to wait for the mountains. Not long after the Impala moved onto the four-lane road, it began gathering speed. That was the first step in his plan to send the car hurtling against one of the granite overpasses that cross the highway or into a truck or even an eighteen-wheel "semi." Trucks are not permitted on the Taconic, but Herrin was unaware of the prohibition and kept scanning the virtually empty road for a giant vehicle to act as a suicide target.

But the courage to kill himself was not as readily available as Herrin had imagined. As he pushed his bare right foot harder on the accelerator and the dotted line markings on the highway began to blur into a solid white stripe, he had second thoughts. Perhaps the Impala's hood was long enough to absorb the impact of a crash: He would be brutally hurt, even crippled, but not killed. If he did run into a truck someone else might be hurt, and there was no reason to draw others into his suicide. As for the overpasses, they were racing by too fast for a perfect death. Herrin lifted his foot from the gas pedal and slowed the car.

Herrin's thoughts moved in desperate spasms. Why not slash his wrists? He would pull the car into a secluded area, open his veins, and lock himself in the trunk. But he had nothing sharp enough to slice through the layers of soft tissue.

The green dashboard lights cast a glow across Herrin's bearded face as he stole glances away from the roadway to find a weapon. Broken glass, he thought. Reaching up, he pulled the rear view mirror from its socket, and laid it beside him on the seat. He tied his red bandana around his arm, believing it would help squeeze out the blood and bring on a swifter death. When the time comes, I will break the mirror and cut my wrists, Herrin decided. But the time never came. It seemed only to pass like the dark stone running beside the window.

As the car moved northward on the 106-mile road that ends some twenty miles south of Albany, Herrin was not conscious of the passage of time. He had left the Garland home sometime near 2 A.M., but now as one abstract mile merged into the next, he had no idea what hour it was. He had left his watch in the Garland house. There was a clock on the dashboard, but not once during the early morning ride did he notice it. Chronology and immediate memory had ceased.

He was obsessed with the desire to die, but his mind refused to dwell on the reason why. Between 2 A.M. and the present, there was no recall, no rush of painful events, no thought of Bonnie, no specter of horror, only the racing engine, the continuous white line, and the hope of a painless death. Herrin was also unaware of any physical sensation. Neither cold nor sleepiness troubled him. Only the feeling that he was totally covered with blood gnawed at his numbed consciousness.

As the car drove on, the road continued higher up into the hills. Its shoulder began expanding and its corners widening until it seemed to drop away and open, finally, onto a panorama visible even in the night. Before him and to the left was a dark valley punctuated by sparks of light, a relief to the eye after ninety miles of blind driving, a break in his desperate dialogue with the road. Had he not slowed the car at the summit, Herrin would have missed the reflectors of the small green and white sign: Rip Van Winkle Bridge.

In midsummer the Hudson River flows easily below the almost mile-long bridge which stands 150 feet high above the water. From its opening in 1935, it has been a favorite spot for jumpers. The local paper had even run a photograph of the body of a winter suicide who had fallen the full distance onto hard-packed ice. Herrin pulled onto the two-lane roadway of the bridge and when he was sure there was no traffic, he stopped the car. For the first time Herrin got out of the Impala and, still barefoot, walked over to the side rail of the bridge.

Herrin peered down into the Hudson River. With the lights from the bridge's deck, he could see the deep, dangerous grey water. The sight struck a chord in his mind, an old, unrelieved fear. As a child Herrin had been plagued by nightmares of drowning, and had even invented a memory, which relatives told him was untrue, in which he was pulled sputtering from the ocean by his uncle.

He had tried often enough, but had never learned to swim. As an adult, even putting his head under water in the shallow end of a swimming pool would tighten his chest. Herrin looked down at the water once more, then backed away from the steel railing, got back into the car, and drove on.

Moving more slowly now, Herrin passed through a shadowy town of clapboard storefronts and then into an open area of flat riverside farmland that ended in a tree-lined residential area of modest white houses and wide front lawns. He followed the street past colonnaded front porches to the corner of Mansion and Washington Streets in the village of Coxsackie, where his thoughts were suddenly interrupted by the sight of a church steeple.

As it rose above the houses and the trees, the friendly image pierced Herrin's suicide-obsessed mind. He read the sign beside the front steps—Saint Mary's Catholic Church—and decided to put his life in God's hands.

For the first time that night he glanced at the car clock

and saw that it was 6 A.M. He had been driving for four hours since leaving the Garland home. As he brought the car to a stop in front of the large red brick building, the sky was beginning to lighten to his right. Richard Herrin told himself that he didn't want to be in charge anymore.

ABOVE THE ENTRANCE to Saint Mary's Church, the Virgin Mary stood serenely in a tiny niche, guarded on each side by a long-haired angel carved of white stone. The three statues seemed to be watching the movements of the man rattling at the front doors below them. Herrin tugged for a few moments at the wrought iron handles but the church doors were locked.

The lights were off in the white colonial house next door, which Herrin assumed was the rectory. He started toward the house, but hesitated, deciding not to wake anyone up. Instead, he moved up the narrow walk between the two buildings to the canopy-covered stairway leading to the priest's entrance to the church, where he tried the door. But that too was locked. Exhaustion rolled over him as he curled up in the shadow of the sacristy and closed his eyes.

Less than an hour later Herrin awoke from his nervous sleep, cold and disturbed by the noise of birds. The cement steps of the church, covered with an itchy green outdoor carpet, were hard. Herrin was anxious to escape the chill scratching at his bare skin and to unload the hours of failed suicide. Richard Herrin was no longer thinking of his own death; now he had to talk to the priest about what he had done.

For a few more moments Herrin shivered against the door of the church as the rush of horrible memory began to engulf him. The reality that he had rejected for four interminable hours now began to press painfully back into his consciousness.

FATHER Paul Tartaglia was usually out of bed by 6 A.M.

Fifty minutes later he would be stepping down the back stairs of the rectory, then walking the few paces to the side entrance of his church, the same route he had traced almost every day for seven years.

There was an exception to the routine on Thursdays, when the Mass was celebrated in the evening. But "Father T," as the sturdy young priest was known in the village of Coxsackie, enjoyed the early mornings, and even on his day of rest he awoke early. This Thursday he had already been up for twenty minutes, relaxing in bed, when the church bell next door began to ring.

It marked seven o'clock, time for the Angelus prayer, the thrice-daily Catholic remembrance of God appearing to the Virgin Mary. Around the world the religious prayed: "The angel of the Lord declared unto Mary and she conceived of the Holy Spirit. Hail, Mary, full of grace, the Lord is with you; blessed are you among women and blessed is the fruit of your womb, Jesus. Holy Mary, mother of God, pray for us sinners, now and at the hour of our death."

Another bell rang, this one from downstairs at the front door. Tartaglia was used to the odd-hour caller. He threw on his black cassock and padded down the stairs. The translucent glass of the front door was covered by curtains which blocked his view of the visitor, but even as he swung the door open, Father Tartaglia did not recognize the unkempt young man who stood on his front porch wearing only trousers. The visitor's face was drained of energy, his expression distraught, almost disturbed. Despite the warmth of the July morning, he was shivering.

It must be an emergency sick call, thought Tartaglia. Someone had been in a car accident or had had a heart attack and the young man had run out only half-dressed to fetch the priest. In his nineteen years as a man of the cloth, he had seen enough of those.

For the moment the priest left the screen door closed. "What can I do for you?" he asked.

Herrin stood almost a head taller than the priest. A full beard and mustache covered his face, and the hair on his chest ran up to the bottom of his neck. A look of exhaustion filled his eyes.

"I need to talk to someone." His tone was soft but urgent.

The priest thought the man looked enough like one of his parishoners to be his brother. "Are you related to Sam Smithif?" the priest asked.

"No." Herrin shivered. Again he asked to talk to the priest.

"Sure." Tartaglia listened to the young man's voice, gauged his expression, then calculated that whoever he was, the fellow was not going to rob the rectory. The priest pushed the screen door open and motioned Herrin in. Tartaglia pointed down the narrow hallway to his office and as Herrin followed him, he asked, "What happened? What is the trouble?"

For five hours Herrin had been wandering without sensation, with only the thought that he had to kill himself. Not until he woke from his fitful sleep on the church steps did he feel the possibility of recapturing the sense of time. Not until the moment when the priest asked what had happened had he thought about what he had done before jumping into the Impala and fleeing. Herrin looked at Father Tartaglia and said:

"I just killed my girlfriend."

The words tumbled out in a heavy whisper before he had reached the office door. The guy's on drugs, the priest thought. He must have been high and now he's coming down, very low. He must be hallucinating.

As soon as the word "killed" left his lips, Herrin winced as images of Bonnie's face in deathly sleep surged through his mind. Tears moved to the edge of his eyes. Richard felt his body, which had supported the weight of his guilt throughout the night, suddenly yielding. But as he felt the first touch of the tears, he held back.

Tartaglia looked intently at the young man who had just claimed to be a killer. He was obviously in his early twenties and relatively attractive, his jet black hair cut long over his ears. The priest noticed that the young penitent was tall and large enough to be an athlete, but his shoulders sloped downward and he walked with a stoop, as if trying to hide his size. Tartaglia's attention moved to Herrin's face where he saw the deep-set dark eyes and full eyebrows.

As Tartaglia stared at the young man, probing for hints to his inner being, he ignored the evidence of blood on Herrin's body. The priest showed Herrin into his office and motioned him toward a cushioned, straight-backed chair. Herrin immediately slumped into it, exhausted.

"How do you know you killed her?" The priest was probing calmly, not wanting to panic the man, still unsure of him.

"She must be dead," Herrin mumbled, staring down at the worn brown carpet under his bare feet. "I hit her in the head with a hammer." He shrank back suddenly as if recoiling from a sharp blow.

It looked to the priest like a completely involuntary jerk. The movement convinced him that Herrin was not hallucinating, but he was sure that some terrible image was flashing through the young man's head. Herrin seemed ready to cry.

The priest sadly realized he might have to be the one to carry the tragic news to somebody. "What is the girl's name?" he asked, reaching for a pad of paper and a pen at his desk.

"Bonnie Garland." Herrin was now sitting straight, looking at Tartaglia.

"Where does she live?" The priest was writing as Herrin gave him the address in Scarsdale and added the three-digit area code and phone number.

"Do you think they know about it by now?"

Herrin remembered the terrible gurgling noises Bonnie was making as he left her room. They had seemed so loud. Even then he had been afraid that her parents, or her brother Patrick, just next door and a few steps below, would hear. An image of blood trickling through the floorboards and waking up Bonnie's grandfather in the room below stabbed at his mind.

"Yes," he told the priest. "I'm sure that they have—that they have found that out." He was also sure that "they" would know that he was the one.

At the Garland home in Scarsdale, Patrick was roused from sleep by a knocking at his door. It was seven o'clock in the morning when he heard his father's voice. Patrick had awakened once before during the night, and seemingly without reason had looked at the digital clock next to his bed. It had read 4:30 A.M.

This time he heard his father telling him he had left the door unlocked and the lights on outside the house overnight. Patrick remembered performing those chores and explained that he had locked the door and turned off the lights.

His father told Patrick that it was all right, but instructed him to make sure that he did it next time.

Patrick went back to sleep. Just after seven, his father left for work in New York City.

"I feel very cold," Herrin told the priest. Despite the mild morning temperature, the long night had covered Herrin's broad bare shoulders in a wintry gooseflesh. Tartaglia left the office and returned with a black sweater, but the stocky priest was only five foot seven inches tall, almost six inches shorter than Herrin, who had been a high school football player. The sweater didn't fit. He left again and this time returned with an old afghan from the parlor sofa, which he calmly lay across Herrin's shoulders.

Whatever fear the priest may have had was now gone. In Herrin's expression, he saw what he believed was sincerity. The priest's instincts were leading him to compassion, but Tartaglia wanted to know more before taking action. He was more concerned about frightening the shivering man than of his own safety. They talked: Tartaglia gently questioning, Herrin low-key, almost polite, responding.

As Father Tartaglia set his notes aside, he thought he saw in Herrin a slight relief from the contorted expression he wore on the front porch, a kind of barely perceptible transformation noticed by men who have spent their lives looking hard at the many faces of guilt. Since his ordination, Tartaglia, a stout olive-skinned man, had worked the common fields of the Catholic terrain, mainly as a parish pastor. But in his nineteen years as a priest, Tartaglia had never confronted a man confessing a killing.

Of guilt, Tartaglia believed he knew something. Though he never stood to the face of murder, he had an inkling that the nature of the transgression mattered little in its capacity to enrage the soul. Guilt, the priest believed, was one of the most destructive elements in human experience. Unremoved, it would eat away at people like a cancer. As with Macbeth, Tartaglia thought the guilt could be so strong that were the offender to wash his hands in the seven seas he could see the water turning incarnadine, the color of blood.

The priest was curious why Herrin had come to Coxsackie, of all places, over one hundred miles from Scarsdale. Herrin described his all-night drive and the failure of his repeated attempts at suicide. He looked up at the priest, then flinched at the memory of the long night. "I didn't have the courage to kill myself," he confessed. Tartaglia saw that Herrin was again on the verge of tears.

"Would you like the sacrament of reconciliation?" the priest asked. The question was second nature. At his ordination Tartaglia, like all priests, was given the power to remove sin in the name of God. It was a power that Catholics believed was passed by Christ to his disciples when he appeared to them after rising from the dead. "Peace" was his first word. Peace, the opposite of the turmoil of guilt.

In the old days the sacrament was called "confession." For Catholics it meant the tiny cubicles in the shadows of the church, the kneeling alone in darkness until a small shuttered panel rattled open. The somber voice of an unseen priest whispered "go ahead," while the communicant took an anxious breath before losing his sins to God.

"Would you like the sacrament of reconciliation?" Father Tartaglia repeated to Herrin, reasoning there was nothing to lose. If the fellow were a Catholic, he should know what was meant. If not, he should not be offended.

Like most men who had sworn themselves to secrecy when handling the affairs of God, Father Tartaglia had often wondered what he would do in such a situation. Even if never confronted with a murder confession, it posed an agonizing dilemma. Does the priest respect the sacred oath to be solely God's messenger, or does he honor a temporal obligation to tell society? When the duties to God and to Man conflict, to whom does the priest owe ultimate allegiance?

Richard was a devout Catholic who had made his first confession in Los Angeles at age seven, but the offer of "reconciliation" now had no meaning to his clouded mind. At church in Los Angeles, and at Thomas More House Catholic Chapel at Yale, the sacrament of Christ's forgiveness had usually been called "confession" or "penance." He had always taken church seriously, but as an adult Herrin was less attentive to the sacrament. At Yale, he made his penance only a few times a year, face to face with the priest rather than in the traditional confessional box.

He did not know how to react to the priest's offer of "reconciliation." Herrin stared vacantly forward as if he were thinking about something else, and gave no response. Tartaglia dropped the subject.

"What is it that you want me to do for you?" the priest asked.

As Herrin was telling his story to Tartaglia, he realized the enormity of the tragedy. He now wanted to be handed over to the police, to be arrested, bound, imprisoned, and punished. "I want to turn myself in," Herrin answered in a low monotone, "to the police."

The priest felt relief, for he would not have to wrestle

the angels about his oath of confessional secrecy. He could now turn the matter over to someone else.

"Are you sure?"

It crossed Herrin's mind that if he told the priest he was only joking about the killing, he could walk out. Father Tartaglia, it seemed, was offering him a real option, letting him know that he was under no obligation to turn him over to the police. The decision was Herrin's, and the priest would abide by it.

"I—I do want to turn myself in to the police."

Tartaglia now felt assured, but still did not want to panic Herrin by jumping right to the phone. He asked if Herrin would like a cup of coffee. When the young man nodded, the priest left the room, went to the kitchen, returned, then calmly reached for the phone.

COXSACKIE'S Superintendent of Public Works, Ed Young, was often the first to arrive for work at the Village Building, a small two-story brick and wood structure that housed all the government offices: the mayor, the highway department, the public works department, and the police. A few minutes after seven that morning Young, alone in the building, picked up the police telephone line. It was Father T, friend and pastor of Young's church. When he asked for Police Chief Ronnie Rea, Young explained that Rea had not yet arrived but that he could locate him if it was important. It was urgent, the priest said, that Rea come to the rectory immediately.

Moments later, Rea's wife watched the blood rush from her husband's face as he talked with the priest on the phone. As Rea hung up the phone and started to breathe nervously, his wife asked, "What's the matter?"

"I gotta go, honey. Some guy over at Father T's says he's killed a girl," panted Rea as he kicked on his clothes and rushed out. It took less than fifteen minutes for Rea to dress, hop in his gold Chrysler Imperial, and drive from his Hudson river-view apartment to the rectory on Mansion Street. The priest had asked him to drive silently, without lights or sirens.

By 7:15 A.M. the young policeman was being ushered past the rectory parlor toward the small office at the rear of the house. He knew Father T well. He had even spent some time in this office when his wife talked him into taking catechism lessons for a possible conversion to Catholicism, but he had never "transferred over."

Rea towered over the priest with his nimble six-foot six-inch, 250-pound frame. At twenty-nine, he was a lifelong resident of the village, as were his ancestors dating back to the sixteen hundreds. He had already been police chief for four years, and during his first three months in office he had enjoyed the unofficial honor of being the youngest police chief in the nation.

Rea had never used the small .38-caliber pistol holstered on his right hip, and sometimes forgot even to load it. As he would tell anyone who asked, "I use these," and he would hold up his two giant hands. "I'm a black belt in karate."

Rea had seen little serious crime in his tenure as chief. There had once been a $20,000 cigarette-smuggling operation, and a few years before the Mafia had dumped a body, its hands cut off, in the outskirts of the village. But in his memory, there had never been a homicide in Coxsackie.

The tall policeman stopped at the office entry, filling the doorway, his chief's hat brushing the top of the jamb. "Chief Rea," said Tartaglia, now standing with his hand on Herrin's shoulder, "I'd like you to meet Richard Herrin."

Rea's excitable nerves crackled a bit. He was close enough to level the man with a lightning kick if need be, closer than he had ever been to a killer. But the young man in the chair seemed more pathetic than dangerous. He was sitting sideways in the chair in a twisted posture, his head bent down and tilted to one side, his shoulders hunched over. His elbows were resting on his knees, and his face was buried in his hands. Almost reluctantly, as the priest began the introduction, Herrin turned his head toward Rea and sat up.

The chief saw the blood immediately. From the top of his chest to his belly, Herrin was covered with dried, caked-on blood. It was crinkled on the dark hairs of his chest and arms, on his hands, the tops of his fingers; it spotted his beige corduroy pants and the tops of his bare feet.

Rea stepped forward and shook Herrin's hand. "I understand you want to talk with me."

"Yes, I do." Herrin's voice was slow and deliberate. As he spoke, he clasped and unclasped his hands. "I want to turn myself in to a police officer. I just killed my girlfriend Bonnie."

"Wait a minute," Rea stopped him. For the first time he was aware of being anxious. The word "killed" flashed warning signals in his policeman's mind. "I have to read something to you." He removed his hat and reached inside for the small yellow Miranda card that always sat under a plastic band.

"Richard," he began to read, "you have the right to remain silent and refuse to answer any of my questions. Anything you do say may be used against you in a court of law. As we discuss this matter, you have the right to stop answering any of my questions at any time you so desire. You have the right to a lawyer before speaking with me, to remain silent until you can talk to him and to have him present with you while you are being questioned. If you desire a lawyer but you cannot afford one, one will be provided to you without cost."

The importance of these Miranda warnings had been hammered into Rea at a half-dozen different police schools and training sessions. The warnings date to 1966 when the U.S. Supreme Court freed Ernesto Miranda, an Arizona man already convicted of kidnapping and rape, because police had failed to advise him of his constitutional rights. Many cops hate the time-consuming formality, but they know that the Miranda warnings can be ignored only at the risk of losing a case. Ronald Rea was not about to take that risk.

"Richard," he continued with another section of the card, "do you understand each of these rights as I've explained them to you?"

"Yes."

"And now that I've advised you of your rights, are you willing to answer my questions without an attorney?"

"Yes." For Herrin it was an unnecessary formality. He wanted desperately to be believed. To rid himself of his guilt he had to convince the policeman of his crime.

Rea put the card back in its slot in his chief's hat. "Now Richard, you say you've killed your girlfriend, Bonnie? Bonnie who?"

"Bonnie Garland." Herrin shifted stiffly in the chair as Father Tartaglia handed Rea the notes from his earlier conversation.

"Richard, how do you know she's dead? How do you know you killed her?" Like the priest, Rea found it difficult to believe that the young man in front of him was telling the truth. His voice was soft and gentle. He was well-spoken, obviously bright, and educated. He was respectful. Except for the blood, Rea would have pegged him "not guilty." Drunk perhaps, maybe on some kind of drugs or medication, but not a killer.

"She has to be dead," Herrin answered with difficulty. "I hit her in the head with a hammer."

Rea looked incredulously at the young man. "How many times did you hit her with the hammer?" he asked.

"At least three times, maybe more." As Herrin answered, he dropped his composure, and for the first time since he ran from the Garland home, he cried, his body heaving in short spasms.

"Take it easy, Richard." The priest put his hand on Herrin's shoulder. As the sobs subsided, Rea resumed his questions. His date of birth: December 16, 1953. Bonnie Garland's date of birth: February 20, 1957. Her parents' phone number. His mother's name and address: Linda Ugarte, Los Angeles, California.

"Can I call your mother?"

"No, not now." Herrin had decided that as much as he could contain it, the mess would be his own.

Had he been drinking? No. Was he on drugs or medication? No. Was he okay? Yes, fine. Had he ever been arrested? No.

Why did he do it? Herrin first looked blankly at Rea, then answered. He had killed his girlfriend because she wanted to date other men. She even wanted to sleep with other men. "I couldn't live with the thought of her sleeping with other men," he explained to Rea. "I couldn't share her with anyone else."

Herrin had answered all the questions with his head downcast. Finally, Rea said, "Let's go, Richard. I'm putting you under arrest."

Herrin rose and extended his hand in front of him, anticipating handcuffs. "I don't think that's necessary, is it?" said Rea, now fully trusting of Herrin's meek good will.

"No, it isn't," Herrin answered. "I want to cooperate with you." The policeman glanced at the priest and nodded as if to say, "No problem, no problem. No handcuffs, no chains."

Tartaglia looked at Herrin and assured him, "You can trust Chief Rea. He'll be good to you." Rea then led the way out.

At the door, Herrin turned and put his arms around the priest. Then he stepped through the door, tripping on the threshold.

"Get hold of yourself," said Rea, reaching for Herrin's elbow.

IT WAS A DRIVE of only a few hundred yards down Mansion Street to the Municipal Building. It was toward the Hudson, into the bright rising sun pushing through the great oaks and maples. Inside the police station, the two men walked into a spartan room on the eastern side of the building which measured barely fifteen by twenty feet. Rea asked Herrin to sit on a wooden armchair facing his desk.

The village had no jail. There was an old two-cell jail out behind the D. N. Hamilton Firehouse, but it had been condemned in the late 1950's, to be used only once since, as a movie set. Rea complained that he didn't even have a temporary lockup, a little cage for one man that could stand in a corner of the room.

A small dispute arose when Deputy Chief Baker arrived. Baker lived across the street and Rea had called him as soon as he brought Herrin in. Baker, a slightly crimson-faced, bellied, and balding man in his forties with six children, was from the "old school." He remembered all too well wrestling with a suspected drug dealer on a Coxsackie street and ending up in a neck brace for two weeks. Baker was, as he described himself, "a great one for not gettin' hurt."

When he saw Richard Herrin he noticed that he was "a big guy." And after listening to Rea repeat Herrin's story, he now saw "a big guy" who had "just beat the shit out of a broad" and was sitting in a chair without any police restraints.

"You better put the cuffs on him," he told his younger boss, already starting toward Herrin to do it himself.

"What the hell you doin'? I brought him in here without 'em on," Rea complained.

"Well, you know the procedures. You set 'em."

"Yeah, I know; but this case is sensitive. He doesn't need to be handcuffed."

But Baker stood his ground until Rea gave in, finally shackling Herrin's left hand to the arm of the chair. The suspect made no protest.

Rea sat down at his faded gun-metal desk, picked up the phone, and dialed the number Herrin had given him of the Garland home in Scarsdale. It was 7:55 A.M. The phone rang four times before it woke Joan Garland. She picked up the phone and answered, "Hello?" The voice sounded cheerful.

"Is this the police station?" Rea asked, pleased at his subterfuge.

"I'm sorry. I think you have the wrong number," replied Mrs. Garland, who hung up the phone. Rea's instincts told him he had reached the Garland home. But it was obvious from the woman's voice that, if indeed her daughter was hurt, she didn't know about it.

Rea immediately dialed the Scarsdale police and asked for the highest ranking officer. "This is Chief Rea, Coxsackie P.D. I got a suspect here who says he killed Bonnie Garland. Could you respond to the Garland house? And I don't think the parents know anything about it."

A few minutes passed before Rea's phone rang. It was Scarsdale informing the chief that a squad car was on the way to the Garland home. Rea was told he would be kept informed. Ten more long minutes passed before the phone rang again and a Scarsdale policeman identified himself to Rea.

"There's no murder," he announced. "Bonnie Garland is still alive."

"Alive?" As Rea repeated the word, Herrin looked up sharply.

"She's in bad shape," the Scarsdale officer explained. "Her head was bashed open and her larynx smashed. We're rushing her to the hospital now."

Rea hung up, and looking across the desk he repeated the message to Herrin.

"Richard, she's not dead."

"No! It can't be! She has to be dead. I don't believe it," Herrin shouted, smashing his foot against the floor. He jerked his head up, and with eyes opened wide with shock he screamed at Rea:

"She has to be dead. Her head split open like a watermelon. The hammer stuck in her head and I had to pull it out." Herrin buried his face in his hands and started to cry. "Oh, my God! What have I done?"

CHAPTER TWO

The Barrio
and the Establishment

LOOKING LITTLE LIKE the bearded Richard Herrin handcuffed to a chair in the Coxsackie Police Department, a clean-shaven youth of seventeen walked slowly onto the Yale University campus laden with two valises and a battered guitar case. It was a drizzly day in September 1971 when young Herrin, buoyed by the great expectations of a scholarship student coming to the Ivy League, paused for a moment to set down his suitcases.

He smiled as he looked around him. Yale presented an exciting vista for the unsophisticated teenager from East Los Angeles. Behind him rose the Harkness Tower, which he had seen in photos reigning over the Yale campus, festooned with tracery, gargoyles, and stone-carved figures of such alumni as Noah Webster and James Fenimore Cooper.

This was Richard's first journey away from home, three thousand miles with a single leap into a prestigious Gothic parkland. Ahead of him, the cement walkway led by the bronze statue of Abraham Pierson, the first rector of America's third oldest college, then branched out across a great esplanade green with lawn and lofty elms. It was the size of a football field and surrounded by an almost unbroken line of massive stone buildings with the unflappable look of timelessness. Even the ivy that climbed their sides looked as if it had been there forever.

With his first gaze he felt the overpowering contrast between Yale and the community he had left behind only eight hours before: the Hispanic neighborhood where the architectural landscape groaned with human foible and deterioration, with worn stucco houses, cinder-block grocery stores, tin and steel taco stands, and store fronts littered with graffiti. Yale was different.

Herrin tightened his big hands around his baggage and walked toward the imposing five-story structure that girdled a rain-sleeked courtyard. He hurried between two bronze lions, crossed the courtyard, and disappeared into one of the portals of his freshman dormitory, Wright Hall.

The new student had only a vague notion that he was tracing the steps of generations of famous men. A few hundred feet from his new home in Wright Hall was the bronze figure of alumnus Nathan Hale, hero of the American Revolution. The school song, "Bulldog," had been composed by undergraduate Cole Porter. When Kingman Brewster, Jr., resigned the Yale presidency in May of 1977, he was sworn into his new office of ambassador to Great Britain by Secretary of State Cyrus Vance, Yale class of 1939.

Yale promised the people who studied there a key to future success, possibly greatness, and with amazing consistency it delivered. The problem faced by many would-be kings of democracy was getting the key to Yale. Each year thousands of the brightest students from around the world competed for admission and most were disappointed.

At Herrin's school, Abraham Lincoln High in East

Los Angeles, the students were too intent on surviving to worry about being rejected by Yale. Most didn't go to college at all. Those who did attended schools like Pasadena City Junior College or Los Angeles Trade Tech where they could study auto-body repair or welding or, for the more ambitious, bookkeeping or nursing. The Lincoln Heights neighborhood, which sprawled over 2000 acres on the northeastern flank of downtown Los Angeles, held 36,000 people, mainly Hispanics cut off from mainstream America by their language. In an area where three out of four adults had never finished the twelfth grade, Abraham Lincoln High School *was* higher education.

Survival meant not only a struggle with the Anglo majority and its strange culture and competitive economy. The youngsters at Lincoln High also had to contest their own peers, either by avoiding or joining one of the gangs that had marked the school as its turf.

Monday mornings, when the word was out that the East Siders were gunning for the Hazards or the Clover Boys were after the Hoyos, the school faculty was put on a "gang alert." A half-dozen of the more *macho* teachers on "Petino's posse"—named after the vice-principal who directed it—raced down the hallways to prevent gang war. They usually succeeded within school grounds, but outside the gangs staked out territories by spray-painting their names on storefronts or the walls of abandoned houses. Rivals who dared trespass on the graffiti-marked turf would be beaten, even shot in the leg or the head with a cheap handgun.

Dickie Fritas fought and survived in Vietnam, then came back and was killed in Lincoln Heights. Vernon Fritas, Dickie's younger brother, had been shot to death six years before. Richard's classmate, Ray Zamorra, a star athlete, was killed by a shotgun blast while he stood outside a house on Hancock Street. Willie Munoz from Herrin's class of 1971 was blown away by a .45 during an argument over a taco in the local Jack-in-the-Box.

Few students anywhere in America faced as many obstacles to education. Every week two or three kids had to be carried out of the stucco-faced school on North Broadway, casualties of too many "reds" or barbiturates. That only made the achievements of Richard Herrin seem all the more miraculous. Richard navigated the violence without taking drugs, fighting, drinking, or swearing, yet was respected by teachers and gang members alike. His 220-pound frame intimidated the toughest of his peers, who also respected the fact that he played defensive tackle on the school football team.

"A" was Richard's usual grade. He was always first in his class. Teachers thought of him as a bright touch in the midst of academic desperation. Not only did he have an IQ of at least 130, but his dedication and apparent grasp of the majority culture was impressive. In addition to playing on the football team, Richard was president of three student clubs and city-wide bowling champion one year. He worked for his stepfather at flea-market swap meets after school and on weekends, played the guitar, loved the Beatles, and went to Mass at the Catholic Church every Sunday. Amidst the barrio's daily defeats, Herrin was the promise of tomorrow.

More confident of his abilities than he was, Herrin's teachers urged him to try for the best college education the nation could offer. Early in his senior year, with little thought of success, he gathered together the necessary forms and mailed them off to Harvard, Princeton, Williams College, the University of Pennsylvania, and Yale. The competition was statistically forbidding: More than nine thousand students applied for the fewer than two thousand places at Harvard, almost nine thousand for the thirteen hundred openings at Yale. As a backstop, Richard also applied to Occidental College in Los Angeles.

The following spring the mailbox at 2435 Johnston Street filled with acceptances from Harvard, Yale, Princeton, Pennsylvania, and Williams, each with an offer of a scholarship. In predominantly Mexican-American Lincoln High, where the average senior was reading at seventh grade level, Richard was assuming the proportions of a hero, mentioned in the same reverent tones as Robert Castillo, who went on to pitch for the Dodgers, or Freddie Martinez, who would pitch for the Angels.

Richard did not agonize over his choice of colleges. Princeton and Harvard were offering better financial packages, but Richard elected Yale. It was the only school at which he knew someone. Javier "Harvey" Sandoval, a bright graduate of the year before, had been the second Lincoln student ever admitted to Yale.

On graduation day at Lincoln, Richard, in cap and gown, marched at the head of his class of 415 onto the football field to receive his diploma and be honored as valedictorian. Linda and Manuel Ugarte, Richard's mother and stepfather, took their seats with hundreds of others who were thankful their children had survived high school, the first great hurdle of Anglo society.

The fifteen honor roll students were called to the stage by principal Pete Martinez, who draped a yellow cord around each of their necks as he told the audience where they were going to college. As Richard's name was called the applause was loud and long. Few knew exactly where Yale University was, but everyone understood that it was a gateway to galaxies of which they had never even dreamed. Father Bernie Gatlin, the young pastor of the Sacred Heart parish, looked over the crowd of bronze faces as it celebrated Richard Herrin's admission to Yale and said to himself: "It's as if he were going to the moon."

IF WE ARE TO believe that killers are made, rather than born, we must understand the dual background of Richard James Herrin. Raised in a poor but cohesive Hispanic community, he came to Yale in that fall of 1971 to find his fulfillment, or perhaps his destruction, in this flower of the American establishment.

Richard's first week at Yale was a blur of chores. He had to arrange the papers for the loan, the work-study job, the federal educational opportunity grant, and the book stipend that were part of his scholarship. He had to have his picture taken for his Yale identification card and locate the post office to send his first letter to his mother. There were tours of the campus, orientation sessions, and meetings with the other freshmen on scholarship, who like Richard, had to work in the dining halls for their subsistence. There was a suit-and-tie dinner at Saybrook College, which would be his residence hall from sophomore year through graduation.

Other than his Wright Hall roommates, the first people Richard Herrin met were the "entryway crowd," made up of the students in the dozen or so rooms surrounding the stairwell of his freshman dormitory. This would become a tight social group, not unlike a small fraternity. They would stop to ask directions, make introductions, invite each other to inspect their barren living quarters, meet each other's roommates, pass around a joint, crack open cans of beer, talk about their hometowns. The early fall was warm and everyone's rooms seemed thrown open to spontaneous bull sessions.

Richard drank in the easy air. He was no virgin to the odors of marijuana, but he didn't smoke it and made no value judgments about those who did. He shared a few stories about the gangs in his Lincoln Heights neighborhood and his high school, but he also listened intently to the others. He was absorbing the Yale behind the ivy-covered walls.

Removed from the warm Hispanic culture of East Los Angeles in which he felt comfortable, Herrin now searched about in the Yale community for a new circle of friends.

At first, he was put off by the difference between himself and some other Yalies, particularly those who he feared might be snobbish. *The Yale Daily News* had warned that "your name may have been revered in your community, but at Yale your roommate may have a name like Vanderbilt or DuPont." Within a few days of his arrival Richard actually met a DuPont: Frank DuPont, who lived on the floor below Richard. In his class of '75 there was also Christopher Buckley, son of

William F. Buckley, Jr., one of the country's leading conservatives, as well as the sons and daughters of scores of prominent Americans.

The prep schools—Choate, Groton, Deerfield—were to college admission what Yale was to Wall Street: a passport office. Richard was only the third person from Lincoln High ever to be, accepted by Yale, but to the Yale class of 1975 alone Phillips Academy, Andover, sent twenty-six of its graduates; Phillips Exeter, thirty-five. They sauntered onto the Old Campus at Yale as they would stride into their parents' country homes. The school was their birthright.

Caste and class, the sense of being subtly ostracized by snobbery, was to become a discreetly hidden but powerful theme in Richard Herrin's life. The students who dominated the *Yale Daily News*, the Whiffenpoof singing group, the crowd at Mory's and the senior secret societies—from Skull and Bones to Berzelious and Scroll and Key—had little to do socially with the half Mexican-American from East Los Angeles.

"These were people with an elitist preppie mentality," Richard was later to explain. "I wasn't like that myself and I didn't think I would be accepted into that circle. I sensed that they had a lot of money and felt themselves to be superior. But it wasn't important for me to get to know them."

Social class was not far from Richard's thoughts as he lay on his dormitory bunk at Wright Hall, paging through his copy of the Yale freshman directory, *The Old Campus*. At first it was just idle curiosity, but after meeting a number of his new classmates, his page-turning became an amateur sociology experiment in which he would try to guess a person's personality by the picture and the short biography beneath it.

The fellow with the turtle-neck sweater and sports jacket; the unsmiling, square-jawed kid with three names followed by a Roman numeral; the girl with the lipstick smile and pearl necklace; that one from Andover, this one from Exeter. Richard felt like an interloper, coming to a formal dinner with a counterfeit invitation.

These were people with golden names, some of whom, he became convinced, were as aloof and confident in real life as they seemed staring up at him from the pages of *The Old Campus*. His lonely picture analysis soon replaced any need to meet them in person. He would see someone in the dining hall where he worked, match them with their picture, and stay his distance before they had a chance to stay theirs.

One of Richard's closest friends at Yale, Paul Bardack of New York, saw possible significance in Herrin's reaction to Yale snobbery. "Rich could get along with the more affluent students when they were doing something he enjoyed, as when they were part of a beer-drinking team. But he didn't do so well when they were with their parents and wearing their plaid what-have-yous. Maybe there are some roots here of problems which later killed Bonnie. Perhaps it was a case of not so much that 'they reject me' as 'I reject them—before they reject me.' "

Herrin and the Yale elite avoided each other, but he found friendship elsewhere. Richard had a warm, affable, even empathetic exterior, and an ability to listen to others. More than ever, he began to cultivate this good-natured friendliness as a passport to acceptance.

Herrin soon struck up relationships with freshmen who shared his Wright Hall entryway and who would later move on to Saybrook College where they would live together until graduation. The new social freedom was exhilarating to the seventeen-year-old who had never traveled beyond the *barrio*. Herrin found it easy to move from room to room, finding the other freshmen equally eager for companionship. At times, he brought along his guitar, accompanying himself in his soft baritone, sometimes until the early morning hours. A dedicated Beatles fan, Richard strummed and sang their hits—*I Want to Hold Your Hand, Yesterday, Here, There, Everywhere*—along with the songs of another favorite group, Creedence Clearwater Revival. His musical talent opened the door to still more friendship.

Herrin's new friends represented a spectrum of America, geographically and ethnically. Paul Bardack, from Staten Island, New York, who would later become a White House intern and a Congressional assistant, was a bright, articulate student slated to become Herrin's closest friend. The two entryway pals seemed an incongruous pair. Herrin, at six feet, was almost a head taller than Bardack, and at 220 pounds outweighed him by seventy. While Bardack was a quick-witted and feisty Jew, Herrin was an unsophisticated, reserved, Hispanic Catholic, a "good ole joe."

But once thrown together, they discovered common denominators. They were both fanatical Beatles fans and they both played a musical instrument: Rich, the guitar, and Paul, the recorder. And having grown up in poverty, Bardack shared with Herrin an acute sense of having cracked some impenetrable barrier on being admitted to Yale.

"Rich was one of my best friends," Paul Bardack explained. "I thought he was a great guy, real low-keyed and laid back. I perceived him the same way I perceived myself. Both of us came from the same kind of environment. We came out of a shitty urban high school and finally really made it. Here we were at Yale."

Another entryway friend, Mike DeMaio, was a graduate of a New England prep school and a member of the freshman crew team. Tony Allen from Oklahoma was an economics major. Chuck Cervantes from Corpus Christi, Texas, was a brainy Hispanic who intended to major in molecular biophysics. Ashbel Tingley Wall II, known to his friends simply as A. T., was a brilliant graduate of Phillips Exeter Academy, and reputed to be one of the few Yalies with the magic "double 800's" in the Scholastic Aptitude Test.

At the intensively competitive Ivy League school, Richard's easy manner made him different, and likeable. His friends felt that there was no one so good-natured, or so generous with his time. If boxes of furniture had to be moved for other Yalies, Richard was the eager volunteer. To a classmate who had difficulty adjusting, he listened empathetically.

He was never angry or mean, and if he was torn by internal hostility he was careful not to display it. Herrin seldom argued or confronted anyone, offering a pleasant face to all. His general demeanor was one of non-competition, acceptance, even conciliation.

HERRIN BEGAN to relax in the Yale social environment, at least among his fellow freshmen in Wright Hall dormitory. But the more he learned about the Yale ethos the more he felt an awkward weight pressing down on his boyish enthusiasm. It was the painful awareness of feeling academically inferior. His biology teacher at Lincoln High had told him that Yale would be different. "Remember," he warned, "at Yale there'll be nothing but other Richard Herrins." Richard ignored the warning. Neither did he pay much attention to the special summer issue of the Yale *Daily News* in which veteran students warned the newcomers to beware; you may have been a big fish in your high school, but don't be surprised to find the fish bigger at Yale.

The bright young man from Lincoln High was beginning to feel that all the fish were bigger, that everyone at Yale was smarter than he. As he listened to conversations around Wright Hall, Richard heard the dismaying introductory dialogues that went quickly from "What's your name?" to "What did you get on your SATs?" to "Did you know that my roommate's SATs were perfect?" The Scholastic Aptitude Test had become a short-cut to sizing up the competition.

Out of a possible 800 points on each part of the test Richard had scored an uninspired 580 in the verbal section and a somewhat better 660 in mathematics. His scores were the highest at Lincoln and better than ninety-four percent of the 1.8 million other youths who took the SATs that year. But at Yale the ninety-fourth percentile seemed to scrape the bottom of the bell curve.

Everyone Richard met was talking about "seven-eighty-two" or "seven-fifty-three" or even an occasional "double eight hundred."

His golden East Los Angeles badge of honor had turned to lead in just days. For the first time in his life, he was intimidated by the competition. Instead of being the academic model he was the under-achiever, the poorly-tutored California Chicano in a stronghold of the Eastern establishment.

One of his first classrooms, the law school auditorium, was large enough to hold his entire high school class. Almost 600 students had assembled to hear Robert Fogelin lecture on "The Character of Philosophical Thought." Fogelin stood behind the lectern and explained that this would be a very basic course, nothing trendy, nothing relevant, he quipped. It would cover Plato's *Republic,* Descartes' *Meditations*, Kant's *Prolegomena to Any Future Metaphysics*, and Nietzsche's *Twilight of the Idols.* As Richard listened he felt swallowed up by the mass of people and by the names of books he had never heard of.

Richard left the auditorium floating in a miasma of confusion. His discomfort was not an isolated response; he had much the same reaction to his classes in calculus and chemistry. In high school he had excelled in the sciences, and had organized the school's first ecology club. Richard expected to major in biology at Yale, with the possibility of someday becoming a doctor. But at Yale he soon discovered that professors were not congenial to unknown freshmen. They did not need to spend time trying to prop up an untrained intellect like his. Herrin did not understand that Yale expected its students to take charge of their own academic life.

Herrin was dislocated, bewildered, unable to understand how independence and accomplishment dovetailed in the strange ethic of New Haven. Instead of fighting for survival, he withdrew from competing academically. Richard was not completing his homework assignments, was not opening his textbooks at night. Within a few weeks of the term's beginning, he found that he was passing some tests, squeaking by others, and failing still others. Only a few months removed from being class valedictorian, Herrin was suffering his first defeat at Yale.

"I was always top of my class, but I quickly realized that it wasn't going to be like that anymore," Herrin later explained about his poor performance at Yale. "A lot of people were smarter than me. They *sounded* smart. They even *looked* smart. I was overwhelmed by it, and my competitiveness just seemed to vanish right away. I didn't want to have to be fighting for A's and worrying about grades. I gave up before I gave myself a chance. I sold myself short."

In a way, Herrin had come to Yale at the wrong time, during its era of greatest permissiveness. Ten years before, Herrin probably would not have been admitted to Yale at all. But during the liberal admission period of the 1970's his ethnic background counted as much or more than his SATs. That same approach had created a relatively loose academic atmosphere which tempted the undisciplined. In Herrin's freshman year Yale was still using an experimental system in which the traditional A to F had been replaced by "pass" and "fail" grades.

Herrin knew he could dawdle with impunity, and he did. Since the academic and cultural shock of Yale had destroyed his equanimity, Richard decided he would take a new route. The model boy of East Los Angeles, the pride of Lincoln High, would settle for undistinguished anonymity. At Lincoln, both students and teachers would have been shocked if Richard Herrin delivered less than an A. But in a class of six hundred brilliant Yalies, who cared, or knew about, Chicano Richard Herrin?

The metamorphosis of Richard Herrin was taking place rapidly. At home, the community, the school, his mother, and the church were all authority symbols that gave Richard a sure guide to behavior. At Yale, with a permissive peer group and with no one seemingly in charge, there were almost no guidelines he could follow. For the first time in his life he had no reputation for brilliance or responsibility to uphold.

One casualty of this new freedom was Richard's entire life style at Yale. Not only did he seldom study at night, but he seldom rose early for class. "I never went to breakfast," Herrin recalled. "For me any time I had to get up in the morning was early." His appearance became particularly sloppy; he favored jeans and worn T-shirts, and sometimes wore a sweatshirt with the sleeves cut off. He was overweight, flabby, and often had the grizzled look of not having shaved for days.

Sloppiness was not unusual on the Yale campus, but Herrin's way of dressing stood out. "Just as there was a stereotypical Yalie," a friend remembered, "there was a stereotype of what Yalies aren't supposed to do, like wearing sweaty undershirts. But that's how Rich was most comfortable. He'd come into the dining hall in just an undershirt and dirty dungarees because he hadn't done his laundry. Even for sloppy undergrads that was a bit much. If he were a hippy, it would have made sense; there would have been some cultural consistency. But Rich did it in a way that didn't fit. It didn't fit in with Yale."

In Los Angeles, living under the scrutiny of an admiring community, he had been a near-teetotaler. At Yale, he was becoming something of a drinker. One year Rich was chosen for the Saybrook Tang Team, a group of expert beer drinkers who competed against other residential colleges for the swilling championship. In his heyday Herrin could down an eight-ounce glass of beer in two seconds. Not long into his freshman year, Herrin added hard liquor.

The new Richard Herrin, swallowed up by the total freedom of the Yale ethos, even abandoned his devotion to the Catholic Church. If he did not go to Sunday Mass, who would know? No one in New Haven knew that his mother had been taking Richard to church since he was two weeks old, had escorted him to catechism lessons, taken him to his first confession at age seven, and went to Mass with him every day during Lent. No one cared that Richard Herrin had never missed a Sunday Mass in his entire life. Everyone who did know was three thousand miles away.

He was surprised at how easy it was to discard both the Catholic mantle and the tight-fitting robes of the scholar. There was no sense of guilt, no anxiety about having committed a mortal sin.

HERRIN'S NEW SENSE of freedom was at odds with his strict East Los Angeles upbringing. But he still felt the need for a familiar anchor in the alien environment of Yale. He found it among the Mexican-American students at Yale, most of whom were drawn from the population centers of Los Angeles and San Antonio. The Chicano group numbered about thirty, the smallest minority at Yale and the last to break the ethnic barrier. Most Chicanos kept to themselves; they sat grouped together in the freshman dining hall. When it came time to live and eat in one of the twelve residential colleges beginning in the sophomore year, they often defied Yale tradition. Instead of sharing their social lives with their college buddies—whether at Saybrook, Branford, Davenport, Pierson or the others—the Chicanos hung out together across college lines.

Their parties were noisier and livelier, with not only the usual heavy beer drinking but also a raucous combination of Latin music and rock 'n' roll that often continued into the early morning hours. When a student received a package of *chorizo*, a Mexican delicacy of heavily spiced sausage, the word went out quickly. Much of the Yale Chicano population would soon be gathered at a party arranged to share the prized food.

The inner-city Chicanos felt particularly unprepared for Yale, suffering severe cultural and academic shock. One student recalled that not long after the school year began, five Chicano freshmen piled into a battered Volkswagen, drove out of the Yale campus, and never returned. Some Chicanos were sensitive to charges that the administration had lowered its academic standards to admit them and became convinced that they were the victims of subtle prejudice. Carlos, a Chicano friend of Herrin's, remembered that some Anglo students insisted on calling him Charles, as if the anglicized name were a compliment. When he tried out for the football team, one of the coaches needled him, "It's your turn, Pancho."

Like Herrin, most of the Chicanos were poor, and helped pay their way by working in one of the Yale dining halls. This traditionally included cleaning tables and serving food to other students, but by the time Herrin began work there, the dining hall had been converted to cafeteria style. But having a dining room job was still a signal that a student was financially less well-off.

During his first week at Yale Richard felt the sense of isolation that accompanies being a member of a minority. But Harvey Sandoval, the other Lincoln High graduate at Yale, soon introduced Richard to MECHA, the *Movimiento Estudiantes Chicano-Americanos*, which had been organized to help the Chicano students adjust. Herrin quickly joined. At his first MECHA meeting in the Branford College commons room, Herrin surveyed the two dozen bronze-skinned young people standing in the wood-paneled shadows, listened to their Spanish-inflected voices, and felt more at home.

"Excuse me. Are you in the right room?" one of the MECHA students had asked as Richard came in. Politely, he was offering to help this student who may have wandered into the wrong meeting.

At a glance Richard didn't look Chicano. But once he told someone that he was, he didn't look un-Chicano, either. Like many Chicanos, his nose lay a little flat and fleshy on his face, but his jaw was square and his head angular like his father's European forebears. His hair, short by the standards of the generation, was Indian black and straight, but it had a wave across the forehead and a curl at the nape of the neck. His skin was tinted olive, but in a way that looked more like he had just completed a two-hour sunbath than taken a dip in the Hispanic genetic pool.

Richard could have passed for mainstream American, but he had grown up in a Chicano tributary. He thought of himself as "semi-white"—not as Hispanic as the other kids, but not white either. At Yale his name would be Herrin, crisp, solid, and Anglo. Back home it had often been a Hispanic "Air'een."

He smiled a bit nervously at the shorter man in front of him and answered, *"Si, si. Amigo de Javier. Soy de Los Angeles."*

RICHARD HERRIN was indeed from Los Angeles. But his birthright included no country homes or prep schools, only an inner-city existence and a history clouded by illegitimacy. Almost eighteen years before Herrin came to Yale, his grandmother, Carmen Brown, died suddenly in East Los Angeles, a death which almost snuffed out Richard's life before it began. Carmen's twenty-three year old daughter Linda, a timid woman, was seven months pregnant, and the shock of her mother's death sent her into premature labor. Only the last minute intervention of a doctor prevented a miscarriage.

Two months later, on the morning of December 16, 1953, Linda was rushed to Santa Marta Catholic Hospital where a nun helped deliver a baby boy, Richard James Herrin. The painful birth was complicated by the umbilical cord being wrapped around the baby's neck, but Linda was finally able to hold a fat infant in her arms.

Linda had defied her church by bearing a son by her lover, James Herrin, an Irish-American wanderer who had never married her. But faced with a birth certificate, she created on paper the family that life had denied her, giving the child his father's surname, Herrin. Then, in a petite rounded script, Linda penned a little lie: She signed her own name as "Linda Herrin." The fabrication mattered less than the fact that her son would not be told the truth about his birth.

Linda was the fourth of seven children born to Carmen and Fred Brown. Fred's father had been a German immigrant to Mexico who married a young Spanish woman. The Anglo-sounding surname belied the almost oriental eyes, rusty skin, stout frame, and softly shaped moon face Linda inherited from her Papago Indian mother, Carmen.

Richard's father, James Herrin, was an unskilled rambler who painted, sang, and played the steel-string guitar. As far as James knew, he was born in Cincinnati of Irish parents, but he was raised by gypsy foster parents. His own father had walked out before he was born, and the woman he believed to be his mother refused to acknowledge him as her offspring.

Richard's mother, Linda, grew up among the Hispanic populace of East Los Angeles and might have remained rooted to her *mestiza* background had she not boarded a city bus bound for the wrestling matches in the fall of 1952. On the bus she met James Herrin. Within a month they talked about marriage, but a priest pried a confession from James. He was a divorced man and had a child, and was therefore not eligible to be married in the church.

Although a devout Catholic, Linda clung to Herrin, even following him to Cincinnati, where she lived with him and his gypsy foster parents. They returned to Los Angeles to have their baby.

James Herrin worked as a truck driver and made a down payment on a house, but he soon began drinking. He insisted that Linda get a job, forcing her to leave Richard with her sister. The elder Herrin moved from job to job, and by the time their second child was born, Richard was two years old and his father was in jail. Five weeks later, Richard's younger brother, James Thomas, died of pneumonia. Linda and Richard supported each other, she shielding him from the turmoil while he responded by being a precocious son. The two-year-old was already memorizing bedtime stories Linda read to him, mimicking her narrative to pretend that he too could read.

Linda went back to James Herrin after his release

from jail, but Herrin soon returned to alcohol. One night, James stumbled into the apartment drunk as Linda was putting Richard to bed. He leaned over his son in the crib and commanded the two-year-old to speak.

"Say 'sandwich,' " his father yelled, fumbling with his belt buckle. Richard was silent, as incapable of saying the word as his father was of understanding why he could not. As Richard cowered, James jerked the strap from his pants and raised it over his head. But just as he swung down, Linda jumped between them, catching the snapping belt on her outstretched arm.

"Get out of here," she ordered. "I never want you to hit my son again."

But despite her anger Linda was loyal. It was mainly for Richard's sake, but she refused to give James up. Even when she confronted him about another woman and he exploded in a rage, sending her scurrying into the night with Richard in her arms, she came back. It was James, sober, who finally made the break. When Richard was two-and-a-half, James Herrin announced that he was leaving to live with another woman.

"What about Ricky?" Linda asked. "Ricky needs a father."

James confessed that he had always been jealous of the boy. "Besides," he scowled, "I was brought up without a father; so you can raise him without a father." James Herrin walked out leaving nothing behind but a name stamped onto his son's future.

When his father left, there was only one place for Richard to go: his grandfather's house on East 3rd Street, where little Richard was fawned over by adoring relatives. But after a few months, his mother found work and moved Richard on again.

The next two years were as unsettled for Richard as were the first two, only now he had no father. Linda sought to explain to the child what had happened. From now on, she told him, she would have to be his mother and his father; he would always be "her little man." They moved into a boxy apartment unit in downtown

Los Angeles where Richard was left with his aunt while Linda went to work at a ceramic factory.

Before he was five, Richard was put down one morning onto the seat of a car driven by a stranger. Linda had met Manuel Ugarte at the factory and the newly-improvised family of three were soon living together in a house on Daly Street, a half-block from the main commercial avenue of Lincoln Heights. Richard's new home was a tiny cottage consisting of two rooms, each about twelve feet square. Linda and Manuel were in one room with a tiny bathroom at one end, while Richard slept on a cot in the second room, a whirring refrigerator at his head.

Richard slept poorly, bothered by a recurring nightmare in which he was lost at the beach. Along with nightmares, the boy's sleep was troubled by regular bed wetting. A doctor told Linda to ignore it, but Manuel complained to Linda that her son was too lazy to get out of bed. Not long after, Richard broke out in severe eczema rashes on his feet and legs, a painful ailment which did not yield to treatment. It was a trying period for young Richard, who cried whenever his mother went out, and more than once he confided to her that he feared that the police would take him away.

One trauma after another seemed to be young Richard's legacy. One evening, when Richard was five, Linda hired an eighteen-year-old boy, a seemingly trustworthy family acquaintance, as a baby sitter. When she and Manuel left, the baby sitter sexually abused Richard, persuading the boy to fondle him.

"I hadn't been to catechism yet and hadn't learned that it was a sin," Herrin later recalled about the incident. "I just felt there was something inherently wrong in what he was doing. I sensed it and asked him to stop." Herrin kept the homosexual incident secret until he was twenty-three, when he revealed it to a psychiatrist.

From the time he was seven, Richard's energy was divided between school, which he loved, and work for Manuel which he quietly detested. Soon after moving in with Linda, Ugarte, a Mexican-born workaholic, became a "swapper," Los Angelese for a flea-market entrepreneur. He quickly filled the little Daly Street house with lamp parts and set Richard to work helping him assemble them.

Working seven days a week with Linda and pressing Richard into service whenever he wasn't in school, Manuel built his swap-meet business into a two-van, one-station-wagon enterprise. Eventually he was able to move his new family into a better house on the other side of Broadway.

But Manuel's success did nothing to lighten Richard's work. For years, he worked with Manuel after school, on weekends, during holidays and all summer. He had to load and unload cars and trucks, move boxes, sort clothes, stand in the hot sun selling lamps or "Superman" T shirts, and anything else Manuel wanted him to do.

Richard hated the work. It seemed as if his whole life had been one continuous swap-meet. At one meet, Herrin turned to his mother at the boys' pants table and mumbled, "I'd rather be dead than doing this."

Linda helped Richard escape the drudgery as much as she could. In the summer, when Richard was still in grade school, she sent him off to his grandfather's house for a couple of weeks. Only that house on East 3rd Street, always crowded with aunts, uncles, cousins, and Grandfather Brown, provided an emotional oasis for the child. Unlike the father he never knew, Richard's grandfather had always been there for him, sturdy and affectionate.

Richard worked long hours, but compared to most of his friends in Lincoln Heights, he was well-off financially: He had a record player, a guitar, and a typewriter. These were extraordinary in Lincoln Heights where more than half of the students qualified for the free lunch program. To his friends it seemed that Richard had everything except freedom. They marveled at his ability to work without complaint, and to absorb the shouts of Manuel.

"How can you take that shit?" they asked in amazement. But Richard replied, "Somebody's got to do the work. It's my duty. I have to help."

School became his refuge. Hours there were times of relative peace, free from the orders and the endless tasks. Richard came to love school, which compensated for his not having many playmates around Daly Street. It made up for the teasing he was subjected to when his eczema forced him to wear knee-high stockings and sandals, or sit on the sideline during gym class.

Before long he had been promoted two grades ahead of his peers and had become a favorite of his teachers. To everyone Richard was the model boy: Outstanding student, devout Catholic, cooperative youngster, uncomplaining worker who was generous with his time and spirit. When Lincoln High School staged a three-day fund-raising carnival, Richard Herrin stayed up until 2 A.M. each morning to clean up and close the doors.

His friends suffered in their parents' eyes by comparison. Sigfrido Chavez, Richard's best friend in high school and an aggressive football player who took "no shit from anybody," remembered that he was constantly chided by his mother. "Why," she used to ask, "can't you be more like Richard?"

The man who was to bludgeon Bonnie Garland with a hammer was idolized by a community for whom he performed nothing but duty and selfless sacrifice.

THE MODEL BOY of East Los Angeles soon found Yale to be a more subtle and demanding environment in which selflessness was less rewarded than independence and individual achievement.

At Lincoln High, he had experienced the pride of being Number One. At Yale that specialness had faded rapidly. A few months into his first semester, Richard walked back to his room with an envelope in his hand. It was light, but the official Yale letterhead gave it an ominous look. Herrin ripped open the envelope and watched as a small pink slip fell out onto his desk. It was a matter-of-fact warning: He had to improve or flunk the course.

This slip was for chemistry. The pink slip for calculus had already arrived. Richard knew how poorly he was doing, but the actual receipt of each pink slip dropped his self-esteem even further. He looked out the window at the modern fourteen story Kline Biology Tower and thought that more than ever, it had the proportions of an unassailable citadel.

Herrin was quickly becoming a full-time dawdler, unable to understand the traditional Ivy League balance between hard work and hard play. Yale offered a myriad of ways to avoid studying, and Herrin seemed to seize on all of them. Whether it was bladderball, played with a massive five-foot-diameter ball, volleyball, or twenty-five-cent table-top football, Richard was there, playing.

He was more of a follower than an organizer, but he did get credit for introducing a game called Four Square, which reached the status of a minor fad. The object was to bounce a tennis ball into one of four squares marked on the floor with black electrician's tape in such a way that the opponent could not return the ball. Four Square was so easy to play that the counselor outside whose door the tennis ball ceaselessly bounced called it a "diabolical waste of time."

Time-wasting was becoming Richard Herrin's specialty. For the first time in his life, Herrin had a chance to unwrap the umbilical cord from around his neck. After growing up as a responsible and conscientious only child, he was suddenly living twenty-four hours a day with kids his own age, and enjoying it. There were always some students who didn't study all the time, even a few who didn't seem to study at all. There was always somebody ready to join Richard for a few beers at Jock O'Sullivan's or Old Heidelberg, run up to Broadway Pizza for a late-night snack, or over to Mr. Donut's for a 3 A.M. chocolate.

One night in the fall of his freshman year, Richard's new freedom was interrupted by a telephone call from home. The receiver grew heavy as he listened to the distant voice tell him that his grandfather Fred Brown, his mother's father, had just died. He had adored his grandfather. Richard hung up and walked slowly back into his dark dormitory room, closing the door. He rifled through his desk for his rosary beads and dropped to his knees in front of the bed.

It required no thought. The impulse to pray was his automatic response to crisis. With his elbows pushed hard into the mattress and his hands clasped in prayer, Richard pleaded with God to take care of his grandfather's soul. Pinching the tiny beads with passion between his fingers, he began the rythmic ritual.

It was like a numbing anesthesia. An Our Father, ten Hail Marys, a Glory Be, an Our Father, ten Hail Marys, a Glory Be, an Our Father. With each prayer there was a new bead to hold. In a low, quick, mumbled monotone that pushed away anxiety, the one-ten-one sequence was repeated over and over again.

The next Los Angeles-bound plane from Kennedy Airport had Richard Herrin on it. He brought no suitcase, no toothbrush, no books. He had the clothes on his back and the tightly-clutched rosary which did not leave his hands during the seven-hour flight.

Grandfather Fred A. Brown had died on Saturday, October 16, 1971, eighteen years and one day after his wife Carmen was buried. He was seventy-eight years old and left behind one son, five daughters, and nine grandchildren, including Richard.

Herrin had traveled farther than anyone else to attend the wake. Nothing much had changed since he had only left five weeks before, but the time span seemed like years rather than weeks. Richard moved about slowly in Los Angeles, dividing his time between his house on Johnston Street and his grandfather's home on East 3rd. As a child, Richard had made the five-mile trip to that house so often that it seemed like a second home.

Richard stayed in Los Angeles for a full week, brooding not only over the loss of his grandfather but about what had become of his life in the short time at

Yale. He reflected guiltily about his academic failure, his sudden falling away from the church, and his irresponsible dawdling. Richard had been shocked by the death into remembering that he had always been a good student and a faithful Catholic. In a tribute to Fred Brown's memory, he vowed to become that again.

HERRIN RETURNED to Yale from his grandfather's funeral a chastened young man. He made an attempt to improve his grades but his efforts were half-hearted and short-lived. His new academic vows were soon shattered. He flunked chemistry in the first semester, mathematics in the second. His studies showed no great improvement in his sophomore year, when Herrin decided to become a geology major and began working part-time at the Yale Peabody Museum of Natural History. Yale had reinstituted the regular grade system, and except for an A in the history of science, Herrin did poorly: one F, and C in the rest of his courses. He had made a negotiated settlement with the Ivy League school: He would do only as well as he had to in order to get by.

But religion was a different story. The first Sunday after his return from Los Angeles, he walked up Elm Street toward St. Thomas More Chapel, the Yale Catholic Center, taking his first steps back toward responsibility. The streets were empty except for other church-goers and some half-awake students lugging their Sunday *New York Times* under their arms. On Park Street, amidst a row of neat white homes, he found the small red-brick church. Richard entered and slid into a rear pew.

He immediately liked what he saw. Unlike the other churches he had attended, the More House Chapel was light and unaffected, unadorned by pillars, ornate statues, or darkly glowing stained-glass depictions of scenes from the Bible. Its interior brick walls were painted a misty grey-blue and broken by tall clear windows only vaguely scratched by the faint figure of a saint. As Richard knelt quietly on the padded knee rest, he noticed that the fifteen pews were filled with an almost equal number of men and women, and very few children.

This too was a change. In the Hispanic Sacred Heart parish in Los Angeles, Richard had prayed surrounded by a sea of women and young children. In the Mexican-American culture, church was mainly for women and children. When boys became men, they seldom attended church except on special occasions. Richard had always gone, but like much about him, this, too, was an exception in Hispanic Los Angeles.

Richard looked up at a half-dozen young people gathered around a music stand near the altar of the More House Chapel. They were quietly tuning guitars, shaking a tambourine, and testing their voices. The small church was alive with whispers until a young robed priest in his thirties with a shock of reddish-brown hair and a full beard appeared at the back door.

As the priest started up the center aisle, the congregation rose and the musicians began to play. The chapel woke with a single voice chanting "I place all my trust in You my God." Richard was singing too: "All my hope is in Your mercy."

The young priest invited the congregation to leave their pews and gather round the altar. This was the Mass as Herrin imagined the early Christians celebrated it: standing around a table in someone's house, leaning against one another, sharing food and drink. It was the kind of intimacy that had eluded him in the shadows of the cavernous cathedrals in which he had worshipped. It was also the kind of closeness Herrin hadn't found in Yale classrooms, where he was cowed by icy competition. He had missed something by skipping Mass at St. Thomas More and he knew he would be back.

As time went by at Yale, Herrin's need to believe became stronger than ever. When he heard the power of the guitars at Catholic chapel Mass during his freshman year, he knew that he wanted to play in church. In the midst of the Catholic renaissance of the 1970's, the Mass was a perfect outlet for a Beatles fan who also believed in God.

At the end of his freshman year, Herrin went home for the summer, where he spent most of his time dutifully working for Manuel just as if he had never gone off to Yale. But he allowed himself some free time during which he exhausted his fingers practicing on his new $100 Aria guitar, "Mary." Herrin had been turned down the year before as guitarist at More House, but now fortified by a summer of practice and a new guitar, he auditioned again. This time Richard was invited to play at the Sunday Mass.

Herrin became the most dependable member of the Sunday music group. He would not balk at mid-week rehearsals, and unlike some of the other volunteers, he never insisted on *his* song, or *his* arrangement. Soon he expanded his More House involvement to include Bible study sessions, weekday Mass, community suppers and retreats. Later, Herrin became a Pastoral Associate in a program which gave students a chance to serve as aides to the chaplains.

At More House Richard began a friendship with an assistant chaplain, Sister Ramona Pena. She was the new breed of Catholic nun. In her mid-forties, Sister Ramona had already given up the traditional Flanders habit for modest street dress. She impressed the students around More House as a strong-willed and open woman.

"She wasn't your typical sister," recalled a student member of More House, "but more like a Jewish mother. She was outgoing, informal and didn't like to be treated with kid gloves. Politically she was very liberal, not from the hell-fire-and-damnation school. And she would not raise her eyebrows if you came to talk about boyfriend problems."

Ramona was intensely loyal to her friends and took great pride in her Hispanic heritage, a quality which drew her to Richard Herrin, a fellow *latino*. In Richard she saw a devout Catholic who lived his religion. She encouraged his religious devotion and helped him plan special Hispanic liturgies.

Richard's religious life was also renewed at student prayer meetings. Once a week Richard and his sophomore roommates, Mark Hans and A. T. Wall, joined a half-dozen other Yalies in a student's room, usually around 10:30 at night. They would sing the Beatles' "Here Comes the Sun" or the songs of Bob Dylan or Joan Baez, followed by prayers and discussions about leading a value-filled life at Yale.

Herrin was undergoing an intense religious experience. But then, inside himself, he also heard the first murmurings of religious doubt. Richard was studying the theories of evolution and began to wonder how they could be reconciled with the Biblical account of man's creation. But he avoided full-scale doubt, fearful of losing his solace and his friends in More House.

HERRIN'S RELIGIOUS DEVOTION had provided a substitute for an important failure: his seeming inability to build a close relationship with a woman. Herrin was not to meet Bonnie Garland until his senior year at Yale. In the years before, both in East Los Angeles and at Yale, his failure to make solid bonds with the opposite sex was an early clue to the rage that would later overwhelm him when he felt rejected.

During his freshman year, Herrin did not have a single date. "I didn't go out with any Yale women that year," Herrin later recalled. "I asked one person to go out but she said no, so I didn't try again." The whole subject of sexuality confused him, but Herrin kept it a private matter that he shared with no one. It was not a subject for easy banter with his entryway crowd.

Yale had been nominally coed since 1969, but the number of women was small. In Richard's class men outnumbered their female counterparts by almost five to one and Herrin's social contact with women was fleeting, relegated to mixers where he had little chance to mix. At these weekly dances and beer bashes, girls were bused in from nearby women's colleges including Smith, Sarah Lawrence and Vassar.

Author John Hersey, former Master of Pierson College at Yale, had called these mixers "pseudo dances" where young women were paraded around like "cattle for auction," then back to the Yalie's rooms, then "finally to the buses, just in time for departure." The girl was lucky, said Hersey, "if the fellow who may well have penetrated her vagina after intellectual foreplay had managed to catch her name."

These socially skilled Yalies bore little resemblance to Herrin. The thought of sex was painful for him and the reality elusive. To Herrin, the female sex was distant, unfathomable, and designed more to be worshipped than enjoyed. He idolized women as if they were a separate species, and spent more time fantasizing about relationships than cementing them.

Only drinking gave him the courage to attend the mixers and talk with the women. Herrin had joined a gregarious group of drinkers from Wright Hall. "On weekends I'd go out with the guys, usually to mixers or dances," Herrin remembered. "We might get drunk first or go to the mixer and drink beer all night. If there wasn't a mixer, we would buy orange juice and soda and vodka and just drink in our rooms—get plastered." He took no women back to his dorm room, and often failed to meet anyone at the mixers. When he did, he was often too drunk to make the evening count for more than occasional necking.

Richard had never had a real girlfriend. Not until after his seventeenth birthday did he have his first true date, a Christmas dinner-dance for the boys who worked after school in the Broadway Department Store in Los Angeles. When Richard walked his date to his old red Fury sedan, he was more confused than nervous. No one had ever told him how to act on a date. Do I dance? Do I mingle? Do I meet some of the other guys? The questions nagged at him all evening and reduced him to immobility.

In his last year in high school, Richard and his friend Sig Chávez did double date every other weekend, and on his desk at Yale Herrin proudly displayed snapshots of his Los Angeles dates. But despite the bravura, Herrin knew that most were friends, not girlfriends. The true romantic spot in his life was reserved for a girl he had never kissed, never even dated.

Helen de Romero had stimulated a fantasy in Herrin's mind. At high school in East Los Angeles Helen had been his friend, but she always declined Richard's bashful invitations for a date.

In Helen's high school yearbook, Herrin composed a long sentimental note: "I'll always be thinking of you no matter where I am. And if you happen to think of me once in a while, I'll appreciate it very much. It will be lonely at Yale, at least for the first few weeks. I think you'll be hearing from me. If I don't hear from you, I'll cry. . . . May God bless you, watch over you and take care of you. With more love than I can give. Richard Herrin."

Richard's ardent inscription surprised, even unnerved, Helen. "I was shocked by what he wrote," explained Helen, who is now married. "I was in his computer programming and biology classes at high school. We talked and occasionally walked to class together. We were friends, but that's all. We never even dated once."

The reality did not deter Herrin. From Yale, he wrote Helen frequent love letters composed from the core of his fantasy life. "I love you," he told her, asking that they establish a true relationship. To Herrin, Helen's answer to his letters was encouraging. "She wrote back and said she wasn't good enough for me, but that someday she would be," Herrin remembered. "I felt, 'Oh, wow. What's a little problem like that? I think she really likes me, and I really like her.' " Herrin wrote Helen several more times, swearing his love.

Helen denied ever encouraging Herrin. "I couldn't understand his romantic letters from Yale," she later commented. "He was a very sensitive person, real nice and very intelligent. But I suppose he misinterpreted my intentions. Finally I stopped writing him altogether. His letters were getting too serious."

Despite the rebuff of silence, Herrin persisted. From Europe, where he had gone on a bargain holiday during the spring break his freshman year, he sent Helen endearing postcards showing the great vistas of history so foreign to East Los Angeles. In Frankfurt, Germany, he bought a charm bracelet in a small curio shop. It was not elaborate, just five small porcelain tiles with depictions of German cities. It cost only ten Deutsche marks, less than five dollars, but it was Richard's talisman of love for Helen.

That summer Richard returned home to Los Angeles anxious to see Helen. He climbed into his Plymouth Fury and drove the familiar streets to Helen's home. "I went over to her house and spoke with her," Herrin recalled. "I was surprised when she told me she had shown my love letters to her family. She told me that they used to have a good laugh reading them. 'Rich you can't be serious, can you?' she said to me. 'You're doing this because you want to make people laugh, right?'

"I was hurt. Those were personal letters to the girl I loved, and she was telling me she had been showing them to her family, reading them and laughing. I was going to give her the bracelet, but the way she was treating me, I said 'No. This is not going to work out.' "

Helen's account of the meeting is almost diametrically opposed, like two versions of the same tale from Rashomon. Her recollection makes the incident considerably more innocuous. "My father was very strict," Helen explained. "I wasn't allowed to go out with boys in high school. The only reason Richard could sit on my porch when he came over that summer was because he was Richard Herrin and he was going to Yale.

"We sat on the steps and he told me about Yale and his trip to Europe. I thought he was trying to impress me. I never said anything about showing the letters to my parents. I would never have done that. They were too strict. And I didn't think the letters were a joke.

They were just too serious from someone I had never
dated. I kept them for several years and just threw them
out recently."

Whatever the true source of Herrin's hurt, he felt
rejected and made to look foolish. When he returned
home, he put the charm bracelet in a drawer and salved
his torn feelings by telling himself that someday he
would give the bracelet to his future wife, whoever she
might be.

WOMEN, SEX, AND RELIGION were a confused triad in
Herrin's mind. He was still a virgin and torn between
desire and the strong sense that sex and sin were closely
intertwined. In high school, he had confessed to the
priest after looking through a girlie magazine and
masturbating. Even in college, he felt guilty when he
sneaked a look at photos of nudes.

His first attempt at sex proved to be an abject failure.
During his European vacation, Richard found himself
outside a whorehouse four thousand miles from Yale, in
a dimly-lit alley in Frankfurt, Germany. The proposal
to go to Europe had been the idea of Heraldo Sanchez, a
fellow Yale student. The round-trip tickets from New
York to Luxembourg were cheaper than the ones to Los
Angeles—at least this was the rationale Herrin offered
his mother and stepfather. It had worked. The two
Yalies had gone from Luxembourg by train to Frankfurt, where they stayed with Heraldo's sister, making
side trips to other cities.

Now standing outside the whorehouse in Frankfurt,
Heraldo and Richard squinted at the bright neon sign
that flashed "Crazy Sex," then stepped through the
door. Richard felt queasy. He had avoided telling
Heraldo that he was still a virgin. Herrin suddenly felt
isolated in the midst of women in blouses that were half-
unbuttoned.

All he wanted was someone who was pretty. He decided to choose the blonde leaning against the far wall,
but as he started toward her, he felt as if he had stepped

onto a giant sponge. The blonde prostitute saved him. As soon as she saw that Richard wanted her, she moved toward him, leading him upstairs into a small room furnished only with the essentials of her trade. The fifty Deutsche marks the girl took from Richard were deposited in a box that hung on the door.

Richard realized that he was finally alone with a woman, but the anticipation of her nudity and the sex act stirred more anxiety than pleasure in him. The slim blonde German pushed Richard away when he reached up toward the buttons on her black chiffon blouse. "No, no. *I* do," she said.

The young girl stepped out of her shoes and took off her skirt and blouse, the only two pieces of clothing she wore. She did not look at Richard who was standing immobile at the door, as if looking back on the burning city of Sodom.

She seemed to slide onto the bed. When she embraced Richard, he felt numbly detached from her touch. For the next fifteen minutes, she fondled him but nothing happened. He tried, but could not achieve an erection; he could not, or would not, lose his virginity. Finally the young woman sat up on the edge of the bed and shrugged. "Gee, I guess it's not going to work," Richard mumbled apologetically.

A few minutes later he had joined Heraldo on the sidewalk under the opalescent glow of the "Crazy Sex" sign. "Hey, Rich, how was it? Pretty good time, huh?"

"Yeah, Heraldo," Richard lied. "That was something else."

"I felt like a failure," Richard recalled, "but I certainly wasn't going to tell anyone that I didn't succeed."

Herrin had failed sexually in Frankfurt, but he finally lost his virginity in his sophomore year at Yale in a brief, unsatisfying encounter. One weekend, Richard was alone in his room at Saybrook College when there was a knock on the door. It was a girl he had met at a mixer, a student from a nearby women's college. They had danced and later kissed the night they met, but Richard didn't consider her very attractive. Herrin

politely invited her into his room, where the two talked
for a while. Before long they were rolling on the floor,
kissing passionately.

They were soon in Herrin's bed, undressed, with
Richard on his way to his first sex act. His partner suggested Richard use a condom, but he shook his head. He
was not having a good time. He wasn't sure what to do
and it didn't last a long time, for which Herrin was
thankful. His loss of virginity turned out to be a dread-
ful affair which bathed his body with embarrassment
and guilt.

Immediately afterwards, the phone rang. Richard put
on his robe and rushed out of the bedroom. It was a call
from Los Angeles. His mother, his best friend Sigfrido,
his aunt, and an assortment of cousins had all gotten
together to phone him. Richard always enjoyed his relatives but this night he was overjoyed to talk with them.
He hung on the receiver for almost an hour and was still
talking when the girl emerged from the bedroom fully
dressed. Richard cradled the phone on his shoulder as
he waved good-bye to her.

His first sexual experience had left him confused.
What should he do with the sin? This was not a girlie
magazine, or even Frankfurt. Now he had done the real
thing. Even though the sex was without pleasure, he had
to go to church to expiate the guilt of the sin. Herrin was
too embarrassed to confess at More House where there
were no dark boxes of anonymity into which his soul
could crawl. Instead he sought a local church, where he
confessed to the priest in a traditional confessional.
Richard awaited a rigorous reprimand and penance for
having broken one of the Church's cardinal laws, but
the priest seemed uninterested in the sinfulness of his
act. "Do you realize the medical dangers?" was all he
asked.

Richard was dismayed. His Church had let him down.
He was being told that he was on his own, that there
were no longer any objective standards of sin. For the
first time in his life he was disillusioned about the power
of confession. There were other ways of expiating guilt,

Herrin thought. Other churches believed in the validity of confession without a priest or any other intermediary with God. Richard decided that from now on, whenever it was necessary, he would merely confess to himself.

RICHARD began his junior year at Yale with a new determination: He wanted a steady girlfriend. He was getting tired of the fleeting, infrequent matches at mixers, frustrated by his inability to deal with a woman for any length of time.

"Rich didn't really have any girlfriends," Paul Bardack recalled. "Women liked him, but saying they liked him was different from saying they liked him with a capital 'L'."

This year, Herrin resolved, was going to be different. "I'd like to have a girlfriend," he told his roommates on his arrival back at school. It wasn't a new theme on the campus, but it surprised them that Richard seemed to get his wish almost within the week.

Her name was Diane, and like Herrin she was a Yalie and a Catholic. Richard could hardly believe his luck. After they dated a few times, Herrin knew he had found his first serious girlfriend.

Sexual intercourse was not an uncommon occurrence at Yale where, as one student later wrote, "heterosexual couples who five years before went in for a long series of trips to first, second and third base now gaily screwed on the first date." But Richard and Diane were different. From the beginning Diane told Richard that she was determined to be a virgin until marriage and that they would only have a "college affair" without sex. With unpleasant sexual experiences still fresh in his mind, Richard agreed, feeling that he was sacrificing little.

Meanwhile, he was falling deeply in love with Diane. She seemed to like Richard, but their mutual friends noticed that while he placed all his energy into the relationship, Diane took it more casually.

"Rich would talk about her a great deal when he was

not with her," a mutual friend remembered, "but she would talk about politics when she was not with him. They were an incongruous pair at best. She was an elitist who believed in status and caste. Rich was a poor Chicano from an inner city. She had strong conservative views. Rich had no political views at all."

Richard didn't suspect there was any difficulty with the relationship until the beginning of the second semester, when Diane confided to Richard that she had a shy friend, a Yale man, who was inexperienced in dating. She wanted to help him adjust to women.

As the Yale Prom in April approached, Herrin was shaken by Diane's delay in accepting his invitation. The reason became clear when Diane's roommate pulled Richard aside. "Don't tell Diane I told you this," she said, "but she has been going out regularly with Fred, even pursuing him."

"I don't believe it," Richard said. "Not until I see it with my own eyes."

Flush with jealousy, Richard decided he had to find out for himself. He devised a plan to spy on Diane and Fred. One night he walked out of Saybrook College to Elm Street then around the corner, through the archway, into Davenport College's grassy courtyard. He walked up to the second floor of the Georgian brick Davenport Library, which was now empty, and climbed out onto a small outside balcony overlooking the courtyard. Across the small yard, about forty yards away, he could see into Diane's second-floor living room.

It was ten o'clock, dark, and Richard huddled in the shadows against the wall thirty feet above the ground, unmindful of the cool night air and oblivious of the height. He sat on the hard ledge for almost two hours before he saw Diane come into her room. His mind raced with anticipation as he strained to see. Yes, it was true. She was with Fred. He followed the two of them with his eyes as they walked to the couch and sat down. The lights in the room were low and the scene became clouded as the window frame partially obstructed his view. It was like watching a distant television screen without sound, leaving his imagination to wander about the room. Herrin sat on his stony perch for another two hours, peering forlornly into the low-lighted box that seemed a million miles away.

Herrin finally saw Fred get up and go to Diane's door. Richard now had a better view. He watched as his girlfriend, her back to him, draped her arms around Fred's neck and kissed him. That was the cue for Richard, who had now been waiting in the dark for nearly four hours. He climbed quickly off the balcony, raced downstairs and across the Davenport courtyard toward Diane's room. He had caught her cheating; now he had to confront her immediately.

Richard had not expected Fred still to be there when he arrived. He had no desire to speak with Fred; his problem was Diane. When he saw that Fred was still there, Herrin became unnerved. First, he excused himself to both of them, then invented a crude ruse to explain his sudden presence.

"Diane, may I have a glass?" he asked.

Diane gave him a glass which he carried to the hallway bathroom for a drink. But Fred was there when he returned. "Well, I think I'll get another drink of water," Richard said lamely, returning to the hallway bathroom. He repeated the strange ritual twice more before he saw that Fred had finally left.

Diane and he were now alone. Richard was livid with rage, feeling used and deceived. "You're supposed to be my girlfriend," he complained. "What are you doing running around with this guy behind my back?" They argued, Diane trying to explain that she had never intended their relationship to be exclusive. She thought that Richard understood that.

His answer made it clear that he did, but only superficially. In his fantasy, Diane had become his true, eternal love. Herrin left, hurt and angry, convinced that Diane had lied to him and betrayed his trust. She became the only person of whom Richard's friends ever heard him speak ill. In the jargon of his anger, Diane became simply, "Creepo." The incident was to become an obsession for Richard Herrin. The rejection was to stay with him throughout the years of his fatal romance with Bonnie Garland.

"There were times later that spring, after I got over it, I created scenes when I met Diane on campus," Herrin recalled. "I pretended to be angry just to harass her. It was kind of fighting back. I had been hurt and I was going to make life a little miserable for her now. After that, during my junior year, I didn't go out with another girl more than twice."

Herrin was distraught with jealousy and humiliation, but Diane was surprised at his reaction. She saw the relationship differently, as one that was less committed. "Richard was a nice guy. We liked to dance together, and I thought he had a good sense of humor in an understated way," Diane later remembered. "I dated him that year and broke up with him the same year. I wasn't living with Richard and I wasn't around him constantly. I never knew the relationship was so important to him."

THE JUNIOR YEAR had ended in a failed romance but Richard began his senior year with hope. He was still without a love to fill his fantasy, but perhaps he would have another chance his last year at Yale. His grades were still poor: That year he had received a D in German, and had to drop a physics course after passing his first semester with only a D. But he knew he would graduate, even if near the bottom of his class. And he had his friends at Saybrook, his MECHA, his guitar, and More House.

On an easy Friday night on the first of November, Richard and Paul Bardack climbed to the roof of the Saybrook tower, which soared over one hundred feet high, and began to sing their songs across the Yale campus. They had just been to a midnight showing of the film "Let It Be" and were moved to try a recreation of the Beatles' serenade scene on the roof of their Apple recording studio. At Richard's room they had picked up

Mary, his guitar, and his "Beatles' bible," a notebook that Richard had filled with copies of more than one hundred Beatles songs.

The two Yalies were not John Lennon and Paul Mc-Cartney, but now, in the early morning hours, Herrin with his guitar and gentle voice and Bardack with his recorder were casting their favorite Beatles tunes into the fall New Haven night as if they were. Below them students were roaming the streets seeking a start on the annual "Bladderball" festivities which were to begin the next morning.

The two Beatles fans had been singing for almost an hour when they noticed that they had company. Classmate Steve Cooperman and two girls whom they didn't recognize had joined them on the roof and were singing along. Richard noticed that the tall red-haired girl had an incredible voice, a light but strong soprano that lifted into the air. Her hair was tied behind her head, and even in the dim light her soft, round face seemed to light up with expression. At the final flourishing chords the five Yalies burst into laughter at their spontaneous little concert.

"I'd like you to meet a couple of freshman friends of mine." Cooperman was making the introductions. "This is Kit." Then turning to the redhead, Cooperman introduced her to the two seniors.

"Paul. Richard. This is Bonnie Garland."

CHAPTER THREE

A Yale Romance

BONNIE JOAN GARLAND had come to Yale from a background as different from Richard Herrin's as one could imagine. Bonnie's father was a Yale graduate and a well-known attorney who had spent years practicing in South America. Bonnie had lived in Brazil for twelve years, spoke Spanish and Portuguese, and had traveled to Paris and Athens.

She had just graduated from Madeira, a preparatory school for women noted not only for the pedigree of its student body, but also for its high academic standards. The school was set on a four-hundred acre forested estate overlooking the Potomac River in Virginia. It had a swimming pool, gymnasium, soccer field, hockey field, eight tennis courts, a stable of twenty-five horses and one of the largest indoor riding rings in the United States. Two thirds of the more than three hundred girls who came from thirty different states and twenty foreign countries boarded at the school.

They were the daughters of successful professionals,

politicians, diplomats, and entrepreneurs. In Bonnie's class were B. J. Murchison, whose family owned the Dallas Cowboys football team; Eleanor MacGregor, whose father was head of the Committee to Reelect President Nixon; and Susan Saltonstall, a descendant of the Saltonstalls, early New England settlers. Madeira was the alma mater of such prominent women as *Washington Post* owner Katharine Graham. Jean Harris, lover and murderer of the Scarsdale diet doctor, was later to become Madeira's headmistress.

Like other prep schools, Madeira was known to produce its quotient of young snobs whose pretentiousness was carried as a badge of social honor. But despite her life of advantage, Bonnie was unspoiled, a fresh, good-natured, free spirited and uncomplicated young woman of seventeen who abhorred the cliquishness that affected many of her preppy classmates.

She came to Yale with much the same sexual naiveté as Richard Herrin. Bonnie was a virgin. She had never even had a regular boyfriend; at Madeira boys were something that happened on weekends. Bused in for Saturday night dances from nearby prep schools, they were watched attentively by cautious Madeira administrators. While most adolescent girls attended coed schools and had already adjusted to boys, Bonnie was living with other girls twenty-four hours a day.

Dating was not allowed until the junior and senior years at Madeira, and then only on Friday and Saturday nights, after the girls had introduced their dates to the housemother. But Bonnie was unconcerned with the strict dating regulations. She was more interested in school, her voice lessons, sports, and having a good time with her classmates than in spending most of Saturday afternoon preening herself for the evening dance.

In those turbulent times of the early 1970's, when even girls from prominent families were rebelling against authority, Bonnie Garland was level-headed. She was independent—it had been her idea to stay at Madeira when her family moved to Scarsdale in 1971—but she was responsible. She laughed with her classmates as they planned a midnight pot party, but didn't attend. She was liberal but not revolutionary. At Madeira that meant that she supported George McGovern for President and wore blue jeans.

One of her Madeira classmates, Lisa Huxley, who went on to Yale with Bonnie and later returned to Madeira as a teacher, remembered Bonnie as a near-paradigm. "Bonnie never smoked and never used any kind of drugs, even though there were a lot of people at Madeira at the time who did," Lisa recalled. "She was a very straight-living kind of person, but not prudish."

Bonnie was not a neurotic product of her difficult era. She never seemed to complain, solved her own problems, and even had time for those of others. "Bonnie was never down in the dumps like a lot of us," Susan Brooks, another Madeira classmate, later explained. "She could stand up to the stress at Madeira. At the time, I was in a bad state, depressed a lot. But Bonnie always seemed to be on target. She helped me out with my school work and with my attitude toward life. She was a really pure person."

Her classmates and her teachers remembered Bonnie as a superior student. Retired Madeira headmistress Barbara Keyser, who preceded Jean Harris in that post, considered Bonnie a "serious" student. "I don't mean that she didn't have fun, but she wouldn't let her work go down the drain just to play around," Ms. Keyser recollected in her Long Island home. She remembered Bonnie as "a clean cut girl, with no pretensions about her," who would sometimes drop into her office in the evening just to chat.

Her friends were struck by Bonnie's sense of humor, which could sometimes be zany and uninhibited. One night at Madeira she helped string toilet seats around the grounds in prankish preparation for Father's Day. "Baloooch!" and "Booga Booga" were the war whoops that Bonnie and friends shouted to each other across the spacious school grounds.

Music was Bonnie's first love. She played the guitar and the piano, had been playing the flute since she was seven, and with near-perfect pitch, could cover almost three octaves with her rich soprano. Her voice was so exceptional that her friends were convinced she would be chosen by the WUMS, the school's leading singing group. Instead, she was refused membership because it was feared that her talent would overwhelm the others. With good humor, Bonnie joined the AGONIES, a group of tone-deaf students who regaled the school with satirical ditties.

Bonnie did not excel in one area: neatness. "Bonnie was one of the messiest people I have ever met," said Lisa Huxley, who was her roommate in their sophomore year. "I was the neatnik; her part of the room was like a pigsty. She could never find anything, and at the end of the year, we found her socks and toothbrushes which had been stuffed away under other things."

Bonnie was not unattractive. She was tall and red-haired with a pleasant face, clear, light-complected skin, and a good smile. Her personality was vibrant. But she was plump, and her general appearance had not yet blended into that of a sophisticated young woman. She spent little time on her clothes or her looks, content to be a carefree seventeen-year-old with other things on her mind.

In the yearbook for the class of '74, each senior designed her own page, filling the space with musings about love, revolution, life, and nonsense. Most of the ninety-six seniors chose to use photographs of themselves in pants, mostly blue jeans, almost always outside, swinging on ropes, smiling in a field of daisies.

Bonnie chose three photos for her page, the largest a black-and-white of her looking away from the camera, gazing somewhere far beyond the viewer's field of vision. She is wearing a casual shirt, her hands tucked partially into the tight front pockets of her baggy denims, thumbs resting outside. There is a simple grandeur to the pose. Above the picture Bonnie had borrowed lines from Mark Twain:

When I'm playful I use the mervolians of longitude

and the parallels of latitude for a seine, and drag the Atlantic Ocean for whales. I scratch my head with the lightning and purr myself to sleep with the thunder.

To the left, bleeding off the corner, is a photo of a shadow figure, its arms stretched out as if to fly. Below that are words from Thomas Carlyle:

See deep enough and you see musically; the heart of nature being everywhere music, if you can only reach it.

Almost as a postscript there is a small picture of baby Bonnie, bent over, peering and almost disappearing into a doll carriage. She signed off the page with a *"BOOGA BOOGA,"* a last hurrah to four years of fruitful adolescence.

THAT SEPTEMBER, 1974, Bonnie Garland moved from Virginia to New Haven, from Madeira to Yale. She had applied to Radcliffe, Oberlin, Cornell, and Yale, and had been accepted at all except Radcliffe. She chose her father's alma mater, Yale, where she would major in music, expecting to make "voice" her life's work.

At Yale she moved into the same freshman dormitory Richard Herrin had lived in three years before. Wright Hall, which had since become coed, was directly across High Street from Herrin's new residence, Saybrook College.

Bonnie had been at Yale almost two months when, after midnight on the night of November 1, Steve Cooperman took her and a fellow freshman Kit to the top of the Saybrook tower where Richard Herrin and Paul Bardack were serenading the quiet campus with Beatles songs. When Kit decided she wanted to go back to Wright Hall, Cooperman offered to walk her home. The other three Yalies continued to sing, Richard turning more and more frequently toward Bonnie Garland

and moving closer to her as he played.

Bonnie returned his careful glances, smiling as she harmonized with her strong soprano. Paul Bardack soon left. "Even in the dark," he recalled, "you could almost see the sparks flying between them."

It was almost 2:30 in the morning when Richard, captivated by the young redhead, asked Bonnie if she would help him carry his song books back to his room in Saybrook. There was no single trait that attracted Herrin to Bonnie. It was, as he later said, "an everything-together quality." He liked her long straight red hair, tied back behind her neck, the blue jeans and brown T-shirt, the magical voice, the way she moved. He was even drawn by her enthusiasm for the Beatles.

"Physically, she was attractive to begin with," Herrin explained. "And as I got talking to her, everything she was saying made me like her more and more. It was everything, the talk, the body language, the gestures, the closeness."

Perhaps most exciting to Herrin was that Bonnie seemed to like him immediately. "It had never happened to me before—having someone like that being attracted to me and have it expressed almost instantaneously, within a few hours of our having met," Herrin later recalled about their meeting. "I knew that night that it was a new phase of my life. To have someone like this. It was a highlight, a plateau."

Bonnie was not anxious to leave Herrin's room. She looked about the large spartan quarters, which included a living room with a fireplace that Richard and roommate Chuck Cervantes used only to burn old newspapers, and a bedroom for each of them. She settled on a musty, coffee-colored couch, and sat there with Richard as they talked.

Richard offered Bonnie a drink of his only liquor, a near-empty bottle of Kahlua, from which he filled two Yale embossed shot glasses. It was the kind of no-frills entertainment that Richard enjoyed. Bonnie seemed equally at home with the casual style. Each new bit of information about Bonnie confirmed Richard's first impressions. As they talked, he felt strangely without self-consciousness, unworried about saying or doing the right thing and free of the doubts which plagued him with most women.

Bonnie was relaxed, shy but not nervous, and interested in *him*. She asked about East Los Angeles, about his family and his high school, and he in turn asked about her. Herrin was impressed by Bonnie's background, yet he saw no pretension or stand-offishness in her, none of the aloof self-confidence of the "snobs" he had learned to avoid at Yale. She seemed as uncomplicated as he considered himself to be.

They were both physically imposing. Bonnie was only four inches shorter than Herrin's six feet. Richard had played football in high school and Bonnie was considered a good athlete. Sometime during their second shot of Kahlua, Bonnie taught Richard how to thumb wrestle. With their hands locked together, they laughed as they wagged their thumbs in the air searching for a way to pin the opponent's finger. Richard would remember it as the first time he touched Bonnie Garland. Soon they were wrestling more exuberantly, a coed college romp on the floor in a playful combat that ended in a kiss.

The hours raced by almost unnoticed. The two were still talking and embracing when dawn began to brighten the Saybrook courtyard. Though they hadn't slept, Bonnie and Richard were both filled with the energy that comes from unexpected discovery. They weren't at all tired; nor could they afford to be. It was Bladderball Day, and though it was not yet 6:30 A.M., preparations were already under way. Bonnie remembered that she had promised to help make banners. "And I've gotta go help the guys set up the apparatus," Richard told her.

Bladderball Day had become one of Richard Herrin's favorites. Students began drinking at breakfast and by eleven, when the game officially began, many of them could barely walk. When the campus police finally closed the gates to the Old Campus courtyard and dropped the giant five-foot ball from the top of Phelps Gate into the middle of the throng, all hell broke loose. The giant sphere never touched the ground as it moved from one end of the grassy quadrangle to the other, born aloft by hundreds of flailing hands until finally grunted over one of the gates. There the game was supposed to end but it rarely did. The havoc spilled out after it, policemen being tackled before they could reach the ball to puncture it.

During his freshman year Richard had raced with the crowd as it streamed down Chapel Street, blocking traffic on the New Haven thoroughfare and bouncing the ball from the hoods of cars to windshields to roofs. Another year he had chased through the streets to help deposit the ball on Yale President Kingman Brewster's front yard. It was a few hours of craziness that Herrin loved. It was a time when even the studious "weanies" came out of their library cubicles.

This year Richard was one of the organizers of a Saybrook scheme to steal the bladderball. Richard enjoyed his senior status in the enterprise. He and his friends had constructed a platform of wood which they hoped to suspend across High Street between Wright Hall and the roof of Saybrook tower. With a complicated set of ropes and pulleys the platform would be lowered to a height just above the heads and hands of the crowd. The ball would then be shoved onto the platform by Saybrook team members, who would bring it into the secured college courtyard and quickly paint it with bright, victorious SAYBROOK.

It mattered little that these schemes never succeeded. The joy was in the drama of the plot. The previous year a similar Saybrook plan failed because the students designated to leap out of the bushes and attach a rope to the ball were, at the crucial moment, flat on their backs in the bushes, stoned.

Richard took his job more seriously. At seven that morning he was on the roof helping with the platform preparations when he heard yelling from the street below. Looking over the side he saw a Saybrook classmate arguing with two Branford College students trying to sabotage the ropes. A few other Yalies were also peering down at the confrontation, among them Bonnie Garland, who had been helping with the banners. When Richard saw her, he sensed a rare opportunity.

"I gotta go help Dave," said Richard, speaking loud enough for Bonnie to hear. He raced down the stairs and out to the street. "Hey, Dave, what seems to be the problem?" he asked in an uncharacteristically assertive tone. He could feel Bonnie's eyes riveted on him. "Hey, you guys," he growled, turning to the Branford students, "this is none of your business. Would you kindly leave the rope alone? This doesn't have anything to do with you."

Richard had an intimidating physique, but never before had he had an intimidating manner. He knew where this surge of confidence had come from: Bonnie Garland. His heroics were for her. As he saved the Saybrook platform plan, Richard felt puffed up with a sense of himself as a senior, someone who knew the campus, who could assert himself.

It was the end of a special night for Richard Herrin. In it he felt "the potential," as he later recalled, "for something I didn't think I'd ever had before. Right off the bat: Here is someone who is really, really different—and she likes me."

Richard saw Bonnie the next day at dinner, and again the day after that. He was still reticent about revealing his feelings to her, but he managed to find excuses to visit her room. On several occasions, Herrin came to Wright Hall in his role of More House Pastoral Associate ostensibly to visit a roommate of Bonnie's who was a Catholic. Each time he stayed to talk with Bonnie. That Saturday they went to a mixer together and the next week he visited her room without excuses and invited her to the Yale-Princeton football game.

Bonnie Joan Garland was as taken with Herrin as he with her. He was tall and muscular, had a good sense of humor, loved music, was easy-going in a complicated and competitive environment, and was always considerate of her. She accepted his invitation.

IT WAS A beautiful Saturday afternoon,—November 16, 1974,—two weeks after their first meeting. Over twenty-nine thousand fans were in Yale Bowl for the sixtieth anniversary of the opening of the giant stadium, watching an undefeated Yale team roll past Princeton for its eighth straight victory of the season.

Bonnie had invited Richard to meet her father and brother who had come up from Scarsdale to see the game. Paul Garland and Patrick sat in the alumni section of the stadium, while Bonnie and Richard sat with the students. After the game Richard walked over to Saybrook to change into a pair of corduroy slacks, a clean shirt, a pullover sweater, and his good pair of shoes. It was extraordinarily decent garb for Richard. Today merited special attention because Richard was anxious to make a proper impression on Paul Garland.

Bonnie's father and brother Patrick arrived at her room in Wright Hall just after Richard. They brought Bonnie a gift of pomegranates, her favorite fruit, and were introduced to Richard. Patrick was a lanky sophomore at Scarsdale High School. His father was a solid-looking man, slightly shorter than Richard. At forty-four Paul Garland was both young and successful, with a thriving law practice that at times had employed some fifty lawyers.

There should have been common ground between the elder Garland and Richard Herrin. Paul Garland had gone to Yale on a scholarship as did Richard Herrin; both had worked their way through Yale, Garland as a dishwasher and in the library, while Herrin cleaned tables in the freshman dining hall and worked in the Peabody Museum; Herrin and Garland lived in Saybrook; both spoke Spanish and Garland had written a thesis on the intellectual history of the Spanish-speaking world from which Herrin took his roots. Like Herrin,

Paul Garland had also been very religious; at one point he considered becoming a Protestant minister.

But as Richard later told friends, the evening was a near disaster. He immediately sensed "a cold barrier" between himself and Bonnie's father. Conversation between Paul Garland and Bonnie's new boyfriend was strained as the four went off to eat at a pizza parlor just a few blocks from the Old Campus. They sat at the counter and ate, then went to the local Baskin & Robbins for ice cream. Richard sized up the selection of flavors and ordered two exotic scoops, one pumpkin, the other licorice, placing the orange ice cream on top of the black one.

"Why did you order pumpkin and licorice ice cream?" Bonnie later chided him. Bonnie knew that Richard had failed to make a good impression on her father and felt embarrassed for him. "What's wrong with something simple like chocolate chip?" She also explained that he had addressed her father incorrectly. "My father is a Brazilian lawyer, Richard. You should have called him 'Dr.' That's what they call attorneys in Brazil, not 'Mr.' "

Paul Garland was not impressed with Richard Herrin. As he later explained, he found the Yale senior slovenly in appearance and manners, difficult to talk to, and physically unattractive. Whatever Bonnie Garland's father and her boyfriend may have had in common, it was obvious that they differed in respects more fundamental than age. Their academic records were polar opposites. While they both may have come to Yale on scholarships, Paul Garland had remained a scholar while Richard Herrin always hovered near failure.

In his freshman year, in 1949, Paul Griffith ("Griff") Garland was a "scholar of the second rank"; his sophomore and junior years, "scholar of the first rank" and member of Phi Beta Kappa. He graduated *summa cum laude*, second in his class, and went on to Harvard Law School. Richard Herrin would receive only two A's during his entire Yale career, one in history of science and the other in geology. But he had failed several courses, and in his senior year liked to tell his friends that he not only had the lowest room number in Saybrook, but also had the lowest grade point average.

Paul Garland's interest in Hispanic culture had sprung from high school years spent in Miami and Denver, where he first saw the results of racial segregation and adopted a liberal attitude towards civil rights. For years afterwards, Garland would be a member of the American Civil Liberties Union. At Yale, Garland was active politically and became chairman of the Liberal Party, head of the Saybrook College Council and president of the prestigious Yale Political Union. He even played softball for Saybrook.

Paul Garland had always been a mover, and his Yale biography is as full of ambition and accomplishment as Richard Herrin's is lean. Herrin was not a mover or a shaker. He was only in love with Paul Garland's daughter.

THE LOVE AFFAIR of Bonnie and Richard moved quickly. One day during the week after the Yale-Princeton game Bonnie Garland stayed the night with Richard Herrin in his room at Saybrook, then stayed the next night, and the next. "And one day," a friend remembered, "they simply told me that from now on I could find Bonnie at Rich's place."

Less than three weeks after Richard and Bonnie met, room 912 in Saybrook had an *ex officio* third roommate: Bonnie Garland. Coming from an all-girls dormitory at an all-girls school, Bonnie was suddenly sharing a bed with a man who, despite his brave attempts at conquering his inhibitions, was making a leap from the dark Catholic confessional into what had once been a sure arena of sin.

The transition was made easier by a pliant environment in which no eyebrows were raised, at a university which had stopped passing judgment on individual sexual morality. The university as a surrogate parent, *in loco parentis*, was a thing of the past.

That Bonnie Garland had come to Yale at a time of sexual openness was particularly propitious for Richard Herrin. Coming from the restricted environment of Madeira at age seventeen with almost no experience with men, she was an innocent. Within months after arriving at Yale, she had moved into Herrin's room and bed, and had been transformed almost overnight from a child into a modern approximation of a married woman. It was an arrangement that was only possible in the sexual atmosphere of a contemporary college where students who wanted to share a bed with each other faced no institutional restraints.

"I've never been to Sweden," remarked one student, "but from what I've heard about that country, I'd say it was kind of a Swedish attitude at Yale. Very casual. If you were in the shower and your next-door neighbor was of the opposite sex and he or she needed to take a shower real fast, then he or she would just join you. No sweat."

It was Bonnie Garland's innocence that made her attractive to Richard Herrin. He had lived at Yale long enough to appreciate its social and sexual complexities though he had so far been defeated by them. He was a romantic and an idealist, not a game-player. And in Bonnie Garland he had finally found someone with whom to share that romanticism, someone as young in spirit and inexperienced in sex as he was. Bonnie was a miraculous gift for Herrin, a woman who did not care about his prior rejections and who totally accepted him as he was.

Their attraction was not just chemical: It seemed to make sense at the time. Bonnie felt that she was unattractive, and Richard's attention to her was flattering and reassuring. "Bonnie had big bones and was filled out all over," Herrin later commented on Bonnie's fears about her looks. "I always told her that she wasn't bad looking, but she insisted she was unattractive because of her shape. She was concerned about her weight, but she wasn't into conscious dieting. She would drink diet soda to save calories, then go out for a pizza."

Both Richard and Bonnie had come from hard-working families, but each saw in the other an opportunity to relax, to keep out the rigorous academic demands of Yale. They idled away hour after hour together as if there were no other world and no other needs. They stayed up late together and got up late together, almost oblivious of their studies.

"They spent a fair amount of time in that bedroom that year," remembered Richard's roommate Chuck Cervantes, "I would come out for class at nine in the morning and they'd be there; I'd come back in the early afternoon and they would still be there. And then at two o'clock they would come bolting out and go running off."

Bonnie and Richard were so obsessed with one another that they could not stay apart. What little studying they did was done together. They eschewed the library except when they had no choice because an assigned book was on the closed "Reserved" shelf. In his Saybrook room, Richard would sit at his desk and Bonnie would be on the bed, or vice versa. The room was small and they were never more than a few feet apart. They could concentrate on their books for only half an hour, or an hour at most. Time for a break, Richard would announce, walking across the room and hugging her.

The room was a shambles after their wrestling matches, pillow fights, and shaving cream battles. "It looked like World War III," recalled a friend. Bonnie had fallen into Richard's unproductive life style. She had her own playful side, and now it became accentuated, pushing her Puritan sense of work and study into the background. Living with Herrin, Bonnie the serious student became Bonnie the casual student, willing to just get by rather than achieve.

"Bonnie was bright, and if not for that brightness, she would have had even more difficulty in her studies," commented Chuck Cervantes. "For Rich it was a struggle to be a student at Yale. Bonnie was more of a natural student, but she was spending enormous amounts of time with Rich and not producing as far as school went." Cervantes was perhaps the first to see the flaw in their romance. "They enjoyed lounging around together but they didn't really give each other much strength."

For Herrin, the relationship with Bonnie was becoming life itself, but it was also crippling his last opportunity to excel. "Rich was not dedicated to school anyway, and Bonnie gave him the perfect reason not to work," said Cervantes.

Studies were the least concern to Richard Herrin who felt as if he were soaring "on cloud nine." Bonnie was making him happier than he had ever been. "I hope you don't mind my pawing at you all the time," he told her with an embrace, "but I just can't keep my hands off you."

But they were a unique couple for a sexually active campus. As intimate as Bonnie and Richard seemed, they had never engaged in intercourse. They took this as a confirmation of their love. If they could sleep together in the same bed without making love, it was a sign that their affection was true. Bonnie was a virgin and wanted to wait until she understood how contraception worked. Richard didn't push, for as he later revealed, he would have been "in deep trouble if it was demanded of me right off." He feared that an attack of impotence would jeopardize Bonnie's love for him.

The arrangement was perfect for Herrin, who had always felt sex to be tinged with guilt. Bonnie's love and acceptance were like spiritual cleansing agents. And the longer he waited to have sex with Bonnie, the surer would be the expiation of the sin when it finally took place.

Their sexless cohabitation followed a pattern all its own. Every night they climbed into bed together, kissed, embraced, and fondled each other, carefully avoiding intercourse. They both wore pajama bottoms as a precaution, like cotton contraceptives that would block an unintended erection or a touch of genitalia during the night. It was their way to both ward off pregnancy and to secure their love against the emotional hazards of adult sex.

They were like children playing husband and wife, naive, pure, totally absorbed by the intensity of their relationship, seeking intimacy without responsibility. The two young lovers lived in a world of rare romanticism, somewhere between the supposed puritanism of their parent's generation and the so-called prurience of their own.

Bonnie and Richard were obsessed with their love. As Paul Bardack recalled, "Bonnie-and-Rich was one word."

RICHARD WAS SUCCEEDING with Bonnie, but her parents offered Herrin a sterner test. A few months after they met, Richard boarded a bus to travel the sixty miles to the Garland home in Scarsdale where Bonnie had invited him to spend spring vacation.

The Garlands' world was unlike any he had known. Scarsdale was neat, spacious, clean, and even as winter closed, green. There were few ways of comparing it to his Lincoln Heights neighborhood without risking understatement. The houses were bigger and set farther apart. There was no garbage on the streets, no graffiti on the walls. There were sixteen thousand fewer people in Scarsdale than in his Los Angeles neighborhood, but twice as much land area. Over half of Scarsdale's adult population had completed four years of college; only a quarter of Lincoln Heights' adults finished high school.

In Lincoln Heights the median family income was $7,258 a year; in Scarsdale it was $33,886. Scarsdale had a downtown with the look of an English village. The town boasted seventeen schools, nineteen public tennis courts, nine paddle tennis courts, five golf, tennis, and riding clubs, and a church for every 908 residents. On a slight ridge in the wooded Fox Meadow section of town, the Garlands' home was an image of the elegance that surrounded it, dwarfing anything that Richard Herrin had ever lived in.

At the Garland house, Richard was given the first floor study to use as his bedroom. The walls were lined with bookshelves which he scanned, noticing that Paul Garland had written some of the books. He was impressed, but after glancing at their introductions he went no further. They were about Brazilian business and law, a subject in which he had no interest. It was a normal reaction for Herrin. Though seemingly accepting of others and their lifestyles, he never expended much effort at understanding them, seldom moving beyond his own horizons.

Conversation between Herrin and Bonnie's parents was strained that week. "It was really hard for me to talk to Mr. Garland," Herrin later recalled. "He didn't seem the least bit interested in anything I had to say. When I mentioned that a mariachi album he had included songs that my little group did, I got no response whatsoever. I was trying to initiate a conversation, something that was a positive indication that I was doing something good, involved in music. Bonnie's a singer. Well, I'm a musician, too, and that is what *my* group does. I don't remember even a word in response to that."

The Garlands were as yet unaware that Richard Herrin was anything more than Bonnie's friend. They had no idea that Bonnie had moved into Richard's room at Saybrook, or that the two were in love. They politely asked Richard about his family and about Los Angeles. But it was obvious that Paul Garland did not like Herrin, who struck the lawyer as humorless, unmotivated, and self-centered.

Nor did Richard make much of an impression on Joan Garland. She had raised four children, was a social worker, and had recently received a masters degree in human genetics from Sarah Lawrence College. There might have been common ground on which Mrs. Garland could meet her daughter's boyfriend. Like Herrin, she had experienced a youth without material comfort. Her father was an apartment-house superintendent and her aunt had helped pay her way through

Mount Holyoke College. While dating Paul Garland, Joan Bruder had visited Yale on weekends, and as a Catholic had worshipped at St. Thomas More Church, one of the centers of Richard Herrin's life at Yale.

But Herrin did little to ingratiate himself with the Garlands. When asked if he wanted to go to church with them that Sunday, he declined. They spoke briefly about Joan Garland's collection of geodes, quartz-like rock formations, but Herrin didn't think it important to tell her of his ambitions to compile a Spanish-English geological dictionary. The Garlands thought their daughter's new friend was sloppy, an opinion that was confirmed when Herrin came to the dinner table wearing a Primo Beer T-shirt.

Yet even as he alienated himself from Bonnie's parents, Richard drew closer to Bonnie and she to him during those days at the Garland house. For four months they had slept together with self-discipline, fearful of "rushing" into intercourse.

The first night at the Garland home, Richard and Bonnie finally consummated their love. They went up to her large upstairs bedroom. With the door closed, their privacy was complete and they nudged closer to one another as the night wore on, talking and watching television from Bonnie's bed.

Richard gave little thought to the propriety of making love to Bonnie in her parents' home. Had her parents known about it, it certainly would have resulted in Herrin's expulsion. But if the barriers which he felt between himself and the Garlands were high, so the walls of Bonnie's bedroom were thick and protective. It didn't feel like the act of rebellion that it was—making love to the daughter under the very noses of her parents. It felt like the right moment to sexually complete their four-month-old romance.

"It was a beautiful thing," Richard later recalled. "There was no pressure at all. We had a few months to get to know each other intimately and it was the natural next phase in the relationship. It was good that we waited. I felt secure in the relationship without the intercourse. I was more able to handle it and I didn't feel pressed to perform sexually.''

Once back at Yale, their union took on another dimension, mature sex. For the first time in his life, the chasm between Herrin's view of womanhood as a romantic ideal and woman as a sexual being had been joined. The stain of sex that had once driven him to confession was gone, or at least pushed back into the recesses of his mind. Bonnie was now both his ideal and his sex partner, and the fusing of the two made it possible for him to perform better sexually and to enjoy it more than he had ever hoped.

''We would have sex a maximum of twice in one day,'' Herrin later told a psychiatrist. ''Or we could have sex once a day for three days, then nothing for four days. We used to spend hours cuddling together in bed that year. There were days when we spent the entire day in the room and only came out for a meal.'' As far as Herrin was concerned, the act of intercourse that had once filled him with such anxiety had sealed his bond with Bonnie. It was now as if they were married.

THAT APRIL Bonnie called her mother from Yale with unexpected news. She was flunking two courses. Richard was also flunking two courses and was not going to be able to finish his senior thesis. Bonnie proposed staying in New Haven for summer school and sharing an apartment with Herrin. It all came rolling out in a single conversation, a jumble of quick shocks that made it clear that Richard Herrin was not just a casual acquaintance in the Garlands' daughter's life. ''She had just turned eighteen,'' Joan Garland later explained. ''I was thunderstruck.''

Joan Garland spoke to Herrin on the phone and carefully explained that he was a senior and that his degree wasn't in peril even though he was flunking two courses. But Bonnie was only a freshman and her whole career at Yale was in jeopardy. Herrin answered glibly,

"I've seen these things before and they always work out." Mrs. Garland reminded him that she was older and understood that things do not always work out. The Garlands' opinion of Herrin began to turn to dislike that day.

For the first time in her life, Bonnie was in academic trouble. At the end of her first semester at Yale, fresh from a solid Madeira preparation, Bonnie had received one A, two B's and one C. Now, in her second semester, she was flunking two courses and was far behind in the others. She was on her way to a disastrous record and the reason seemed clear: Richard Herrin. The Garlands rejected her proposal to stay with Herrin that summer, anxious for the day that he would be off to graduate school in Texas and out of their daughter's life.

But Richard Herrin was contemplating action that would postpone his departure from Yale. Before he became seriously involved with Bonnie, he had been accepted at Texas Christian University to study for a master's in geology. But he now had a plan to avoid going there. That spring of 1975, Herrin decided that he would drop out for the one-year leave of absence allowed by Yale, then use an additional six months to complete his degree. That would give him a full year and a half to remain in New Haven with Bonnie.

As Richard explained his drop-out plan to Bonnie, he was faced with the first strain in their relationship. "How easy do you think it will be to get into graduate school after you quit Yale?" Bonnie asked. "I think it will screw up your future. Quitting won't look very good on your record."

There was a hint that their seemingly self-sufficient universe was indeed subject to outside constraint. Bonnie's objection unnerved Herrin, not because he disagreed with her, but because of its implication that they would no longer be together.

"What about our future?" he asked, fearing the question even as he uttered it. "Now that I'm going off to Texas, do we keep it together? Do we stay together?"

Bonnie expressed the fear that the relationship had quit moving forward. "The question of our future hung over us for a while," Herrin recalled.

Up to this point they had had no arguments or differing perception. "We never fight," Richard boasted to friends. Beyond telling him that he shouldn't come to her concerts because it made her nervous, or remonstrating him that it was dumb to use an umbrella in the snow, theirs appeared to be a seamless union.

But did Bonnie now have doubts? Richard wondered.

"At this point, I think she was probably concerned about me as a person," Herrin later admitted. "I think she had already begun to see some flaws in me. Since she subscribed to *Psychology Today*, I figured she knew a lot about psychology. I think she was concerned about my ability to grow."

Herrin's worry about the relationship suffered through two more trials that spring, both prompted by fears that Bonnie might be interested in exploring other men. One day Bonnie suddenly approached Richard to tell him that a male freshman friend had asked her to a performance at the Yale Repertory Theater.

"I'd like to go with him," Bonnie said. "He knows that we're going out together. Is it okay?"

"Sure." Richard gave his immediate consent. Bonnie had made it sound harmless enough.

But as much as he acted with liberated unconcern, Herrin became nervous the night of the play. Just as he had done with Diane, Richard decided he had to see with his own eyes. Taking a book along so that he could feign an errand to the library in case he was seen, he left his room at Saybrook and planted himself in the shadows of High Street. There he would await Bonnie and her date's return from the Yale Repertory Theater. From his vantage point, he could see if Bonnie had told him the truth.

When Richard spotted them, Bonnie and the young man were engrossed in conversation. But Richard was watching for a telltale sign of betrayal. Were they holding hands? When he saw that they weren't he felt a sudden rush of relief. For him, holding hands, the simplest sign of affection, was like a scale model of all intimacy. It was if there were an unbroken line between his thumb wrestling with Bonnie and their first sexual intercourse. For Bonnie to have made physical contact with someone else, Herrin believed, would have demeaned the importance of their sexual union.

Richard went back to his room in good spirits. Bonnie had passed a crucial test. "I never told Bonnie what I did that night," Herrin later revealed.

The second test did shake Herrin's nerve, precipitating a near crisis of confidence. In the spring of 1975, the day after they returned from Scarsdale and their sexual consummation, Bonnie was invited to a party without Herrin. Richard later told the story of that trying incident to a psychiatrist.

"Bonnie came to my room when the party was over and told me she hadn't come straight there because she was too embarrassed for the host. He had escorted her to her dorm at Wright Hall, then embraced and kissed her. She said that it was a kiss of passion on *his* part. After he left her, she waited a few minutes and then crossed the street to my room.

"I started to get dressed to go talk to the guy about what happened. But Bonnie convinced me not to go. I felt very angry and hurt. I asked Bonnie if I would have to go through with her what I went through the year before with Diane. Bonnie said I shouldn't relate anything about us to the relationship with Diane. She was sorry she had hurt me."

It took weeks of long conversations before Herrin decided that he could go off to Texas and still keep the future intact. Together he and Bonnie decided that the relationship could and would continue as strong as ever.

ON MAY 19, Yale played host to hundreds of visiting parents and dignitaries for the graduation ceremonies of the Class of '75. Isaac Stern, concert violinist, was awarded an honorary Doctor of Music degree; novelist

Eudora Welty, a Doctor of Letters; Sidney Dillon Ripley, secretary of the Smithsonian Institution, Thomas Watson, chairman of IBM, and Vernon Jordan, National Urban League director, all became Doctors of Law. Sitting quietly and proudly in the crowd was Linda Ugarte, who had traveled for three days from Los Angeles by bus to be there for her son's graduation.

But for Richard Herrin the ceremony wasn't the cap to his Yale career. He was there with his classmates, but he didn't receive his diploma. Forty-two percent of the class of '75 graduated with honors that May; Richard Herrin would have to go to summer school in order to earn his degree.

Bonnie Garland flew off to Latin America immediately after graduation. She had anticipated the trip with great excitement because she was able to sing with the Yale Glee Club. "It was unusual to take freshmen when we traveled out of the country," Director Fenno Heath recalled, "but Bonnie was so enthusiastic and had a repertoire she wanted to do and had a gorgeous voice. So I said okay."

The Yale Glee Club was one of the most prominent college choirs in the country, an institution that in its 114-year history had entertained thousands of people from California to Czechoslovakia. This would be its first long-term tour of Latin America. For four weeks Bonnie and a score of other student musicians would perform almost thirty concerts on a tour that took them to the American embassy in Mexico City, the National Theater in San Jose, Costa Rica, and gymnasiums and churches in Guatemala, El Salvador, Panama, Colombia, Trinidad, and Puerto Rico. There were uncomfortable bus rides and afflictions of "turista" that left many of them sick and complaining.

But for Bonnie it was a great adventure and a coming home at the same time. She never whined and always seemed ready for a new exploit. With her red hair, and fluent Spanish, she attracted the Latin men. At a bar in Mexico City she spent an evening singing with tequila-drinking mariachis and warding off the *machos*.

"Bonnie seemed to attract people wherever she went," recalled Fenno Heath. "She seemed much older than she was. I couldn't believe she was only eighteen."

In some ways Bonnie did seem older than her eighteen years, in being well-adjusted, well-traveled, well-educated, and well-spoken. But in other ways, she was younger, still unsure of herself, still exploring.

While Bonnie was in Latin America, Richard Herrin was alone in the room he had rented for the summer in a house on Orange Street. He had to remain in New Haven for make up classes in order to graduate from Yale in August, but most of his day was spent in front of the television set, occasionally strumming his guitar, or thinking about the studying he should be doing. Sometimes, he would talk out loud to himself: "I miss you, Bonnie. I wish you were here." He and Bonnie had often joked about their powers of ESP, as if they could reach each other's thoughts. He had been pretending that his brain wave messages to Bonnie were being transmitted and received when the phone woke him from his reverie.

"BONNIE!" He shouted when he heard the crackling voice. "Where are you?" Richard didn't need to ask for he had a complete list of the Glee Club's arrivals and departures at each stop.

"Panama." She sounded closer than that. "How are you, Rich? What are you up to?"

"Just missing you."

"I miss you, Rich. We're having a wonderful time."

Richard was ecstatic. The last thing he expected was a phone call from Bonnie. They spoke for forty-five minutes before Richard said, "Say, who's going to pay for this darned call?"

"Don't worry, babe. My treat."

Reluctantly, they hung up, promising they would soon be in one another's arms.

"Oh, babe, it was so great to talk to you tonight—the proverbial sappy grin is here." Bonnie went almost immediately to her pen and paper to write Richard. "I'm sitting in my room thinking about you and it's almost as

if you were here—the mood is perfect—Antonio Carlos
Jobim on the stereo coming from both sides of this
double bed, it's 3:00 A.M. and the lights are out except
for 1 lamp with a red clear shade, air conditioning,
private bath—it's so sexy and so perfect except for the
most important part—you, my love. But I'll hug my
pillow tight and we'll share this in my dreams. . . . I
think you know what I mean. I love you with my mind,
body, heart and soul and I'm counting those days just
like you babe.''

Richard knew exactly what Bonnie meant. Herrin had
turned his small bedroom into a Bonnie museum. The
walls were dotted with her photos and her gifts to him
were prominently displayed. "Snookums," the teddy
bear she had given him for Christmas, and the frisbee
she had given him that spring, were above his desk. The
nightstand at the head of his bed became a special shrine
topped with more pictures in a plexiglass cube, candles,
knick-knacks, cards, and letters, all mementos of
Bonnie.

It was all waiting for her when she returned from
Latin America at the end of June for the first of their
many reunions. The intensity of the relationship had increased with the month-long separation. For three days
they clung to one another and were suffused with
pleasure as they made love. They drew close to make up
for the weeks Bonnie was away with the Glee Club, but
they were also trying to ward off an imminent and much
longer separation.

THE STRENGTH of their relationship contrasted with the
growing antagonism of the Garland family, who saw in
Herrin a weakness that could only damage their
daughter. The Garlands had forbade her to see him
while she attended a class in music conducting that summer at Sarah Lawrence College, only a half-dozen miles
from her Scarsdale home. Bonnie had not yet told
Richard that for the next month they would have to
keep their meetings secret.

The morning Bonnie was to leave New Haven, Richard helped carry her belongings down to the street as they waited for the Garlands to pick her up. On the way back upstairs Richard commented, "It'll be good to say hello to the family again."

Bonnie was shaking her head. "No, Rich. It's not a good idea," she said. "They don't want to see you."

Richard was incredulous. "What am I supposed to do, hide in the house when they arrive?"

"They don't like my being here with you. They just told me they don't want to see you." When Bonnie saw that Richard was hurt, she shrugged as if to say, "What can I do?"

Richard made weak protestations, but no more. He was too fearful of losing Bonnie to object, too timorous for a confrontation with the Garlands. He felt rejected, but he submitted to the rebuff. As the Garland car pulled up to the curb, Bonnie kissed Richard good-bye and went down into the street. Richard walked over to the window and watched his lover jump into her parents' car and drive away.

Richard was hurt, but he was determined to hold Bonnie despite her parents' attitude. "I know what Mr. Garland thought of me," Herrin later commented. "He thought I was a bum and that I wasn't headed anywhere. And that I was going to use Bonnie and dump her and hurt her. There seemed to be pretty strong feelings there. I was sorry the Garlands felt that way about me, but I wasn't going to let them interfere or tell Bonnie what to do. I wasn't going to let them deter me."

Richard and Bonnie lived sixty miles from each other for the next month, closing the gap with constant phone calls and secret meetings. Twice Herrin took the train into New York City for day-long rendezvous with Bonnie. They met at Trader Vic's in the Plaza Hotel because she had a fondness for the fruity mixed drinks. With Paul Bardack they attended a Judy Collins concert in Central Park and walked the streets of Greenwich Village. They visited Bardack's parents on Staten

Island, and with Mike Greenwald, another Yale classmate, they rode the ferry to the Statue of Liberty. Bonnie led Richard to a Brazilian restaurant and ordered, in
perfect Portuguese, a heaping plate of *feijoada*. Every
moment was suspended as they stretched out these illicit
summer days.

Herrin was in a buoyant mood as he looked forward
to Bonnie's completing her Sarah Lawrence class and
rejoining him in New Haven for a short period before
his departure for Texas. "Hi Babe!" he wrote in half-
inch high letters on July 30. "Now that my paper isn't
due until Thursday, I feel less pressure, but I'd like to
really *try* to grind all weekend. Then, I'll see you again,
and we'll finish off this summer with a bang (!!!) HA
HA!!!" He was still extremely apprehensive about the
impending move to Texas. "I'll need you more than
ever then, love, because it will all be so new and strange.
You will be my link with reality and people."

He was positive even in his fear. Texas, he knew,
would be a lonely place. But he also knew that Bonnie
would carry him through. Even his professional future
seemed more open. He had heard of someone who had
received a Ph.D. in geology and then gone on to law
school. "I had forgotten about that possibility for a
long time," he explained to Bonnie optimistically. In
Texas, he was going to find out who he was. He told her
he was also going to stay in touch with a geologist at the
Smithsonian and boasted of a "contact" he had at the
Museum of Natural History in Los Angeles.

"Who knows what the future has in store for Richard
Herrin and Bonnie Garland?" he wrote with new confidence.

By August Bonnie had passed her Sarah Lawrence
class and received her parents' reluctant permission to
go to New Haven, believing that this would be their
daughter's last fling with Richard Herrin.

For the next two weeks she and Richard were inseparable. As the day of Richard's departure neared, he
once again became anxious about going to Texas where
he knew no one. Most important, he was leaving Bonnie

at Yale, in an environment where she already had friends. He knew it would be wrong to deny her a social life, but he also knew he wanted her all to himself.

He heard himself magnanimously telling her it would be all right for her to go out with other men, as long as she didn't fool around or fall in love. At the time, it sounded reasonable. Male wolves at the door were mere abstractions. Bonnie and Richard promised each other that even apart they would remain faithful and together.

On August 18, 1975, Richard and Bonnie got into an airport limousine at the New Haven Sheraton Plaza hotel and rode for almost two hours, their arms entwined, their mood dismal, to John F. Kennedy International Airport in New York. They grew more sullen as they remembered how happy they had been the day before, driving with Paul Bardack and friends into the hills of Massachusetts. On that warm sun-filled Sunday they had sat beside a stream and sung Beatles songs just as they had done the night of their first meeting on the Saybrook tower.

At the airport, as Richard passed through the security check alone, he could feel the tears beginning. Behind him, unable to accompany him to the gate without a ticket, Bonnie was already sobbing. Richard wanted to comfort Bonnie and tell her he would never leave her, but the plane was ready for boarding.

As he turned and started toward the gate, he saw Bonnie crying. He walked a few more feet and looked back again. Richard finally turned away and walked toward the plane. His own tears had started to flow, but he made sure Bonnie did not see him cry.

CHAPTER FOUR

———————————

The Separation

RICHARD HERRIN moved into the Deauville Apartments on Princeton Street in Fort Worth, Texas, in late August, 1975. He unpacked his belongings in his small bedroom without much enthusiasm. It was what he expected: a new city on the dusty plain of northern Texas, a strange school where he knew no one. And worse, he was fifteen hundred miles away from Bonnie Garland.

Joan and Paul Garland had breathed with relief when he left, hoping their daughter could get on with her Yale education. They didn't know how completely Richard had absorbed their daughter into his soul. He had brought her with him to Texas in spirit, and was already lining the walls of his bedroom with her pictures and starting a new shrine by his bed.

"Bonnie, I'm living every second for you," he wrote almost immediately. "Now I'm in graduate school getting a degree so I can get a decent job someday. For us. For us, babe, me and you. I'm suffering alot by being away from you, suffering by missing your soft gentle words and kisses and touch.''

Coming to Texas Christian University had once seemed like a good idea. He had set the wheels of migration in motion in his senior year at Yale. He knew that the East coast was not his world; he had never fit into the establishment culture. He had not even applied to graduate schools in the East. When TCU accepted him he had told friends with mock scorn, "Everybody else can go to Harvard grad school, darn it, I'm going to TCU."

Texas was closer to the Hispanic Southwest where passion and fellowship were part of the topsoil; community and family, the bedrock. Mentally, he was preparing to move back to his origins. Mexican music, which he once knew little about, had become an avid interest his senior year. He had joined a Yale mariachi group the month before meeting Bonnie, and for the rest of that year had applied himself to playing and singing the songs of his ancestors.

He had also enrolled in a Chicano history class at Yale. Unlike his other Yale teachers who knew him vaguely, if at all, Professor Pedro Castillo remembered Herrin as a "very good student who was especially interested in Mexican music and how important it was to Chicano culture."

Before meeting Bonnie, Herrin had confided to Connie Gaytan, a Yale minority admissions officer, his frustration at not finding a Chicana to date. "His main concern at that point was that all the girls he had liked were not Mexican-Americans," she recalled.

When Herrin met Bonnie Garland, he began to feel the difference between his own temperament and that of the dispassionate Eastern-Anglo world of Yale. His suppressed passion found expression in her. Bonnie became his West, his sunshine; geography and culture no longer mattered. It was like the dream of the *Foto Novellas*, the comic book-like stories read by some lower-class Latins. In their stereotyped plots the poor Chicano boy

falls in love with the daughter of the rich Anglo in-
dustrialist and, fighting all the barriers of caste and
class, wins her love. Herrin was living out the cartoons
of his past.

Texas Christian should have been ideal for Herrin. It
was closer to Los Angeles. He had received a scholarship and would be doing field work in nearby Mexico,
where he already spoke the language. Unlike Yale, TCU
was a relaxed and non-competitive environment. The
school's geology department was very small and informal. Everyone wore jeans, and noon poker games
were traditional.

But being separated from Bonnie had changed all
that. TCU now seemed like a remote army barracks.
During three consecutive nights in early September
Herrin huddled over his desk, pouring out his heart to
Bonnie Garland.

Herrin's letters to Bonnie reveal a Richard Herrin different from the seemingly easy-going Yalie. They are
passionate, maudlin, despairing, hopeful, even suspicious. They rise to rage and drop to simpering romanticism, always pirouetting on the point of passion. Yet
they are often philosophically childish.

In these letters, Herrin gallantly claims that they are
like "war lovers": he, the soldier, going off to battle;
she, the girl, back home dizzy with worry about whether
"her man was alive." He reminisces about the "phe-
nomena" of their first sex and confesses to Bonnie that
their romance has "caused me to look at girls a different
way." He faces their love with unadorned optimism: "I
could go on forever. For that's how long our love
should last." He then shifts to mock playfulness: "Be
reasonable. I only expect a card, letter, phone call or
visit from you about every 6 hours. I'm going Krazee.
Coo Coo. Da Da." He falls to the doubtful and apologetic: "I keep asking myself why you're still with me.
You could find others."

Diane is always there to haunt him. Though it had
been a year and a half since he felt betrayed by her,

Diane appears in his tiny Texas bedroom as his metaphor for pain, and as a standard by which to judge women. One moment he lashes out in anger. "She deceived me and lied to me, and I can prove the lies," he writes Bonnie. In the next moment, he proudly claims, "I forgave her."

Since Diane was still at Yale, Herrin feared that she would try to sabotage his relationship with Bonnie. He imagined her taking Bonnie aside and, woman-to-woman, revealing what she believed was the true Richard Herrin. He needed to warn Bonnie, tell his side of the story first. But as he wrote his long monologues about Diane, whom he now called "Creepo," he was also letting Bonnie know the depths to which he could be hurt by a woman. For the first time, he hints at the extent of the "trauma" if she should ever leave him.

> *Nite*
> *Thurs, Sept 4, 1975*
>
> *My Love:*
>   *Hi!*
>   *As always, I was tickled to hear your voice in real life instead of imagining it. . . .*
>   *Babe, it disturbed me that Creepo is asking you about me. Takes balls to do that, I thought. I guess she's got em! Really, I can understand how she may value my friendship, because I'm such a terrific guy, right? (is that me talking?). . . . She deceived me and lied to me, and I can prove the lies because they were to my face when I knew the truth. What does she want? She'd make an excellent politician because she's not bad at deception and lies. She hated when I brought up Watergate! She was such a big Nixon fan. . . . I have to admit Bonnie that she would make a good wife—for a duck. They could sure waddle well together. Why am I wasting all this valuable ink and paper and time on Creepo? Because now it's on my mind. And it is something which you*

*may be seeing more of. . . . I have this gut feeling
that something is brewing. Just a hunch. I wish I
could discuss pleasanter issues, but bear with me
while I blow all this out my ass.*

*Hey boobie, have I been boring you? It's for
your own protection. Bonnie, I'm living every
second for you. Now I'm in graduate school getting a degree so I can get a decent job someday.
. . . I keep asking myself why you're still with
me. You could find others. Different than me,
but others. There are so many who would like to
have you. You're attractive and likeable and a
very great person, caring and warm. . . .*

*Can you imagine what war lovers had to go
through. . . .*

*In all that time that we've been in love I have
not thought about how I could fool around on
the side. No, you've been my everything, the only
one to get crunched, kissed, even held by the
hand by me in all that time (except for Sister
Ramona and my mom). I can't think about not
having you. The trauma would be great. But
realizing that your love is as strong as mine for
you, I have no fear of such a trauma.*

*Be seeing you soon. Hope to hear from you.
Will you be my VALENTINE?*

> *With love forever
> (at least until eternity),*
>
> >   *Your Ricky*

I miss you darling.

The next day, a Friday night on which Richard again
had nothing to do, he was back at his desk. His loneliness had made him vulnerable. "I can't pretend to be
strong," he wrote Bonnie.

> *Nite
> Fri, Sept. 5, 1975*

*Hello Again, Bonnie
   Why are you hearing from me again so soon?*

Because I want to write to you. Tonight I was all
alone, watching TV, playing cards, looking at
your picture and missing you so much. . . .

Herrin then moves into an apparently serious, if un-
tutored, attempt to woo Bonnie to Texas to study voice,
or to work as a songstress:

I went to the office of the music department,
and they told me that there is no singing in the
summer. . . . During the school year there is a
church choir and an Acappella choir (the Glee
Club). The guy in the office gave me the number
of the "musicians referral service" in Dallas. . . .
I have their number, and I will call them to see
what they can do for you. Also this guy told me
that there is an Italian restaurant which has
singing waiters (and waitresses.) Are you in-
terested? . . .
As I mentioned, the TCU campus is kind of
dead. There aren't posters all over the place ad-
vertising this and that movie and event etc. I sup-
pose you've already been to movies and concerts
and stuff. I'm also sure I approve of your com-
pany. That is, unless you run into Creepo again.
. . . I hope Therese is suitable nighttime com-
pany. All I have are Bobo and Schnookums
(sometimes Jenny the Cat). [Stuffed animals Bon-
nie had given to him.]
I guess I've reached the point of talking about
unimportant things. Hope you don't mind. I need
this kind of release to remain sane.
Always yours,
Ricky

On Saturday night Richard writes five long pages,
giving much of his thoughts over to the rage he still feels
for Diane, and even the "suspicion" he first felt when
he met Bonnie.

Nite
Sat, Sept 6, 1975

Hi Bonnie!

Me again! Gosh darn, talking to you this afternoon was great but afterwards I was getting down on myself. Maybe I was feeling sorry for myself. Maybe I was feeling bad about having admitted my weakness in our separation. I'm not sure what it was, but I was getting bad vibes. And then there's Creepo. Maybe you're correct in believing that surely I couldn't dislike her as much as I do. I'd like to believe that because I've already forgiven her, but the whole thing leaves a bad taste in my mouth. You know, when we first started going out she told me she didn't want to get serious, that it should just be a "college thing," and that she probably would accept dates with other guys. Well, of course I said I'd beat up anyone who asked her, but seriously told her it was okay. Of course, no one asked her for so long I got spoiled. As you know, she finally accepted a date with Marshmallow and it broke my heart. . . . Bonnie, I was very blind. She knew how to use people and I'm sure she still does. How would you feel if I took 2 different girls to proms on 2 consecutive nights and ignored you? Babe, it took time to clear this out of my mind so that it didn't affect me. Much of my revelation didn't happen till after the summer. That's why there was a lot of suspicion and mistrust in me when I first started loving you. Eventually I blew it out of me, and I was happy. I had put the hurt behind me. I forgave her. Its the Christian thing to do. But can you understand why I still feel the way I do about her? . . .

Damn, I keep using you for pouring my heart out. Please don't get sick of me. I need you more than ever now. Its not easy being here alone. I'm not saying its easy for you, either. God, how I wish we could be together. This is the third *straight night that I've stayed up late writing to you. Thinking about you. Trying to clear my mind of troublesome thoughts. Creepo is starting to be troublesome again. Damn it, wish she would leave me alone. . . .*

With all my love, though the word can't express all that I feel for you.

Ricky

In his letters to Bonnie, Herrin claimed that by dwelling on his "betrayal" by Diane, he was "protecting" Bonnie. But there was another purpose served in dredging up the Creepo tale. It was a mini-lesson in personal psychology: why Richard Herrin mistrusts women and how not to incur that same mistrust in the future.

Easy going and complacent about everything else in his life, Herrin could not accept being toyed with by women. "You probably can't believe sweet old me thinks that way about anybody," he wrote to Bonnie after lambasting Creepo, "but I do, Babe, and it's *me*." It was the same Richard who appeared to glide facilely through life, never rebelling or uttering a mean word despite disappointment. He had seemed content to take life as it came until Diane "betrayed" him.

But to Richard, Bonnie Garland was different from the other women he had dated. Bonnie was like the two women in his life whom he could trust unquestionably: his mother Linda Ugarte and Sister Ramona Pena at More House Chapel. They were the only other women with whom he could so much as hold hands. Bonnie was the third essential person of his trinity.

What gnawed at him in Texas was the threat of change. Bonnie was young. His own observations of the sexual jungle of Yale convinced him that she would be "under the gun." She had not yet known Yale except through him; perhaps she didn't yet know that there were "others."

UNLIKE RICHARD, who had gone to Fort Worth and

found it empty in the absence of his sweetheart, Bonnie Garland had returned to New Haven, old friends, and a flurry of activities.

The contrast between the new life styles of the separated lovers was dramatic. While Richard found little to do other than think about her, Bonnie had plenty to do. She missed Herrin, who had been her lover for almost a year, but she also loved music and having a good time. At eighteen, she was not prepared to be a martyr for their relationship. It was as if, free of Herrin, Bonnie could now begin to live.

Bonnie plunged into her musical activities. Two hours, twice a week, she practiced with the Yale Glee Club in the large rehearsal room on the second floor of the old brick Hendrie Hall. It was filled with the memorabilia of the club's extraordinary history. From floor to ceiling, portraits, banners, and poster cluttered the wall space. Past Glee Clubs had entertained royalty, yodeled in Munich and Heidelberg, and sang Beethoven's ninth symphony in Carnegie Hall. Well-known composers had written original music for the group, including Randall Thompson's "Tarantella." In 1913, the soon-to-be-celebrated Cole Porter was the club's president.

Bonnie was on her way to becoming an important soloist for the group. "Bonnie was a soprano, very high, very light, and very good," a friend recalled. She was also a lively addition. "People in Glee weren't as interesting or fun as Bonnie was," another friend remembered. She became a member of the "notorious back row" who stood at the rear of the more than sixty singers at rehearsals, telling jokes out of earshot of director Fenno Heath.

Like the songs she sang, Bonnie's manner was unaffected. At rehearsals, she favored jeans, sneakers, and T-shirts. She eschewed the matched skirt and sweater that were part of the preppy resurgence, and rarely wore make-up except for concerts. Bonnie was large-boned, but when she dressed up for concerts, "she looked stunning," as friends recalled.

Bonnie began her sophomore year with the stage set for a new life. She and eleven other friends were about to become campus sensations as they formed the school's newest singing group. The Proof of the Pudding, as the women undergraduates called themselves, was the brainchild of Adrienne Benton, a member of the Glee Club. The previous spring, Adrienne decided that women vocalists were being cheated. The men had a half-dozen all male groups to choose from; while the women had only one, the New Blue. For the men there were the Spizzwinks (named after mythological bugs which attacked corn crops), the Dukesmen, the Baker's Dozen (who were the Noxious Nine until they added three new voices), the Alley Cats (famous for their rendition of "Sally in Our Alley"), and the Society of Orpheus and Bacchus (known familiarly as the S.O.B.'s).

All were modeled after the famed Whiffenpoofs, those "gentlemen songsters off on a spree" who for almost seven decades had prided themselves on an abiding love for "old ballads and old ale" at "the tables down at Mory's." The Whiffenpoofs were, as a Proof of the Pudding member put it, "more Big Man On Campus than football players. If you were a Whiffenpoof, everybody knew who you were."

Launching a new singing group at a school where minstrelling was as heralded as football was not an easy task. Benton auditioned almost fifty women that spring before choosing eleven. "Bonnie was one of the last to come in," she recalled. "I knew her a little bit from the Glee Club, but she really impressed me at the audition. She sang a classical number that was lovely. Her voice was beautiful. But she could do more than just sing: She could play the piano, conduct, transpose a song. She turned out to be the most talented musician of the group."

That fall Bonnie and her singing colleagues worked overtime to polish their meager repertoire for the Proof's debut at the annual Dwight Hall Jamboree. It was a festival *cum* competition in which each singing group vied to impress the crowd sufficiently to be asked to perform, for a fee, at mixers and parties throughout the year.

For Proof of the Pudding, as a new and unknown group, the Jamboree was crucial to their fortunes. Dwight Hall was packed that night. The Alley Cats, Dukesmen, Baker's Dozen, Spizzwinks, S.O.B.'s, Whiffenpoofs, and New Blue all regaled the audience, but when it was over, the headline in the Yale *Daily News* proclaimed: "Pudding Highlights Jamboree."

A Whiffenpoof M.C. introduced the women while holding a can of tuna, but was soon upstaged. As the *News* commented, Bonnie and her friends "stole the show from the male groups and the women's rival, the New Blue." They sang "Amazing Grace," "In the Mood," and "Two of Us." When they finished, said the campus paper, "the silenced audience broke into wild applause and calls for encore."

"We were really a hit," recalled a Proof member. "Bonnie did the first verse of 'Amazing Grace' solo and she blew them away. They were clapping even while we started the second verse." The success gave Proof instant celebrity. "We've gotten a fantastic reaction from the men's groups," Proof's business manager reported to the *News*. "They've all asked us to have concerts and rush parties with them."

The two weeks of rush which followed the Jamboree, the Yale equivalent of an old college fraternity ritual, turned into a stampede. Proof was swamped by ninety women hoping to be tapped for the ten new places they wanted to fill. "For the men, of course, Whiffenpoof was the thing to be," recalled Laura Kidd, who was one of the ninety to try out for Proof. "But for the women it was now Proof. It was the new thing on campus."

This was the mantle of achievement that Bonnie had shunned her first year at Yale in favor of a lazy love life with Richard Herrin. With the Glee Club and the success of Proof of the Pudding, of which she was now a co-director, she came into a Yale world much brighter than the one she had inhabited with Herrin.

Bonnie's group was quickly invited to Mory's, the venerable eating and drinking club. There "the gallant girls," as the *News* reported, "put away the five red cups sent them by admirers. They sang every song in their repertoire twice before the crowd stopped yelling for encores." The contrast between Richard Herrin's "so dead" Fort Worth and Bonnie Garland's new vitality at Yale was stiletto sharp. Bonnie was beginning to feel, as she told Richard, as if she were living in "two worlds."

It was in the midst of Proof's autumn splash that Bill Breitenbach, who had shared the house with Herrin the previous summer, remarked: "I think Rich is in for a big fall." He later recounted what he had seen on campus. "It was a few weeks after the term began. I was walking down the street in New Haven and I saw Bonnie walking along arm-in-arm with another guy."

After observing Richard that summer, Breitenbach concluded that Herrin's romance with Bonnie was an adolescent infatuation with a built-in fault. "It seemed a pathetic sort of puppy love that wasn't terribly mature," he recalled. "And these long distance conversations—the phone was in the living room—that would go on for three hours and were just kind of baby-talk. When they were together they were always all over each other, cooing in each other's ear. It was a kind of self-absorbed infatuation that seemed more like a seventh- or eighth-grade relationship than what you'd expect from college-age students. That's why I wasn't surprised when I subsequently saw Bonnie with someone else."

Those who didn't know Richard Herrin assumed that he would have been doing the same thing in Texas, walking hand in hand with a TCU coed. Instead, he was spending much of his energy imagining what Bonnie Garland was doing in New Haven. Each time Herrin and Bonnie talked by phone, which was usually three times a week, he asked for reassurance that she was being faithful.

Herrin was now having trouble sleeping at night. He

got nervous when Bonnie said she was going out occasionally with other men and wouldn't calm down until she assured him there was nothing to worry about. But when Bonnie told him that Henry Howser had taken her out a few times, Herrin's anxiety resurfaced.

"I don't like it," he complained to Bonnie on the phone.

"But it's just on a friendly, casual level," she responded. "Don't worry."

But Herrin was worried. "Don't even go out with him," he pleaded.

"Please, Rich, I know what I'm doing."

When Herrin hung up, for the first time since he had left Yale, he was not reassured. It was the last Sunday in September and they had been separated only a little more than a month. The tenuous nature of a long-distance love was becoming hauntingly clear. For a few hours Herrin wrestled with an array of fearful thoughts, then finally picked up the phone and called Bonnie again. He was apologetic. He said he was ashamed of himself for not trusting her, and as they talked, Richard began to cry.

He was falling into an agonizing trap. If he demanded that Bonnie not date, or if he continued to want to pass judgment on every man who asked her to Broadway Pizza, she might just become angry and leave him. But at the same time, he told himself, one of these Yalies might easily sweep Bonnie off her feet.

"Inside of me there was the fear that maybe she was going to go off with somebody and fall in love with him and I'd be left out in the cold," Herrin later confided. "I couldn't really say to her, 'Bonnie, I don't like you going out with other guys because I'm afraid you'll leave me.' I tried to convince myself that I didn't mind that she was going out, as long as she wasn't fooling around or falling in love. I agreed to it, but I really did mind."

Herrin was in a double bind situation to which he could see no worthwhile alternative. Whatever he did, other than accept things as they were, he would be admitting that he did not trust Bonnie. Just as he believed that mistrust was the flaw in his romance with Diane, trust was what made his relationship with Bonnie so ideal. To doubt was to admit the possibility of mistrust. Herrin pushed out of his mind as unthinkable the possibility that the two romances might culminate in the same way.

"Dearest Bonnie," Herrin was at his desk the next evening. "Sorry to throw a heavy letter at you so soon, but I haven't been able to concentrate on anything else the entire day," Herrin wrote. He had a lot to get out of his system. After the phone calls of the previous night, he was beginning to figure out what was happening to him, to analyze why he was so suspicious of Bonnie and how he might change.

Inevitably, the rejection by Diane kept intruding into his psyche. It now seemed to control his mind. In this letter to Bonnie, appear the first signs of self-analysis, including the use of psychological jargon. By its end, Richard had successfully transposed any mistrust of Bonnie onto himself, and absorbed blame for the "hang ups" that had led him to doubt her fidelity:

> *Monday nite*
> *9/29/75*
> *Fort Worse, Texas*

Dearest Bonnie,

I've been recalling things you've said in the past, things which clearly indicate to me that I should stop acting like a worried parent whose beautiful daughter is on her first date, and the guy is the biggest mover in town. This kind of parent knows their daughter has high moral standards, etc., yet they're afraid because of the guy and his reputation. Well, thanks to you, last night I straightened out a lot of my twisted thinking. I believe a part of it was leftovers from the Creepo Nightmare. If there's one thing I wish I could

*completely forget, its the Creepo Nightmare. I
mean, there are some things I'd like to forget and
there are other things I'd really like to forget, but
I'd really really truly like to forget the Creepo
Nightmare!!!*

*Time will heal that wound, Bonnie, but not as
fast as I'd like it to. In the meantime, it keeps
sneaking in and grabbing me. When I think of
how I felt knowing I had been deceived and lied
to, I'm really happy for you that you will never
experience that feeling, because as a human being
I could never want to see another person go
through the same thing.*

*I've also pinpointed the reasons for some of my
other disturbances, but I won't bring them up
because the solution lies within my own head and
not anything I'd want you to say.*

*When I think of the times we've held each
other and professed our love, and pledged our
hearts, minds and bodies to each other, I can't
understand why I'm still so messed up. . . .
Countless times you've told me that you love
me, so why this internal conflict when I know
you'd never hurt me?. . . . When you make a
mini-analysis of me, for example by telling me
how paranoid I am, it's as new to me as it is to
you. We're both learning about me as we go
along. . . .*

*Have no more thoughts that I don't trust you,
Bonnie. . . .*

*I don't want you to change anything you're
doing, because changes have to take place in* this
head in order to keep things smooth. . . .

I love you very much.
Forever, Ricky

The new maturity of Herrin's psychological "breakthrough" that would banish his "paranoid" thinking
created a veneer of stability. But underneath Richard
Herrin felt his precious Bonnie slipping away. The more

he thought about it, the more he realized there was only one solution to the gnawing dilemma. He had to marry Bonnie Garland. And the sooner the better.

HERRIN ADVANCED his scheduled trip to New Haven by two weeks, afraid to delay his proposal of marriage. He · arrived at Yale in time for Proof of the Pudding's October 16 triumphant debut at Mory's. Herrin had written Bonnie about the fact that he lived in "one world" centered around her, while she lived in "two worlds," his and Yale's. It was the perfect opportunity to dive directly into Bonnie's other world: her new friends and her status as part of the new campus singing sensation.

Instead, when he arrived at Yale Herrin tried to recreate their old world. At a Proof rehearsal he was almost oblivious to the other women except for a nod. "He sat by her at the piano," recalled a member of Proof. "When the others would talk to Bonnie, he'd just sit there and stare at her and not participate in the conversation, not even laugh when something funny was said."

Most of the Proof women had not known about Bonnie-and-Richard until Herrin appeared at Yale. Unlike some Yale women who talked openly about the men in their lives, Bonnie was reticent. Not once had she mentioned Richard Herrin to the others. This was part of Bonnie's world from which he had been excluded. Now, sitting in the midst of it, he wasn't even participating.

Alone with Bonnie it was different. For a few precious days at Yale, it was once again Richard-and-Bonnie, one word, one world. Except for her rehearsals, they were together constantly, suspicions buried, doubts cast aside. They spent most of the four days in Bonnie's room in her new sophomore residence in Saybrook College just under the tower where they had met. Bonnie convinced Therese Ohnsorg, Bonnie's best friend and roommate, to sleep in the living room while

Richard was visiting. The two lovers treasured their privacy as they passed the hours doing what they never seemed to tire of, what Richard had longed for in his letter: "hugging and kissing and crying for joy."

But that Saturday night, Herrin's faith in Bonnie was suddenly threatened. At a dance in Woolsey Hall, he met an old friend, Liz Morris, who had been a Pastoral Associate with Herrin at More House the year before. Liz thought well of him, as a warm, sincere, religious person with a sense of humor.

Their lives had also intersected because Liz had dated Hank Howser the year before. That night, Liz and her new date were standing on the steps of the Woolsey rotunda, listening to the Whiffenpoofs, when Herrin approached. After exchanging pleasantries, Liz teasingly commented, "Hey Rich. I hope you've been keeping an eye on Bonnie. I think she's been getting attention from Hank Howser."

As Liz remembered, Herrin suddenly flipped. "He immediately grabbed my arm and said 'What do you know?' I was stunned. I told him 'Calm down, Rick. It was just a casual remark.' I had never seen him upset like that. Then he started asking all these questions 'Exactly what do you know?' 'What have you seen?' and I said, 'Really nothing. I just saw them together in the dining room.' We had a fifteen minute conversation about it, and he kept asking me questions over and over. Finally, he told me that he had already talked to Bonnie about Howser, and that she had assured him that they were just friends. He added that Bonnie wouldn't lie to him. When he left he was fairly agitated."

The next morning, at Sunday brunch in the Saybrook dining hall, Herrin sought out Liz as she got up to get her food. He looked calmer, as if he had resolved his problem. "I just want you to know that Bonnie has assured me that she is not sleeping with this guy," he told as astonished young woman. "I made her swear on a Bible that she hadn't gone to bed with him."

Liz felt dismayed, conjuring up the bizarre image of

Herrin using the Holy Book to confirm his girlfriend's sexual faithfulness. "We were both religious people, and you just don't go around using the Bible so lightly," Liz recalled. "I thought it was very odd."

But for Herrin it was the reassurance he needed. Now satisfied with Bonnie's sexual fidelity, on Sunday afternoon Richard decided he could no longer hold back his secret of marriage. "It was nice and peaceful and quiet," Herrin remembered, "and we were all alone. We were sitting in the living room on the couch talking. It just seemed like the right time to bring it up."

He turned to Bonnie and asked if she would be his "eternal sunshine." He paused and added: "Will you marry me?"

Without hesitation, Bonnie answered, "Yes."

Herrin had no engagement ring to offer, but he reached into his travel bag and pulled out the small five-dollar bracelet that he had bought in Frankfurt and had saved for the woman he was going to marry. It had stayed in a bureau drawer at his home in Los Angeles until August, 1975, when Herrin retrieved it. He carried it with him to Texas, knowing that one day he would offer it to Bonnie.

The day of their engagement, October 19, 1975, was the emotional peak of Richard Herrin's life. He wanted to run to the top of Saybrook tower and shout, "Hey! Guess what everybody." But Bonnie convinced him that it was best not to tell anyone.

"She was adamant that our engagement not be made known to people," Herrin recalled, "that it would be kept just between the two of us. In her circle, what she had learned is that it's not proper to announce an engagement if the wedding is more than a year off. I had never heard that before, but she knew all these rules of etiquette. I went along with it because that was a rule she had learned and was telling me that's the way it was done. All right. Fine. It doesn't matter as long as *we* know."

Herrin would have liked an immediate marriage, but he bowed to practicality. They agreed that at least one of them should first finish school. Since he would not receive his master's degree in geology from TCU until the spring of 1977, it put the marriage off at least a year and a half.

But Bonnie's "yes" was all he cared about. A few days after he returned to Fort Worth, Richard received a letter from Bonnie confirming her promise of marriage. "Hey Babe," Bonnie wrote. "You know what? You are a beautiful person and I am the luckiest woman to be a part of you and your life and to have you as part of me and my life. We may not complement each other academically but as people I think we complement each other very well. . . . I look forward to our marriage for it symbolizes the strongest bond and commitment of love between a man and a woman."

SEPARATED BY HALF a continent, Herrin's day-to-day life was miserable. But the image of Bonnie sustained him.

For Bonnie Garland it was the opposite: It was only the living and breathing Richard Herrin whom she loved. Absent, he became only "a voice on the phone." Bonnie had grown up in an environment of privilege, but one which encouraged seeing the world as it really was. She did not need to romanticize her world to make it bearable, as Herrin did. Richard wanted to be her war lover, but could such a fantasy satisfy her? Her steady boyfriend was in Fort Worth, not in a foxhole in Vietnam. Bonnie was at Yale in 1975 where men and women were actively experimenting in real life: studying, singing, dancing, even sleeping together.

To Henry Howser, whom Bonnie continued to see even after Herrin's warnings, Bonnie confided that she "missed Richard a lot." But Howser later recalled that Bonnie also had her doubts about Herrin. "She was worried that he wasn't aggressive enough. Something was missing in the relationship and she didn't know what."

Bonnie and Howser dated throughout November and

December of 1975, Bonnie's sophomore year. At first it was an easy relationship without involvement. Bonnie felt loyal to Herrin and Howser had another girlfriend. But they soon realized that they had become more than drinking companions. As they became closer Bonnie worried about Richard. "I said, 'Why don't you just tell him you're dating me?' " Howser remembered. "She said she was afraid he'd hit somebody, either me or her." Bonnie felt torn between the two men, one who was fifteen hundred miles away to whom she was secretly engaged, the other real and present.

Howser remembered Bonnie beginning to talk about breaking up with Herrin and going with him. "I said that was a bad idea. I had another relationship," Howser recalled. "She got mad at me because I didn't have guilt feelings and that terminated our relationship."

Her misgivings about Richard temporarily laid aside, Bonnie wrote to Herrin in mid-December about the coming vacation. Herrin was going to Los Angeles for Christmas and Bonnie was going home to Scarsdale. But afterward they would meet in Washington D.C., where Bonnie was to perform in a Yale Glee Club concert.

Jennifer Clark and Connie Crawford, two former Madeira classmates of Bonnie's, got together with Bonnie for a small reunion at which they met Richard Herrin. Bonnie's chums were unimpressed with her new boyfriend, who seemed to be little more than a conspicuous tag-along.

"Within a half hour of meeting," Jennifer remembered, "we were all kind of uncomfortable, because almost instantly I picked up something from him. I think Bonnie must have felt our reaction toward him. He didn't talk. There was nothing coming from him, no personality. He was just a wimpy guy. Afterwards, when we said goodbye to them Connie and I just couldn't believe that Bonnie was going out with a guy like that."

But Bonnie, conflicted as her life was, seemed to love

"a guy like that." Bonnie visited Herrin in Texas a number of times in 1976 and 1977. It was for these visits that Richard Herrin lived. Academically, his life was unremarkable, "fair to middlin' " as a classmate remembered it. Socially, it was remarkable for its sterility.

Jack Edmondson, Herrin's roommate for two years, recalled that, except for the frequent phone calls from Bonnie and his mother, "only on one or two occasions in the course of two years did a phone call come for Rick."

"I never knew *any* human being who was one hundred percent devoted to anybody," Edmondson later asserted. "But that was how Rick was to Bonnie. There was never a wandering eye at any other female, never a lecherous quip about some teen starlet on television. Every desire or need he had was wrapped up in Bonnie."

And the wrapping was tied even tighter when Bonnie visited. Without telling her parents, Bonnie flew to Fort Worth for two weeks in early March of 1976. The Bonnie Garland who stayed at the Deauville Apartments was not the same Bonnie Garland who was dazzling Yale crowds with throaty solo renditions of "Amazing Grace." As soon as she arrived, she retreated into a silent world made up almost exclusively of Richard Herrin and television. "Bonnie was quiet to the point of being strange," Edmondson recalled.

Bonnie and Richard withdrew into their impervious cocoon. Herrin awoke and went to school while Bonnie slept late, not infrequently until noon, then emerged from the bedroom and watched television soap operas and games shows most of the afternoon. When Herrin returned to the apartment at about five, he and Bonnie changed into bathing suits and played for an hour at the Deauville's bathtub-sized swimming pool. Then they came inside, watched television, prepared dinner. A favorite dessert was "Snackin' Cake," which they devoured whole at a single setting, plunging their forks directly into the nine-inch square baking pan. If Herrin didn't study after dinner, they watched television until going to bed. If he did study, Bonnie watched television by herself before joining Richard.

Their love-making remained an important part of the relationship. While admitting to Henry Howser that she had reservations about Herrin, Bonnie had confided that "she was very happy sexually with him." Sex was a pleasurable new experiment for the young Yale coed, its intensity elevated by its secrecy.

For Herrin sex was more complicated, for it also included omens of defeat. His first sexual encounter in a Frankfurt brothel had ended in impotence; his second, with the embarrassment of premature ejaculation. Diane might have been his third, but she had refused him. The failures ended with Bonnie Garland. To a friend in Los Angeles with whom Herrin spoke openly, it seemed that "Richard loved Bonnie so much because they had something good sexually. He didn't have too many sexual encounters. With Bonnie I guess it was different because he loved her and it was like the first time for him."

In Bonnie, he had minted a golden sexual coin that gave him curative joy. But the coin had two sides. "I had intense fear that if she got involved sexually with somebody, that would destroy her love for me and her need for me," Herrin admitted.

But by themselves they seemed content. That summer Bonnie stayed in Fort Worth for almost two months, living in Richard Herrin's world, far from Yale and Scarsdale. In early August, they flew to Los Angeles, where Linda and Manuel Ugarte openly accepted Bonnie into the family. There could hardly have been a more radical leap for Bonnie Garland than the one from Scarsdale to the barrio of East Los Angeles.

Linda Ugarte, Richard's soft-spoken mother, adored Bonnie. When Linda went to New Haven for Richard's graduation, "Bonnie was with us all the time," she recalled. And when Linda had had a breast operation, Bonnie had called from Yale to wish her well. "Bonnie was a fine woman," said Mrs. Ugarte. "She was a warm beautiful girl. I just loved her."

Richard and Bonnie kept a busy schedule in Los Angeles. On Saturday they went to the wedding of Richard's oldest friend, Sigfrido Chavez. On Tuesday and Sunday Bonnie got to see how Richard had spent his youth as they worked with Linda and Manuel at the swap meets. Manuel took Bonnie to supply outlets to buy her gifts to take home, including several shirts for Paul Garland.

"When she was finally ready to go," Linda Ugarte later tearfully told a crowded courtroom, "she was crying all the time she was packing. She really didn't want to leave. And so, just before she went outside the door, she was—she was crying and she came up to me—" Herrin's mother broke off, sobbing, "with tears in her eyes, kissing me on the cheek."

As THE 1976–77 school year began, there seemed to be a new urgency to their relationship. Bonnie was determined to increase her junior year class load at Yale so that she could graduate early and join Herrin.

In December, as soon as he finished his fall semester at TCU, Richard was on a New Haven-bound plane. He stayed with Bonnie in her Saybrook room, then, a few days later, they boarded a train together for Boston, where Richard had arranged an interview for the Ph.D. program in geology at Boston University. From there, they flew to Rochester, New York, where Richard had an interview at the University of Rochester and Bonnie at the Eastman School of Music. These were the first concrete steps taken to create a permanent union.

"Bonnie told me more than once that she and Rick planned on getting married," remembered Elaine Moss, Bonnie's junior year roommate. "She looked forward to it, even though she wasn't ready for it at the time. She spoke of having children." Elaine believed that with Bonnie it wasn't a question of *if*, "it was a question of *when*."

On December 23, 1976, Richard and Bonnie arrived in Scarsdale for the Christmas holidays. Bonnie's parents now understood that Herrin could not be ignored. Bonnie's younger brother Patrick picked them up at the nearby Westchester Airport. Patrick and Herrin got along well: They played backgammon, went bowling together, wrestled on the Garland couch, and talked baseball and football.

But Herrin felt he was only being "tolerated" by Mr. and Mrs. Garland because of Bonnie. He presented the Garlands with a Hawaiian flower arrangement and a Christmas card wishing them "peace and happiness," awkward attempts to break what he called "the barrier" between them. The gifts were not unlike the swapmeet shirts that Richard's stepfather had given Bonnie for Paul Garland, shirts that the Scarsdale attorney never wore.

Breaking the Garland family tradition, Richard and Bonnie exchanged gifts on Christmas Eve instead of the next morning. Richard had a special present for Bonnie. In private, Richard handed Bonnie a small box, to which he had affixed a note in Portuguese: "This is the first, but not the last." Bonnie was excited as she tugged at the wrapping. For weeks Richard had dropped clues about the gift, an engagement ring.

But as Bonnie opened the box, Herrin noticed her averted eyes with dismay. "From that first look on her face I could see that she was disappointed," Herrin recalled. "It was my own fault."

As Bonnie picked up the forty-dollar opal Richard had bought on the installment plan she tried to cover up her disappointment, but it was too late. "I felt inadequate because I couldn't afford a diamond," Herrin remembered. "My eyes started welling up and I started to get emotional. And she felt bad too because she had caused me to do that. And we both wound up crying."

Herrin could neither conquer his weaknesses nor keep from displaying them. His "engagement ring" had been a failure. But even in his unfortunate performance, Richard still saw hopeful signs. "In some ways it was encouraging to me that the relationship was still strong enough that she would be expecting an engagement ring.

Even though I was hurt and felt inadequate, the positive part of it was that she's still expecting it." It was another battle in his strategy of victory through failure. Herrin seemed to be winning in the muddy trenches.

That Christmas, the Garlands realized that Richard Herrin was not going to walk out of their daughter's life. However distasteful the thought, he might be a future son-in-law. They were convinced that Herrin was selfish and had little true interest in Bonnie's welfare, but saw her rather as a life raft for his own inadequacy.

"He seemed very smug," Joan Garland remembered. "He felt he had Bonnie in his pocket." As Richard sat on the sofa with his arm around Bonnie, Joan Garland confronted Herrin, hoping her daughter could look at him from a different perspective. "I asked him, 'Do you encourage Bonnie to get in touch with people in music?' He said, 'No.' 'Do you keep in touch with your own field?' He said, 'Yes.' It was a very direct confrontation. 'Rick, the thing that worries me about you is that I don't see your concern for Bonnie's career.' He had no answer. 'Suppose someone said Bonnie needed to go to Europe for a year?' He said, 'I'd have to think very seriously about that.' Bonnie was listening and, I hoped, absorbing the differences between his approach to his career and his approach to hers." Joan Garland was sure that eventually her daughter would see that Herrin "had no concern for her welfare."

IT WOULD NOT be easy for the Garlands to win their daughter over to their view of Herrin. A few days after she returned to Yale in January, 1977, Bonnie wrote to Richard, "My love will always look to expand its depth and meaning. With all my heart I wait for our reunion."

But there were also warning signs in her letters. "I'm in for a rough ride. I didn't go to school today—I really don't want to go back at all," Bonnie told Richard. "Already there is so much to do—applications, the new opera 'Peter Grimes,' this Proof record and jamboree, not to mention figuring out what I'm going to do next year."

Bonnie's rough ride was an understatement. Not only had she signed up for five and a half courses, almost double the normal Yale class load, but she was practicing twice a week with the Glee Club, twice a week with the Saybrook Madrigal Singers, taking private voice lessons, singing in the Battell Chapel Choir, and, without telling Richard, dating other men.

Bonnie was soon sleeping through classes, eating whole cheese cakes at one sitting and ballooning towards a size sixteen. She was pale, nervous, and depressed. Fenno Heath, the Glee Club director, remembered her "coming into my office quite a bit, sitting on the couch and telling me about all kinds of troubles she was having and very often just crying."

Only a few weeks into the new semester Bonnie called her parents with a dramatic announcement. She could no longer go to classes. She was temporarily dropping out of Yale. "She was mentally and physically exhausted from trying to accelerate and do extracurricular work," her mother later recalled. "She didn't withdraw officially until spring break because she wanted to stay with the Glee Club, with her music. But she just couldn't go to classes." Bonnie agreed to see a psychiatrist.

One of the first people to feel the fallout of her strain was Richard Herrin. The pace of her correspondence had slackened. He was dialing her number more often but finding her less and less often in her room. Bonnie, in turn, was beginning to complain to friends that Richard Herrin was bombarding her with phone calls, often on Saturday nights when she wasn't in. Once again, he was acting extremely suspicious. When he did get through to her he invariably wanted to know who she was out with and what she did.

"I'd call her up because I was lonely and not doing anything," Herrin later explained. "If she didn't answer, I'd call later. Some nights when I was in really bad shape, I would just keep calling and calling and calling until she came home. I might spend a whole night calling her room. What else did I have to do?'' But if it were loneliness that first prompted Herrin's calls, it was fear that fired his persistence.

In late February Richard made a phone call to Bonnie which rekindled what she had called his ''paranoia.'' ''We spoke for what was to us a short period of time, maybe ten or fifteen minutes,'' Herrin remembered. ''She said at one point, 'someone's at the door. I have to go.' I asked her who was at the door. She said, 'I'm expecting Stephanie to come by.' '' When Herrin asked if he could talk to Stephanie, ''Bonnie refused to even answer the door. She told me she had to leave, and that she was doing to hang up.

''I objected. I told her not to hang up, and she said she was hanging up, because she had to go, and she hung up the phone. I called her right back. I was disturbed, upset. I couldn't understand why she was doing this. But now the line was busy. I remembered Stephanie's last name. Stephanie was a girl in the singing group Bonnie was with. I called Yale for Stephanie's phone number, and I called Stephanie's room.

''A woman answered, and I asked if Stephanie was there, and the reply was, 'This is Stephanie.' So I hung up. I felt that I had been lied to. I was very suspicious as to why she wouldn't answer the door while I was there on the phone. I felt that there was something wrong, something that I didn't know about, and I wanted to find out what it was. I also felt that, perhaps, the relationship was in some kind of trouble. No matter how minor the trouble, the best way to patch it up would be to do it in person. I made a reservation to fly to New Haven the next day.''

But Herrin couldn't wait for the next day. Within a half hour he was back on the phone with Bonnie, who admitted she had not gone out with Stephanie. ''I figured you might check up on me,'' Bonnie explained, adding that the person at the door was just a male friend of hers with whom she sometimes went out to get something to eat.

"I was hurt when she hung up," Herrin explained. "She had never done this to me. Realizing that she had hurt me, she apologized for that. She was sincere and promised that it would never happen again. And as far as I was concerned, the whole issue was settled that night on the phone."

It had taken a single phone call to rekindle his fears of losing Bonnie Garland. But it also had taken only one call to pacify him. Richard Herrin wanted desperately to believe.

BONNIE GARLAND was trying not to hurt Richard Herrin. But even as she was reassuring him, she was experiencing the freedom of a nineteen-year-old in a sexually open society. "One night in February," Bonnie's junior year roommate recounted, "a fellow Yale student came over to the room and ended up spending the night with Bonnie. And he ended up spending most of the nights for the next couple of weeks in the room with Bonnie."

Day by day Bonnie Garland's life was becoming more complicated. She had dropped her classes, but stayed in her room at Saybrook College for a while. Eventually, she moved into the basement of the fraternity house of her friend Hank Howser. Her days were spent mainly at her new job, baby sitting, from nine to five.

Depressed by her increasing weight as well as by her problems with school and love, Bonnie was seeing a psychiatrist. She was beginning to feel increasingly guilty as she dated other men while fielding nightly phone calls from a man to whom she still felt committed. "Bonnie in some ways could be lazy," recalled a friend from Proof to whom Bonnie often confided her troubles late at night in the Broadway Pizza. "As far as Rich Herrin was concerned, she didn't want to deal with the situation. She seemed very depressed about where she was going. There was nothing out of the ordinary about 'fooling around' a little. At a coed college you're supposed to explore other people, learn what you like.

Everybody did it. Bonnie was just unfortunate enough to have a guy who still believed in monogamy, who went strictly by the book—and I mean *the* book, the Bible.''

On Valentine's Day, 1977, Bonnie sent Richard a love poem which she had translated from the Italian. She did not know that she was scribbling prophecy:

> Before leaving, my sweet love,
> I should have to see the mountains walk,
> the day be forty-eight hours long,
> and the sea turn to stone.
> If all this cannot happen,
> I always want to keep you in my heart;
> if all this cannot occur,
> before leaving you I should have to die!

In early March, Richard called Bonnie from TCU and confided that he too was having troubles. He was receiving nothing but rejections from the graduate schools he had applied to, two book publishers had turned him down as a Spanish translator, and he was doing poorly in classes.

Despite her seemingly divided loyalties, Bonnie performed like a true friend, even a wife. She immediately quit her nine-to-five baby sitting job, took the savings she had accumulated from it, and flew to Fort Worth. She stayed with Herrin for two weeks, helping him type papers, consoling him, encouraging him. But during the fortnight visit she touched one sensitive nerve.

"Richard, I don't think you're in touch with your deep feelings," she told him one day. "I'm seeing a psychiatrist, and I think you should do the same." If he couldn't afford it, Bonnie suggested a public counseling agency.

Richard was taken aback. He had forgotten about the "hang-ups" he had admitted to over a year before. He reacted coolly to the idea of probing either Bonnie's or his own psyche, fearing the exploration.

When he had first heard that Bonnie was seeing a psychiatrist, Richard became suspicious. "What if you learn that you don't need me?'' he had asked plaintively.

Now faced with Bonnie's request that he too see a psychiatrist, he brushed it aside. ''It's hard to believe, but that was my response to her,'' he later confided. ''I said, 'You're wrong. I know who I am.' ''

Herrin was not prepared for the next onslaught, one which was to prove that he literally did not know who he was. Least of all did he expect that its source would be his beloved mother.

Linda Ugarte arrived in Fort Worth for a visit shortly after Bonnie left. Richard told his mother about his plans to go to the Yale Prom in April, showing Linda the check Bonnie had sent him so he could buy shoes for the big event. At one point, as the conversation turned to marriage and divorce, Richard asked his mother a question that had perplexed him for twenty-three years. Why had she divorced his real father, James Herrin?

''I looked at him'' Linda Ugarte later revealed, ''and I told him I had never married his father. He just looked at me, and he asked me how come I had never married. I told him it had not worked out the way we wanted it to.''

Herrin stared blankly at his mother, but his innards tightened as he heard the news that he was an illegitimate child. He held back his true reaction. His mother already felt guilty enough, he figured. But as soon as Linda Ugarte had left, Herrin called Bonnie, the only one he could still entrust with his deepest feelings, and he cried into the phone. ''I felt worthless,'' Herrin later related. ''I felt that I had been betrayed by not having been told before. I was twenty-three years old. For a few days after, I felt that my mother had been hypocritical. She had been a woman of such great faith.''

HERRIN came to Yale for the Spring Prom in mid-April 1977 with news of a quick upturn in his prospects. He had been accepted conditionally into the Ph.D. program at George Washington University and even had a possible employment contact with a geologist at the Smithsonian Institution.

Bonnie was pleased, but she had more pressing concerns. She was praying that Herrin wouldn't run into any of the men she had been dating that winter and spring. "She went out with about three or four different guys that spring," recalled a friend of Bonnie's. "Not a lot by Yale standards, but certainly more than she ever had before. Bonnie was just starting to think of herself as an adult, beginning to find out about herself, beginning to enjoy things."

One of the men she had been dating with increasing frequency was Jim Lawrence, a handsome member of the Whiffenpoofs. Lawrence seemed to be pulling Bonnie slowly away from Richard Herrin. She had confided to Henry Howser that she was totally confused. "Bonnie loved Jim and she loved Rich," Howser explained. "She wanted to break off with Rich but she thought it would destroy him completely. And her concern for Rich outweighed her concern for herself and Jim."

Proof of the Pudding performed the night of the Prom, as did the Whiffenpoofs. Lawrence knew all about Herrin and Bonnie, but didn't know that Richard was at the dance. Bonnie was working feverishly to keep the two men apart, in a scenario not unlike an old Hollywood movie. When Lawrence looked for Bonnie, she ran right past him. "I went off with some friends," remembered Lawrence, "but then I said, 'Goddammit, this is stupid!' I went back to talk with Bonnie. When she saw me coming, she thought there'd be trouble and dragged Herrin out of the dance."

Herrin had no idea that he came within a few feet of confronting, in the flesh, one of the innumerable faceless fears that he had lived with for almost two years. All he remembered was that "at one point Bonnie said she was hot and that she wanted to go outside for some fresh air. So we went outside for awhile." Bonnie had played her role, keeping her two men apart, with aplomb. "I don't remember any panic on her part," Herrin recalled.

IT WAS THE first week of May when Bonnie Garland casually wondered over the phone whether Richard wouldn't want to date other women. It was a hypothetical question, she said. Just suppose. What would happen? Richard quickly asked Bonnie how it would be possible to go out with someone regularly "and not end up in bed."

It seemed obvious to Herrin. Ever since he had gone to bed with Bonnie Garland, sex had existed on one long undifferentiated continuum that stretched from holding hands to intercourse. He had lived for almost two years by such a credo, unable even to hold hands with another woman. He constantly asked Bonnie whether she held hands with the men she went out with. Did she kiss them? That had been important to him. The more he thought about Bonnie's suggestion, however hypothetical, the more disturbed he became.

He told himself that the issue had come "out of left field." But what he was feeling came from dead center. He worried for two days about why Bonnie had brought it up before he called to tell her he was "very upset."

"Oh, I didn't mean anything by it," Bonnie responded. "Don't worry about it. It was just something I happened to bring up."

Once again Herrin was relieved. But it was the last reassurance he would ever get from Bonnie. He went back to feeling "on top of the world," ready to buckle down to get the A he needed in his sedimentary petrology class, finish his thesis, and look forward to seeing Bonnie as soon as she returned from Europe with the Glee Club. He wrote to Bonnie to remind her to send him her itinerary so that his cards and letters would arrive on time.

"I'll be thinking of you every single day while you're gone," he wrote her. "You know that wherever you are or whatever you're doing, I'm sending my love in full force. I want you to feel my love and tremble with excitement when you look forward to being with me again—in my arms, bodies intertwined, love pouring out all over.''

THE YALE GLEE CLUB and the Whiffenpoofs left the United States together on May 17 for their six-week tour that would take them to London, Amsterdam, Geneva, Zurich, Munich, Copenhagen, Oslo and the fjord country, Notre Dame in Paris, and Chartres.

Bonnie Garland was beginning to look like a different person. She had changed her hair style, bought a new raincoat, restocked her wardrobe, and lost weight. "I'd never seen her as consistently happy as on that trip," Fenno Heath, the Glee Club's director, later stated. "Before she had always been up and down, unpredictably moody, worrying about whether to drop out of school, worried about not getting credit for voice lessons, sitting on my couch crying, an unhappy girl."

Professionally as well, Heath thought, Bonnie was turning the corner. On the tour Bonnie was an important soloist, singing with her lyric soprano Benjamin Britten's "A Ceremony of Carols" and "Festival Te Deum." "I had the feeling she was on the verge of taking things more seriously," Heath later recalled. "She had certain potential. The charm was there. She was just beginning to get it together." But Heath wasn't sure whether the change was because Bonnie no longer had the pressure of school or whether it had something to do with Jim Lawrence, the Whiffenpoof who had become Bonnie's constant seatmate during the tour.

At every stop, as Richard Herrin promised, there was one and often two letters waiting for Bonnie. In Paris there was a postcard of Odilon Redon's "The Birth of Venus" with the comment "Now I understand a little bit more about classical beauty, because that is you." In Geneva, Bonnie read, "You know sweetheart, as of today (Saturday) I still haven't heard from you. 10 days!!! I can't stand it. Why me?!! . . . I really do hope to start receiving your cards or letters soon, babe. I love you and need you always.''

In Munich, Bonnie heard from Richard: "Hi babe, I'm sad, sad, sad; lonely, lonely, lonely; depressed, depressed, depressed. Today is Saturday June 4th, and I still haven't received any word from you. I didn't expect the mail service to be so slow, because it's tearing my guts out.''

The problem was not the mail service. For the first time in their relationship, Bonnie was not writing to Richard. After a while on the tour she even stopped opening his letters. For three months she had been putting off telling Herrin about Jim Lawrence and herself. Not writing was one way of getting a message across, but Bonnie still had to find a more definitive way out of her classic love triangle.

On June 8, three weeks into the six weeks Glee Club tour, Richard Herrin sat down in his Fort Worth apartment on Lowden Street and wrote three identical letters, addressing one to Bonnie in Denmark, one to Bonnie in Norway, and one to Bonnie in Sweden. In each one he said, "Hi, Remember me? June 8 and still no mail from you. . . . I'm sending [these three letters] all at once, which means they'll say the same thing: that is, nothing. You probably won't get them anyway. I at least hope you're safe. I'm not angry with the Postal Service, yet, and I hope they're the cause of the delay in me hearing from you. But, 3 weeks? I'm depressed and confused, and at times I feel like I'm getting fucked over. By the postal service or whatever. I'm sorry I can't be more cheerful. 3 damn weeks.''

Herrin had now moved into a tiny house in Fort Worth with two rooms and a kitchen. He was house-sitting for friends who were away. The bed spring and mattress were on the floor. Herrin had a radio but no television, no phone, no roommate. And now no word from Bonnie. After two weeks of not hearing from her, he told himself that it was the mail service's fault. After three weeks, Herrin knew he couldn't blame the post office any more.

He turned over a number of possible explanations in his head. Maybe she was too busy singing and shopping to write. Or worse, maybe she had met someone on the tour and wasn't thinking about him. Maybe she had eloped and he'd never see her again. Herrin began to work less on his thesis now, staying by himself in the little house, moping. A friend asked him if he had heard from Bonnie, but he didn't respond, ashamed, as he says, "to admit that I hadn't heard from Bonnie."

He then told himself that Bonnie would be back on June 30. She would explain everything and reassure him as she always did and they would carry on as before. But after four weeks of not hearing from Bonnie, Herrin had all but stopped his laboratory work, his research, and his reading for the thesis. He began to go to the Stables, the local bar, in the afternoon to watch television and have a couple of beers. He was thinking about Bonnie all the time, even during the brief moments when he tried to work.

It was then that the "little nightmares" began. They would just "pop into my head," he said. "Bonnie and I were in a car or in my truck. The truck went into a lake and we drowned or we crashed into a barrier and were killed." The thoughts immediately repulsed Herrin and he tried to push them out of his head.

But another "little nightmare" popped into his head to take its place. "I could see Bonnie lying naked with her breasts and genital area having been mutilated with a knife," Herrin said. Snapping to consciousness, he felt ashamed for allowing such "horrible" thoughts to enter his mind. But they came back.

To a psychiatrist, Herrin later confided that it was the thought of Bonnie's being unfaithful to him that stimulated the unconscious hostility. "If I found out that Bonnie had slept with another man, I would cut out her genitals, and cut off her breasts, but not kill her. This would flash into my mind and I would say to myself: How can you have such thoughts?" Herrin's fantasy of vengeance was to remove the parts that had been violated. At this point, the psychiatrist believed, Herrin unconsciously sought not to kill her, but to purify her.

A secretary in the geology department noticed that Herrin was coming in to the office irregularly and looking as if he had slept in his clothes. Leanne Watson, a friend with whom Herrin had consulted about mail delivery to Europe, asked him occasionally if he had heard anything from Bonnie. The first few times Richard just said "No" and shrugged. Then one time Herrin didn't shrug. He glanced up quickly and gave her a rude, intense response, "I don't think you ought to ask that anymore."

In the middle of June, Herrin flew home to Los Angeles for ten days. He went to the wedding of an old high school friend, but told no one about his depression. Just before he left he mailed a postcard to Scarsdale, where Bonnie was due home in less than a week. "My life has been empty without you for these last 5½ weeks," he told Bonnie. "I have missed you terribly and have reached the pits. I want you more than ever. I've never needed you so much."

As he flew back to Fort Worth, Herrin encouraged himself with a pleasant fantasy. Since he had been away for a week, there would be a little pile of mail in the box when he got back. And in that pile there would be something from Bonnie. He went from the airport directly to his mailbox, but there was nothing from Bonnie.

BONNIE GARLAND, Jim Lawrence, and Fenno Heath had captured a small corner table in the Norwegian roadside cafe. They were on the final leg of their tour, taking a lunch break on their way from Oslo to the fjord country. Bonnie sat at the table toying with a small envelope. It was a vital letter to Richard Herrin.

"She had been trying to write that letter to Herrin for most of the trip," Fenno Heath later recounted. "We'd talked about Herrin before on the trip. She was always in a bit of a quandary about what to do and we'd sort of joke about it. So over lunch in the cafe she had the letter in her hand. She said, 'Well, I guess this is it.' "

The men kidded Bonnie about what Herrin would do after receiving the letter. Jim Lawrence suggested that Richard would be waiting for her at the airport when the plane landed in New York.

Bonnie disagreed. "No way," she answered. She then looked at both men, and in a half-chuckle that disguised its seriousness, she said: "When Richard gets this letter, he'll probably kill me."

Fenno Heath would later recall Bonnie's remark with a shudder. "It will stay with me as long as I live."

———————

CHAPTER FIVE

The Rage of Richard Herrin

Thursday, June 30, 1977

Though he had already memorized it, Richard Herrin looked again at the final entry on his copy of the Glee Club itinerary:

Thursday, June 30	*Oslo–London–New York*		
Oslo SAS 511	lv.	8:15 AM
London	arr.	10:20 AM
London British 509	lv.	1:00 PM
New York (JFK)	arr.	3:35 PM

All his hopes were now on the last line, on Bonnie Garland's arrival in New York. He had calculated the time it would take to travel from Kennedy Airport to Scarsdale. With customs, baggage, goodbyes, and the thirty-mile drive, he estimated that it would be six o'clock when Bonnie drove up to her home. He wanted the timing to be as perfect as possible, to reach her just as she was coming through the door.

He ached for this phone call. After six weeks of agonizing silence, it was his first chance to hear Bonnie's reassurances that the absence of news had not been her fault, that her love for him had not diminished.

For Herrin the past six weeks had been misery. He had given up all work on his thesis. Richard continued working at his job in the geology department a couple of hours a day, but even there the secretaries remarked on his grizzled and distracted appearance. His beard was untrimmed, hair uncombed, and his clothes rumpled.

Herrin would wander to the library and glance aimlessly through books that had nothing to do with geology. He spent hours huddled under the air conditioner in the two-room house, playing his guitar and reading through the stack of old letters from Bonnie that he kept by his bed. He kept asking himself the same questions: "What is going on? Why haven't I heard from her? What could possibly be wrong?"

He listened to baseball games on the radio to distract himself, but when there was no baseball, the radio only depressed him more. As if taunting him, it seemed to play only songs about lost loves: "It's Sad to Belong to Someone Else When The Right One Comes Along" or "Torn Between Two Lovers." They were popular that summer, but for Herrin they were slow torture. "There's been another man that I've needed—and I've loved," he heard. He angrily snapped off the radio.

It was now almost five o'clock, six in Scarsdale, and Richard's anxiety was increasing. Bonnie would be home soon, probably right now driving the final miles of the Bronx River Parkway. He would hear her voice in minutes.

Richard had no phone in his house. He picked up the stack of dimes and quarters that he had been accumulating for this call and walked the few blocks to the geology department's pay phone. What would Bonnie have to say? How would she explain everything? Could he tell her that he had been dying for six interminable weeks?

Richard dialed the familiar number of the Garland home. He was trembling when he heard the voice of Bonnie's mother. "Mrs. Garland, this is Rick. May I speak with Bonnie?"

It took only an instant for his expectations to deflate. Bonnie wasn't home, Mrs. Garland told him. She had called from the airport to say that she was going to New Haven with some friends for a couple of days.

Richard was silent. In all his preparations, he hadn't considered the possibility that she wouldn't come directly from the airport. "Do you have the number there?" he asked hopefully.

"No," Joan Garland replied. Bonnie had only said that she would be home Saturday night. There was no message for him.

No message? What the hell was happening? Was the whole world turned upside down? Where was his Bonnie?

They had always called each other after a trip. Why had she not even bothered to leave a number for him with her mother? Why had she ignored him? His mind was somersaulting.

"Do you suppose," he finally asked of Mrs. Garland, "that she doesn't want to speak to me?"

But Joan Garland couldn't help. "I don't know," she replied.

Richard told Mrs. Garland that he was running out of change and had to hang up. He could now almost visualize his worst fear. "She was going to New Haven because she was with a guy from the Glee Club, and they were going off to spend a few days by themselves," he thought. After three years, he had been deserted. Bonnie was with another man.

Richard tried to convince himself that it was just his wild imagination. Diane was one thing, but it hurt too much to think that he had been jilted by the woman he was going to marry. There had to be a more reasonable explanation, he hoped. He invented one that wasn't so painful. Perhaps some of the people on the tour wanted to have one final party together in New Haven before they all dispersed and went their separate ways. He didn't believe that, but he thought it sufficiently rational that he could, as he later said, "give that story to anyone who asked about Bonnie, since several people knew she was due to arrive that day."

Richard didn't know what to believe. His mind whirled as he walked to the nearby Pizza Hut, where a friend worked. He ordered a Coke and stood around the counter not quite knowing what to do. Finally, his friend arranged for him to wash dishes, a mundane distraction which allowed Richard to lose his pain in gushes of steam. He washed until closing time, then went home to his apartment. With thoughts of Bonnie and another man piercing his brain, Herrin thrashed around on his bed for hours before falling asleep.

Friday, July 1

It was shortly after nine when Richard awoke and went straight to the mailbox as he had done each morning since arriving in Fort Worth. Even after six weeks without news from Bonnie, he had persisted in his habit.

But when Herrin peered into the small compartment this morning, the envelope with the blue-and-red-striped border shone like an invitation from royalty. He grabbed at it. There was the familiar, neat script, and the stamp from "Norge," the Glee Club's last tour stop. With the letter in his trembling hands, Richard ran back into the house and tore open the envelope. For weeks he had begged Bonnie to write. Now, as he read this singular response to his repeated pleas, Herrin began to cry.

> *Dear Rick,*
> *I know it has been an unforgivable crime not to have written you all this time but I have been*

trying to postpone action on something very important which has come up on this tour. I still don't know what to do but I must at least tell you what has happened. I have spent almost all my time on this tour in the company of one specific man, someone I saw off and on during the semester. To make things short he has fallen in love with me. I am in a total state of confusion because I know I still love you just as much, but I feel an infatuation, at least, for him. I did not want to tell you because I thought it would all be over when the tour ended. But now I am not so sure. It makes me sick to write this letter because I know how you are going to react. But I couldn't lie and I didn't want to tell the truth, so I just haven't written. You remember those conversations we have had about being constrained and feeling like I hadn't had a social life—well, in a way I think the elastic finally broke into this. I can hardly believe that this is happening and I hope to straighten things out with the help of my shrink when I get back. I need time by myself to think, but also hope you will not turn your back on me. I know you feel hurt, betrayed, alienated, but you have always said that if it happened, you would want to know. I wish now more than ever that you will seek psychiatric help to help you deal with a flood of emotions which is probably beginning to overwhelm you. I hate this letter and this mess, but please be patient and I'm sure things will work out because I still love you and I need your love as much as ever—please don't desert me. I'll be back soon and we can talk. I've missed you a great deal.

Love,

Bonnie

Hopelessness engulfed Richard Herrin as he finished reading Bonnie Garland's letter. He fell onto his bed weeping uncontrollably, clenching his teeth to keep from screaming, closing his hands into fists to stifle the exploding pain. For the next several hours Herrin lay on his bed, weeping, reading the letter over and over, telling himself one moment that the relationship had ended and the next that it could be salvaged.

Herrin was convinced that "another guy" had taken Bonnie away from him, that the woman he loved more than anything else was deserting him. Still sobbing, he examined the letter again, searching for clues that his dismal interpretation was incorrect. ". . . I still love you just as much. . . . hope you will not turn your back on me. . . . things will work out because I still love you. . . ."

Perhaps there was hope after all. "It doesn't say anything definite," he told himself. "I'll see her soon. I'll get it all fixed up. There is nothing to worry about." Then on rereading the letter he found evidence that his worst fears were in fact justified: ". . . thought it would all be over when the tour ended. But now I am not so sure." Herrin went back over the edge into despair.

The only thing that seemed definite was that Bonnie Garland seemed to have pegged her man well: "I know how you are going to react. . . . I know you feel hurt, betrayed, alienated."

Perhaps she knew him too well to torture him with the full story. Better than anyone else, Bonnie understood the powerful currents of emotion that ran under Richard's controlled surface. Her letter was mild by "Dear John" standards. Far from saying goodbye, she had asked Richard, "please don't desert me." Knowing that he would be overwhelmed with a "flood of emotions," she hesitated to land the crucial blow: that of telling Richard that she had slept with another man.

Bonnie knew how close to the surface were his nerve endings of anger and jealousy. She had seen them. There were the inquisitorial phone calls at one or two or three in the morning. There was the sometimes angry questioning about whom she had gone out with and what she had done. "Bonnie once went to a movie with a male friend," recalled one man Bonnie had dated.

"Rich happened to come up the next weekend and got upset when she told him about it. He asked, 'Did you kiss him?' Bonnie said, 'No, but I held hands with him.' Rich got mad and cried. He was very jealous. She said he had 'a typical macho outlook.' "

Bonnie always tried desperately not to hurt her first love. Jim Lawrence, Bonnie's constant companion on the tour, recalled that "it was Bonnie's impulse to protect him. All the delay was designed to protect him. It certainly wasn't done to save her any trouble because the longer it went on, the harder it was for her." Bonnie was too inexperienced to know the consequences of her protective instincts or the hazards of indecision, too young to appreciate the depths of Richard Herrin's obsessive love.

It was hours before Richard finally stopped crying. His mind was now racing to find solutions: the word, the action, the key that would enable him to keep Bonnie. His first thought involved New Haven. He decided not to study for a doctorate in Washington, D.C., and instead to find a job in New Haven, near Bonnie. He would even start seeing a psychiatrist as she had asked.

Richard went to the geology department office to put a plan into action. The secretary got him a telephone WATS line and Richard dialed the Yale Medical School's Primates Research Unit. His academic interest had recently been moving towards primates. In May he had written Bonnie that "a personal goal is to know more about apes than any other person alive!!!"

Ann Stoddard, the secretary at the Primates Unit who listened to Richard's request that afternoon, recalled: "He was very interested in coming to work at Yale. He was willing to do any kind of work at all. I took his name and address, and actually I was hoping he would get the job, because he seemed so interested in it."

Richard felt relieved for a moment after the call. He collected himself and ate the pizza which was his payment for the dishwashing. But at home that night Richard couldn't concentrate. The letter from Bonnie and the phone call to Mrs. Garland kept playing over in his mind. It was like another of his "little nightmares." But this time it was real.

What was she doing with the guy she mentioned in the letter? He could almost see it. "She's gone to New Haven with someone she's probably been sleeping with." What he had lived in constant fear of for two years might now be happening. He couldn't believe it. His wife-to-be was making love to another man while he was sweating in a desolate room in Texas.

Saturday, July 2

For most of Saturday Richard was suddenly and curiously calm. He tried to pretend that the hopelessness wasn't there. That morning, as if nothing had happened, he drove his old Chevy pickup, "Twuk" (as he and Bonnie had nicknamed it), to the muffler shop for some scheduled repairs. He seemed to be operating on two levels, alternating between illusion and reality.

Only the week before he had called his mother and asked for three hundred dollars to overhaul his truck in preparation for a trip that he still planned to take with Bonnie. As Linda Ugarte later recalled, "He wanted to make sure that the truck was in running condition because Bonnie was going to come and spend the summer there with him. Then they were both going to drive together up to Washington, D.C." Now Herrin was keeping the appointment as if nothing had happened. He was still going back East, he reasoned, either to Washington, D.C., at the end of the summer, or to New Haven as soon as he got a job. It felt better to feel reasonable.

Twuk had its brakes and exhaust pipe replaced while Richard waited in a small anteroom of the shop, reading. His paperback companion was *Sybil*, the true account of a woman possessing sixteen different personalities. "That there was a seventeenth self to supplant the depleted waking self was testament that truth is internal, the surface a lie,'' Richard read. He closed the book not thinking about Sybil Dorsett but about the futility of life without Bonnie Garland.

After the truck repairs were completed, he went to get a haircut. A new plan was taking shape in his mind. From the barbershop he drove to the geology department and called American Airlines to book a seat on a New York-bound flight. Calmly, he mapped his route. Bonnie was due home tonight, so he would give her Sunday to rest. He made a reservation for Monday. ''I planned on calling her Sunday morning,'' he recalled. ''I would say, 'When would you like to see me?' And then I could say, 'Good. I'm coming up the next morning.' ''

He was striving to think rationally, to anticipate everything, including Bonnie's responses. He would get Bonnie to invite him up, act calm, give her a day to be alone with her parents. Having formulated a reasoned plan, Richard went back home relieved.

But once he was alone in the empty house, confusion again caught up with him. Confidence in a rational scheme gave way to fears that Bonnie wouldn't respond accordingly. He hadn't eaten all day; all he could think about was her letter from Norway. As he contemplated spending all of Sunday with himself and his thoughts, he panicked.

Richard ran back to the geology offices to change his flight plans. He would leave as soon as possible for New York. He booked passage on flight number 759, leaving Fort Worth-Dallas on Sunday at three in the morning, less than six hours away. Forget Bonnie's day of rest. She would have no chance to say, ''Don't come.''

Richard prepared for what he knew was the most important trip of his life, what he was beginning to think of as ''a rescue mission.'' Everything he did now was precise and unhurried. He gathered together a couple of shirts, a change of underwear and socks, anthropologist Jane Goodall's text on primates, his special container for loose change, and his checkbook for buying a ticket back to Fort Worth.

In the pressure of his eroding world he was supported by the order of detail. He took a bath and then lingered for a long time in front of the mirror while he trimmed his beard. He went to his stuffed animal collection and picked up a small Saint Bernard that he had won for Bonnie at an amusement park in Los Angeles. The little dog even had a plastic brandy barrel around its neck—an appropriate symbol, Richard thought, for his rescue mission.

Everything was falling into place. To win Bonnie back he would have to be confident and cool. How would he act when they first met? He juggled the different poses he might assume in this all-important scene. "When we first saw each other, the first few words would be very important. I was trying to decide whether I should be very submissive, if I should try to make her feel sorry for me, or if I should demand that she explain the whole thing." He would be whatever was necessary to win Bonnie back.

But what stance would Bonnie want from him? Submissive? Victimized? Demanding? He had been all of these and Bonnie's elastic had still snapped. For two years he had been the simpering victim. He had cried when he was hurt and frightened whenever the relationship was threatened by everyone from ex-girlfriends to psychiatrists. Bonnie had chided him for being paranoid, for not being aggressive enough, for not being in touch with his emotions. If Bonnie was moving out of his orbit because he was wimpy, he would show her that he could be a man, stable and strong.

When Richard sat down to compose the short note he would give to Bonnie in Scarsdale, it was as if he were inventing a new personality. He wrote not in his tightly-packed script, but printed each letter, made each larger than usual, and left more space between the words. There were no triple exclamation points or question marks, signs, as he had once written to Bonnie, "when I start using !!! you know I'm returning back to normal!!!" Neither was there a salutation. It was almost as if he were addressing himself, as if Bonnie were writing to him, trying to cheer him up.

> REAL STRENGTH INVOLVES CONFIDENCE IN ONES ABILITY TO MEET WHATEVER PROBLEMS ARISE WITHOUT OVERREACTING, TO BE ABLE TO THINK THROUGH THE SOLUTION RATHER THAN PANICKING. CONFIDENCE COMES FROM BEING IN TOUCH WITH YOUR OWN FEARS. REAL STRENGTH MEANS UNDERSTANDING YOURSELF AND YOUR CAPABILITIES AS WELL AS YOUR FEARS. I WILL BE NEAR YOU FROM NOW ON, ALWAYS WITHIN REACH, TO GIVE YOU ALL I CAN. I WILL NEVER DESERT YOU, WILL ALWAYS, ALWAYS LOVE YOU, BONNIE.

He folded the letter, put it in an envelope and wrote Bonnie's name on the outside. He had now decided on how he would greet Bonnie. "I figured when I first saw her, I would have the dog with me, and I would give her the dog, and she would read the note, and that would kind of be an ice-breaker."

It was after midnight when Herrin, his flight-time quickly approaching, hastily scribbled another note. This one was as despairing as the earlier one had been hopeful. The unconfident Richard Herrin had resurfaced, and as he confused the month of the year, from July to June, he gave the first evidence that he was contemplating something drastic, ostensibly his own suicide.

> *If I do not*
> *return from New York soon,*
> *(departure—June 3)*
> *I will never be back. The*
> *enclosed letter will explain why.*

He left the note unsigned, but taped it to the letter Bonnie had sent him from Norway and left it on a desk in the living room. Looking around the room, Herrin fixed his gaze on a long length of rope tied around a box of books. Should Bonnie not come back to him, the rope would be his means of escape. He hurriedly grabbed the rope, stuffed it in his flight bag, and left the house.

Sunday, July 3

When Bonnie Garland returned home Saturday night her parents welcomed home a new daughter, a changed person from the constantly sad and confused young woman of the past two years. She had lost weight. She had a new zest for life. And she had a new boyfriend.

Almost as soon as they met Jim Lawrence, Joan and Paul Garland knew that they had seen the storm through. Not only was Bonnie happier, but her new companion seemed to be everything that Richard Herrin was not. Jim Lawrence was a real Yalie: bright, articulate, and self-assured. He was a Whiffenpoof, an honors graduate, and on his way to law school. He was a delight to have around. On Sunday morning Paul Garland invited Bonnie and Jim to go boating with him, a family activity that Richard Herrin had never been asked to share.

Joan Garland remained behind that morning to be with her father who was recuperating from a stroke. Just as she was about to step into the shower, the phone rang. On the other end of the line was the soft voice of Richard Herrin, who asked immediately to speak with Bonnie.

"She isn't here," Mrs. Garland told Richard. "She's out boating with her father and I don't know when she'll be back. Probably several hours."

Herrin spoke nervously. As with the call he made to the Garland home Thursday, he had planned this one for hours. "Mrs. Garland, I'm not calling from Texas," he announced. "I'm calling from the Hartsdale station."

Joan Garland was astonished. The Hartsdale station was only a few hundred yards away from the house. Richard Herrin was at their door again.

"Well," Mrs. Garland began, "as long as you're in Hartsdale, I think I should tell you that there is a young man staying here at the house."

The words bent him in two. No longer could he attribute his fears to his "wild" imagination. This was real, the first affirmation that someone had taken his place.

Mrs. Garland suggested that as long as he was so close he should come up to the house for lunch. The back door would be open and he could let himself in.

Herrin hung up, shocked by another punctured expectation. Nothing in the last three days had followed the scenarios he was constantly trying to write in his head. Only the fears kept surfacing, always more real. In return for his carefully-timed phone call to Bonnie on Thursday he had learned only that she had gone to New Haven without giving him a thought; in answer to his entreaties that she write him from Europe, on Friday her lone letter of response had made him shudder; and now, after his impulsive all-night flight to New York, the long-awaited reunion was aborted on Bonnie's doorstep.

Herrin knocked on the back door and walked in as Mrs. Garland had suggested. When he saw that there was no one in the breakfast room, he dashed up the back stairs to Bonnie's bedroom. Setting the toy Saint Bernard on her bed, Herrin extracted the note that he had written the night before from his flight bag and with a roll of scotch tape he had brought along, he attached the envelope to the dog's plastic barrel. At least he still had the power to implement this small part of his plan.

The Richard Herrin who greeted Joan Garland in her kitchen this sunny Sunday morning was not the one who seven months before had sat in the Garland home nonchalantly fielding questions from the Garlands, his arm confidently wrapped around their daughter. He was now a supplicant instead of a victorious lover. Richard declined Mrs. Garland's offer of food, but said he might have some coffee.

Though Richard had never felt welcome by the Garlands, he had begun to believe that Mrs. Garland had softened toward him. Earlier that year she had offered to help him draft a *curriculum vitae* when it seemed he would not be accepted into graduate schools. "Mrs. Garland actually wrote directly to me," he later recalled. "I tried to express to her that maybe I did have a lot of shortcomings but I was trying to work on them, and maybe I was a late bloomer. And I remember that she referred to that later when she wrote and said, 'There's nothing wrong with being a late bloomer.' "

Joan Garland was never pleased with Richard Herrin, but as a mother and social worker her inclinations were toward compassion. She talked with the young bearded Chicano for almost two hours that morning. Facing Bonnie's mother he could be solicitous, but he also had to act mature and rational.

"I mentioned that I was aware that Bonnie had gone out with Yale men throughout the two years that I was in Texas," Herrin would later recall of this conversation. "But I didn't feel threatened by that because she assured me that nothing was going on, that she needed to have some social life."

But Joan Garland was hearing something different in the same conversation. "He said that all through the last semester he had had to pry out of her who she was going out with," recalled Mrs. Garland. "I said to him that if he was afraid that she wouldn't speak to him on the phone and he had to pry out of her who she was dating, that as much as he wanted to believe the relationship was something else, there really wasn't the trust that there should be."

Richard was discouraged but he held tight to his mask of reason and nodded in meek agreement. "Even if I held Bonnie now," he offered hesitantly, "it would be different."

Mrs. Garland agreed that it would be different, explaining that Richard and Bonnie would now come together as adults. Joan Garland had watched Bonnie's academic slide at Yale after meeting Herrin. In her sophomore year Bonnie had seemed constantly depressed. She had always rebelled against her parents' dislike of Herrin, but as Joan Garland had asked Bonnie, "If Herrin is so great, why aren't you happy?"

Not until Bonnie tried to accelerate during her junior year and buckled under the weight of the studies and her extracurricular load did she begin to take stock of herself. That was five months before. When Joan Garland finally saw Bonnie return from her European tour with a new boyfriend and a new appetite for life, she knew that Richard Herrin was finished as a suitor for her daughter.

Mrs. Garland was trying to prepare Richard for the letdown. "I said that Bonnie was now older and she would meet him now as an adult," Mrs. Garland explained. "She was twenty. She had only been seventeen when he met her. And he had been her first boyfriend."

"I wouldn't want her back out of guilt," Richard said after they had finished their coffee. Despite the emotion surging through him, Richard wanted to appear like an adult.

"No, you wouldn't want that," Joan Garland reassured him, "because eventually, it would work out badly."

It was now past noon and Mrs. Garland thought it would be awkward if the boaters returned while Richard was in the house. Richard had even less desire to be there when his fiancée walked in on the arm of another man.

Joan Garland helped Richard track down the phone number of Mike Greenwald, a Yale classmate of Richard's who lived on Long Island. Herrin thought he could stay for a few days, but he made no move toward the phone.

"Mike was a friend of mine," Herrin explained. "He also knew Bonnie very well. And I would be too ashamed to tell Mike that Bonnie wanted to leave me, that there was another guy, or that she just didn't want to continue the relationship with me. I felt I would lose my self-esteem having to admit that.''

Joan Garland suggested that he could tell the Greenwalds that he had come to Scarsdale but that ''nobody was home.''

It was such a simple way to preserve his dignity. He called the Greenwalds, told them he was at the Hartsdale station, and they invited him right over, his self-esteem still intact. It raised his spirits to have taken some positive action and have a place to stay until he could see Bonnie. After all Bonnie and he had shared, it was impossible that she was leaving him so abruptly. If he could only see her, everything would work out.

When he left the Garlands' home Richard walked back to the Hartsdale station, took a train into Manhattan, and boarded another train for Long Island. He was picked up at the Syosset station by his former classmate and greeted warmly at the Greenwald home. It was like touching down in a friendly foreign country. No one knew about his problems with Bonnie, and no one would know.

At the Garland home later that evening, as Mrs. Garland was preparing dinner, Bonnie came into the kitchen with a quizzical expression on her face.

''Was Rick here?'' she asked her mother.

Not wanting to ruin the day, Mrs. Garland had planned not to tell Bonnie about Herrin's visit until after the Fourth of July fireworks that evening. ''Yes. How did you know?''

''He left something on my bed.''

Bonnie gave no more details, but Joan Garland was curious. Later she went to her daughter's room to see what Richard could have left behind. On the bed she saw an envelope with ''BONNIE'' printed in big red letters across it. Inside was Richard's plea: ''I will be near you from now on, all ways within reach, to give you all I can. I will never desert you.'' Mrs. Garland picked the envelope up and was about to look inside, but stopped and put it back on the bed. Had she read it, she might have wondered how it could have been written by the same timorous young man with whom she had spoken that morning.

At the fireworks display that night Bonnie was unusually quiet. When Jim Lawrence finally asked her what the trouble was, she answered, "Rick is in town. He left a present on my bed."

Lawrence wasn't surprised. "I hate to say I told you so. What are you going to do?"

"I'm going to see him," Bonnie replied.

Monday, July 4

Richard seemed to relax in the company of the Greenwalds over that lengthy Fourth of July weekend. He played volleyball and sat in the backyard, building his reserve of confidence for his ultimate talk with Bonnie. He even waited until five o'clock that afternoon before trying to phone her, not wanting to appear anxious or upset.

Bonnie's brother Patrick answered the phone and went to get his sister. Richard took a long breath. The next voice he expected to hear was that of his redheaded sweetheart. But it was Patrick who came back on the line reporting that Bonnie was asleep.

"Would you mind trying again to make sure?" Herrin asked Patrick. It was his third attempt in five days to reach Bonnie. She had always been reachable before; now she was avoiding him.

Patrick returned. Yes, she was asleep.

Richard didn't want to let go of the phone, and tried to engage Patrick in some trivial conversation. They kidded each other about whose favorite football team was better. Richard defended his Los Angeles Rams, who were always being edged out of the conference championship; Patrick was proud of his Oakland Raiders, winners of that year's Super Bowl. Patrick said he was going to a Pink Floyd concert in Madison Square Garden that evening and offered Richard a ticket, but Herrin declined.

Patrick volunteered to try Bonnie again. But when he came back this time, the report was even more confusing. Bonnie didn't want to talk with him right now. He should call back at ten.

Richard hung up, sure that Bonnie was lying. She wasn't really asleep. "The other fellow was still there," he told himself in dismay, "and that is why she didn't want to be disturbed." It was the Diane Nightmare all over again, but now on a grand scale. He had never been engaged to Diane, had never made love to her, never proposed to share his entire life with her.

For the Greenwalds, Richard kept up the appearance of stability, telling them only that he hadn't been able to get through. But only a few hours later, Mrs. Greenwald summoned Richard to the phone. For a moment he was startled. No one knew where he was but the Garlands. It was only seven o'clock, and he wasn't supposed to call Bonnie until ten. Still he was anxious as he picked up the receiver.

"Hello?"

"Hi, you nut. What are you doing here?"

Bonnie Garland's first words in over six weeks almost pushed Richard's depression the fifteen hundred miles back to Texas. She was as buoyant and jovial as ever.

"Sorry for being so tired before," she said, "but I just wasn't up to talking over something so emotional."

"You don't have to apologize," Richard assured her, avoiding any mention of the other fellow. "I just want to understand how you feel. But you shouldn't feel guilty." As much as he wanted to recount the horrors of his panic, he held back. He would strain against every inclination to cry out, if only he could win her back.

"Let's not talk about anything that's been going on," he told her. "When will you be ready to see me?"

"Right this minute, if possible."

It was the scenario he would have written. After two months of a daily ache to hold Bonnie in his arms again, he couldn't have fantasized it better.

But Richard propped up his ego as if to demonstrate his new confidence. "I can't right now," he said soberly. "I told Mike I'd help him cut down some trees in the backyard tomorrow. But I can come tomorrow evening."

Tuesday, July 5

Not once at the Greenwalds did Richard even hint that his world might be coming unstuck. He created for the Greenwalds an idealized, even fictional portrait of Richard Herrin's life: successful school work, good job prospects, a beautiful fiancée.

The act was perfect. "Everyone who met him that weekend," Mrs. Helen Greenwald said later, "commented about the sweetness of Richard and how nice it was to see a young man who knew where he was going."

Richard was always the first one up in the morning. When Mrs. Greenwald heard him stirring around, she came downstairs and they talked at some length. To Helen Greenwald it seemed that everything was meshing for Richard. "He told me that he was finishing his thesis, he was going to be taking his doctorate in Washington, working at the Smithsonian," she recalled. "He said that Bonnie was going to be studying music in Baltimore, so they could be together, and he was going to save up for an engagement ring for her, and that marriage was in the future."

Even Mrs. and Mrs. Garland were mellowing, Herrin said. "I knew that Bonnie's parents didn't approve of him, and I asked him about that," Mrs. Greenwald continued. "He said he thought they were beginning to accept him. He just felt their feelings toward him had changed because he was straightening himself out."

Richard never let on that events were burning up his world. Instead, he played volleyball, chatted with guests, went with the family to see "Star Wars" on Monday night, ate well. On Tuesday, he helped Mike cut trees. And just before six o'clock he said goodbye.

With a package of brownies from Mike's sister, Richard boarded the train for the seemingly endless ride to Scarsdale. The Long Island interlude had raised his hopes, as if the stories he had told the Greenwalds were true. Temporarily, he had buried the pain of thinking that Bonnie had slept with another man.

He felt no anger toward his rival. "I wasn't considering him at all because he wouldn't have been able to take her unless she was willing," Herrin later explained. Towards Bonnie, Richard now assumed the pose of father-confessor. He was beginning to see her as something of a fallen angel. And in that fall he had the moral advantage because he was in a position to forgive her infidelity. It made him feel powerful, and pious, to think that though Bonnie had been unfaithful to him, he still wanted her back.

"I had no despair," he later told a psychiatrist of his thoughts just prior to seeing Bonnie. "I felt proud of conquering my fear and jealousy and would be able to forgive her. I had already forgiven her in my mind for anything that happened with Jim—if she had sex with him. I honestly felt I could forgive her and be understanding of the fact that she was away a long time on tour and needed companionship. On Long Island I thought about it, and I decided that I could try to forget about it if she would forget about it."

And if she didn't?

It was a pleasantly warm evening when he arrived at the Hartsdale station just before eight o'clock. Despite his newfound pride, Richard could not muster the strength to march straight into the Garland home. Instead, he went to a phone booth to call Bonnie and ask that she come to meet him. It was too important a meeting, too fraught with uncertainty, to risk having other people around.

After hanging up, Richard walked up from the small declivity where the station sat and onto the narrow brick-surfaced overpass that spanned the railroad tracks and the busy Bronx River Parkway. It was open space, a kind of no-mans-land between the wooded hills of Hartsdale and those of the Fox Meadow section of Scarsdale where the Garland house stood. From the bridge Richard saw Bonnie as she walked down the slight incline of Fenimore Road and emerged from under the great canopy of leaves. She looked better than he had ever seen her.

Their embrace was anxious and distracted. Richard's mouth felt miserably dry as they kissed. They complimented each other about how well they looked as if they were old acquaintances, not the wartime lovers of Richard's dream. For him the encounter was sadly superficial, but he was powerless to make it any different. They walked self-consciously back to the Garland house, arm in arm, but without much conversation.

Richard felt the tension as he and Bonnie walked in the front door. Her parents were home and greeted Richard amicably. When Bonnie had asked if Richard could stay a few days, they gave their consent, thinking it a polite farewell for Richard Herrin. Mr. Garland shook Richard's hand and asked how he was. "Okay," Herrin replied. He then greeted Mrs. Garland, but didn't stay for many pleasantries.

Richard excused himself, put his plastic airline bag in the den where he was to sleep, and went upstairs with Bonnie to settle his fate. As they closed the door behind them, Richard didn't know how to begin. He sensed the presence of the other man. The entire six-week tour was avoided. For Herrin, everything about the trip was tainted with the shadow of Jim Lawrence.

Finally, Richard gathered enough courage to begin. "What's happening to our relationship?" he asked cautiously.

Bonnie replied without much hesitation, "I don't know exactly. I still love you. But I also want to be free to go out with other guys for a while."

It sounded like a refrain from the hated letter. Now he was hearing it personally from Bonnie, who was sitting only a few feet away from him. He could reach out and touch her. "And how long is 'for a while'?"

"It could be a week, a month, several months. Or several years. I can't tell. I just want to know what it's like to be a single girl for a change."

It was all so confusing. He looked at Bonnie. It was the same beautiful Bonnie, but he sensed that he was face to face with a disintegrating fantasy. She was not going to run back to him apologizing for her mistake. A single girl? What could that mean? Only that she wanted to be free of him.

"You mean you want to go out with this other guy?" Richard asked.

"Jim wasn't the reason for the letter. It was that at the beginning of the tour I suddenly felt that I had to experience life without commitments. And soon. Jim will definitely be someone I will be seeing, but he won't be the only one." Bonnie paused, searching for a broader perspective. "Remember, Rick, I went to an all-girls boarding school, and I met you as a freshman. I didn't have an opportunity to meet anyone else before you."

But that had been the whole idea, Herrin thought. Bonnie had been as young and naive as he was. They had been contagiously happy together and promised one another that it would stay like that forever. But now he was experiencing the unhappy result of his decision to go to Texas and leave Bonnie at Yale. It was what he feared during their two years of separation: that she would grow up and go away from him.

"Now," Bonnie continued, "I just want to be able to go out with different guys. Maybe I want to sleep with different guys."

Richard could not believe what he was hearing. His love for Bonnie was sacred. They had first had sex in this very room, and made it into a holy ritual, the center and symbol of their relationship. Her body was like a religious shrine to him. Her love was all that made him a full person, a complete man.

Before, he had cringed whenever someone had threatened to violate their union with so much as a kiss. And in Texas, just a month ago, when he thought about Bonnie sleeping with another man, he had manufactured the gruesome image of Bonnie with her sexual organs mutilated. Now Bonnie was casually discussing sleeping with other men.

As he cringed inside, Richard stretched for his new paternal, rational pose. "Won't you get a bad reputation by sleeping around?" he asked.

"Rick, you should know me by now. I would be very selective." Knowing that she should tread lightly about the subject of sex with other men, Bonnie added, "Up to now I've been exclusive in my selection of lovers."

Exclusive? Richard was sure that he heard her correctly. He was certain that she meant that he had been the only one to make love to Bonnie; that she had been faithful and had not soiled the purity of their love. But why did she say "lovers," using the plural form? Richard didn't pursue it. He needed to believe that Bonnie had not had sex with anyone else. It freed him from his nightmare.

Bonnie was speaking to him from a world whose language he could not comprehend. It was a modern world, one which had lifted the burden of confession and forgiveness from premarital sex, or, from his view of their relationship, from extramarital sex. For Bonnie the term was "single girl"; for Richard it was "sexually loose." Between the two was a fatal semantic chasm.

"The fact remained," Herrin later said, "that she still had this desire to see other men and not be committed." Only a short while before they were vowing eternal love and promising to marry. Now Bonnie wanted to sleep with other men. How could it be reconciled?

"What about marriage," he asked her. "Is that still in the future?"

"Yes, definitely. But I can't guarantee that it will be with you. I just don't know at this point," Bonnie answered.

Richard reminded Bonnie of their many conversations about her wanting to have someone else. He had told her that she could have another man if she wanted to, but if she did, he would just walk away.

"Well, now it's different," he told her. "I want to win you back. That's why I flew up here. And I've decided to put off going to George Washington University for a semester so I can move to New Haven, to be near you. I'll be within reach anytime you need me.''

Richard was making his gallant offer, but it was snubbed. "Rick, you'd be making a mistake if you did that," Bonnie said. "Your school work is important. You don't have to move to New Haven." Bonnie convinced Richard to think of his schooling first. It was the only mutual decision made that night.

Tiring of the intense argument, Bonnie and Richard agreed to change the subject. Drained of the evening's anxieties, they soon fell into a routine familiar to both of them. The television set went on. Richard went down to the den and brought up his package of brownies. They drank milk, ate all the brownies, and watched the television until Bonnie signaled her readiness for bed. She fetched Richard the sheets and pillowcase for his bed in the den, then undressed and climbed into her own bed.

Richard stood mutely holding his bedding. What was he supposed to do? In his other visits to the Garland home, he usually had slept with Bonnie. This was the bed in which they had first made love, the touchstone of their relationship. He felt awkward hovering over it now, with Bonnie under the covers. If he went downstairs, it would signal the end of their love. But Richard didn't want to say goodnight. He wanted to hold on to this room and Bonnie for a while longer.

Bonnie was still sitting up in bed. Finally, Richard set the sheets down and walked over to her. He leaned down, intending only to kiss her goodnight, but Bonnie returned his kiss with such warmth that he couldn't pull away. He felt all the tenderness that he had known before, and the passion that only Bonnie could arouse in him. All the old feelings—the good ones—came rushing back as if there had been no bad ones. Bonnie was accepting him; she seemed to want him in her bed.

They pulled each other close, Richard's nightmares melting away as they made love as tenderly as they ever had. For Richard it was a sign that he had won Bonnie back. "She expressed the same emotions that she did when we made love before. In fact, she seemed anxious to make love to me, as I felt anxious to make love to her. Everything seemed forgotten. She was warm, loving, responding. She was as passionate and loving as ever."

They lay for a long time afterward, just holding each other, not saying anything. Eventually, as he usually had done, Richard got up and went back downstairs to the den. Everything bad was forgotten. His despair had lifted, and for the first time in weeks he went to sleep without the heavy burden of depression. He was convinced that he had brought his Bonnie back from the brink of infidelity.

Wednesday, July 6

The day for Richard Herrin dawned with Bonnie Garland hugging him awake in the den. His Texas isolation was forgotten in Bonnie's embrace.

"Time to get up, Rick," she whispered playfully. "Time to get up."

Bonnie was on the sofa-bed, fully dressed, smiling. She lay down next to Richard and cuddled up close. They kissed, and then playfully wrestled on the sofa-bed for a few minutes. "It seemed like the same old Bonnie. It was like nothing had ever happened," Richard recalled.

"You want to come to Columbia today?" Bonnie asked eventually. "I've got to register for my summer class."

"Sure," Richard replied, welcoming any opportunity to be with Bonnie in these crucial hours. Herrin was ecstatic. He had made love to Bonnie the night before. It was now a new day.

Richard dressed and went into the kitchen with Bonnie to find something to eat. They took their breakfast upstairs to the television room and relaxed with the mid-morning game shows until Mrs. Garland arrived to give Bonnie a check for her tuition and some cash to fill the car with gas and oil.

"Is Bonnie going to drive that car to school every day?" Richard asked Mrs. Garland, feeling a rush of new confidence about his place in the family. He expressed his concern about the poor condition of the 1974 Impala and suggested boldly that, if Bonnie were to be driving to school every day, the Garlands' either buy her another car or let her use the Valiant or the MG.

Joan Garland was so surprised by Herrin's forthrightness that she found herself going into detail about the car's new tires, its excessive oil-burning and poor gas mileage, and the plans to sell it at the end of the summer. She reassured Richard that it was all right for the few months that Bonnie would be using it. The explanation seemed to satisfy Richard, but when they were ready to leave, he told Bonnie that he would drive.

"No, that's okay," Bonnie said. "I want to get the practice and get to know the route."

With Bonnie in the driver's seat they started off for Manhattan shortly after one. For the first time that day they picked up their conversation from the previous night and began to talk about their relationship. Richard was in an ebullient mood, believing he needed only to tie up the loose ends for his victory.

Within a few minutes he couldn't believe what he was hearing. As if nothing had happened the night before, Bonnie was restating her commitment to be romantically and sexually uncommitted, and to see other men. By implication, she was denying the importance of their sexual union the night before. The realization that she still wanted to sleep with other men was a shattering blow to Richard's identity. All the love, religion and sex that seemed so perfectly embodied in their union, that he felt he needed for his very survival, was now more confused than ever.

"I couldn't believe it," Herrin later explained, "considering our experience, you know, the night before, and that morning when she woke me up. Everything had seemed to be coming back together again. And all of a sudden, my world starts to fall apart again."

It was Herrin's first real confrontation with Bonnie's

new identity. Unable to maintain his mask of reason, Richard rejected it out of hand. "There is no way I can be a part of this," he exclaimed, "after being the only person in your life for two and a half years. Can't you understand that I couldn't possibly be just one of many."

"No. I can't understand," Bonnie shot back.

"Put yourself in my shoes and just think about how I would feel. Think about what you're asking me to do." Richard was almost pleading.

But Richard was speaking from a past that no longer had a hold on Bonnie. He was spiritually a married man; she was a single woman. He lived in a monogamously unified world; she in a sexually pluralistic society. By asking him to be one of her lovers Bonnie was asking him to give up everything.

"Don't you see the inconsistency in your interest in Jim? It would be another commitment."

"But I don't have any commitment to him," Bonnie answered. "And I wouldn't have to make one. He isn't possessive like you."

Richard had heard the criticism before, but never in such a confusing context; never with Bonnie saying that she wanted him and others. "Well, if this is what you really want," he said, "I definitely cannot be a part of it. No way."

"You're only refusing to go along because of what other people will think."

"I agree. They'll think I'm a fool," Richard commented.

"I don't care what others think," Bonnie replied.

Richard knew that he was losing fast, and decided to play what seemed like his last card. It had worked in the past. Whenever he had told Bonnie that if she wanted other men, he would leave her, she had promised him he would be the only one.

"If you're really serious about this," Richard said, offering his trump, "don't be surprised if I don't want to return to you after you get fed up with the new phase of your life."

But the rules had changed. "If that's how you really feel," Bonnie replied, "then I'll have to take that gamble. I didn't intend it to be that way. I still love you. But if that's what you want, then I'll have to go along without you."

By now the big Impala was moving into the maze of highway signs on the final approach to Manhattan, and Richard and Bonnie realized that they were getting lost. They had to drop their frustrating dialogue and concentrate on getting to Columbia.

Richard had failed in his attempt to win Bonnie back, but he managed to shelve his problems while he and Bonnie walked around the Columbia campus. "We had a good time, both of us cheerful and hugging and kissing on occasion, as we went around to the different buildings to complete Bonnie's registration. It was as if we were back at Yale."

On their way home their mood had changed back again. Richard could think of nothing else to say that would influence Bonnie. For most of their return trip, including dinner at a Friendly's Restaurant in White Plains, Bonnie and Richard were silent.

When they arrived home in Scarsdale, they stopped in the television room to talk with Joan and Paul Garland. Bonnie's parents asked how the registration had gone, if she had any problems with the tuition. The Garlands were avoiding confrontation with Richard Herrin. They knew that Herrin was on his way out and they were leaving it to their daughter to end the love affair amicably. Richard soon excused himself and continued upstairs to Bonnie's room.

When he left, Joan Garland turned to her daughter. "Has he made his reservation back to Texas yet?" At Mrs. Garland's suggestion, Richard had agreed to leave the next day, Thursday. She wanted Bonnie to have three good days of rest before beginning her summer class on Monday.

"No," Bonnie told her mother. "But I'll speak to him about it." She left and went upstairs. Joan Garland, who thought she had just helped arrange for the final departure of Richard Herrin, had said her last farewell to her daughter.

Almost as soon as Bonnie entered her bedroom, Richard picked up his unrelenting pursuit of the eternal "yes." The argument had become frustrating, when it was interrupted by a knock at the door. As Patrick came in, he saw Richard sitting on the bed with his back against the wall. Richard was somber and made no effort to say anything. To Patrick, who knew why Herrin had come to Scarsdale, it looked as if Richard were getting nowhere. He turned to Bonnie, who sat quietly on the couch, and asked if she and Richard wanted to go out for dinner. Explaining that they had already eaten, she declined.

When Patrick left, they resumed their argument, which by now had become circular. Richard felt trapped. Though she was only a few feet away from him, Bonnie seemed a million miles distant, locked in an idea he was unable to penetrate. He kept trying to reach out to remind her of the way it was before, but she always faded before him. He wanted some relief, but he could now think of no other way except to surrender.

He would go to George Washington University in the fall, he finally told Bonnie, not at all sure that he really believed what he was proposing. He would start his Ph.D. work and give her his address and phone number, and he expected hers in return.

"You can call me anytime," he said halfheartedly. "And we can see each other on occasion." But even as he admitted defeat, Herrin was telling himself that he would have all day tomorrow, Thursday, to reconvince Bonnie.

"Rich, my mom wants you to leave tomorrow."

Richard could have leaped off the bed. There was to be no tomorrow, no more chance to win Bonnie back. He knew that Thursday had been the agreed day of departure, but he had always expected that if he asked, he could stay longer.

"If I can stay another day or two," Herrin implored, "we can be sure of our decision."

But Bonnie didn't reply.

A little later Bonnie went downstairs and brought up two glasses of milk and some cake. It was a signal that they would put their differences aside for the night and resume their traditional routine in Bonnie's room. They turned on the television. It was a warm July night, and they stripped to the waist and climbed onto the bed to watch the set.

Richard leaned against the headboard while Bonnie nestled between his legs in front of him. Richard had his arms around her and Bonnie was holding his hands. Once again, it seemed just as before. It was the same bed. The same television. They kissed and petted as "Baretta" and "Charlie's Angels" moved across the screen.

It was the same as before except for Richard Herrin's monumental confusion. In a single day he had been pushed from despair to celebration and back to despair. Bonnie had told him she wanted to sleep with other men, then Tuesday night had made love to him as passionately as before. As he held Bonnie again it was apparent that "sex" and "love" now held different meanings for Bonnie than they did for him.

As they kissed, Richard felt the urge to make love. But almost as quickly he felt awkward about it, as if he were holding a strange person. She was in his arms, but farther away than ever before. He let the urge pass. Bonnie had rejected his love, had belittled it by saying it could be transferred to others.

Tonight could be the same as Tuesday night, but now there was a difference. Bonnie was inviting him to her bed as she had invited him the night before and as she would invite others. She had betrayed him Tuesday night by sleeping with him. She had sex with him without eternal love, as she would do again. All this was spinning within Richard's head as he touched Bonnie's soft white skin. With her beautiful body pressed against his, she was deceiving him openly, flaunting her strange new ethic of sex.

They listened to Johnny Carson do his opening

monologue on "The Tonight Show," then Bonnie turned off the set, telling Richard that she was sleepy. "It's probably from the medication that I'm taking for the sickness I got in Europe. But I think I'm going to bed," Bonnie said.

It was not yet midnight, which by Richard and Bonnie's old standards, was still early. "I'm not tired yet," Richard said, getting up off the bed. "I'll join you when I get sleepy." Richard felt no fatigue. He moved over to the couch and watched Bonnie as she got up and removed her clothes.

"Where did you get those?" he asked, staring at Bonnie's bare legs. There were three bruises, no bigger than half-dollars, on Bonnie's left thigh. He hadn't noticed them the night before, but he had not watched Bonnie undressing Tuesday night before they made love. Now he looked at her nakedness as if for the first time. "Did I do that to you last night?" Richard tried to make it sound like a joke. He knew he hadn't caused the bruises, but he was trying to coax from Bonnie something that would stop her naked body from laughing at him.

"Sorry," she said. "They're from boating." On this warm summer night, Bonnie fell into bed without a nightgown and covered herself with only a sheet.

Richard watched her from the couch. "I'm going to read for a while," he said. Then he got up and stepped over to the bed. "Will it bother you if the light's on?"

"No," said Bonnie, nudging her head into the pillow.

Richard bent over and kissed Bonnie Garland goodnight, his black beard brushing for the last time against her pale skin. "I'll be with you shortly."

Thursday, July 7

It was a few minutes after midnight early Thursday morning, when Patrick came home. The high window on the side of the dark house was like a white eye that seemed to stare down on Patrick for the full twenty-five yards that he walked up the driveway, mounted the steps to the backdoor, and disappeared into the breakfast room.

Behind the window in the lighted room, Bonnie had turned over on her side away from the light. With the television off, the room was still except for the sound of Richard leafing distractedly through the pages of *Sports Illustrated*. He had resumed his sentry-like position on the couch near Bonnie. She had turned her back to him and he could now look at her with complete freedom. He saw only her red hair and the gentle outline of her body under the white sheet.

He tried to read the magazine, but his eyes were drawn back to Bonnie. She was asleep, the sheet barely moving as she breathed, torturing Richard with her betrayal. He had entrusted her with his entire sense of well-being. She had soothed him, accepted him with all his insecurities, and given him a manhood that he could never achieve on his own. She had cleansed the awful sinfulness of sex by making it the summation of her complete love for him. With Bonnie it had become unnecessary to confess his sin of premarital intercourse because in his mind they were married. Theirs had been the perfect union, of mind, body, and soul.

Now she was making it all sordid again, turning sex into frivolity, the search for pleasure without the pledge of eternity. Bonnie, once his sunshine, had become his source of greatest pain. She had ignored his letters of love as did Helen, the first woman he had tried to love. She had gone off with another man as had Diane, his second love. All these years he had thought Bonnie was different, that she would never hurt him like the others. But then she had hurt him more. She had accepted him completely, so her rejection was complete. He had trusted her blindly, so her deception had cut out his eyes.

Back and forth, Herrin glanced from the magazine to Bonnie, his nightmare growing. She had rejected him and then invited him back into her bed. She now wanted him in her bed as she wanted others, to mock his love, to laugh at an entire life built around her.

"It" suddenly came to him. He had to kill her. Once the thought entered his mind, it settled down like a cloud covering all anger, all resentment, all despair. There was no panic or anxiety, no past or present, no right or wrong. Neither law nor religion, no prison, no purgatory or hell entered his mind. There was no fear and no debate. "I have to kill Bonnie, then kill myself," he thought. It was as if the killing of Bonnie Garland had always unconsciously been part of him, just as had been her love.

Richard Herrin felt as suffused with calm as he had when he kissed Bonnie goodnight. But he was no longer looking at her. He now glanced around the room searching for something to kill her with. He thought of slashing her wrists, slashing his, then climbing into bed with her to die together. But he abandoned the idea because she might wake up before dying. He looked at the mug on the table, which they had drunk milk out of earlier that night, but decided that it wasn't heavy enough to be effective as a club.

Hanging over a chair was a pair of stockings that he believed might work as a garrote. No, she would wake up and scream, bringing in the whole Garland family before she suffocated. She would defend herself, and she would recognize him. He didn't want her to know that he was her killer. He looked into the closet, but saw nothing to suit his purpose. As he looked out the window to his left over the driveway, he saw there was no one there. Patrick Garland was in his room, next door to Bonnie's, with his door shut and the stereo turned on. He was reading as Richard Herrin walked softly down the stairs outside his door.

Richard knew that the stairs squeaked, but it couldn't be avoided. He risked it, successfully, without alerting anyone. Downstairs in the kitchen, he turned on the light to aid his search for a deadly instrument. He didn't consider the drawers that held the knives. Instead, he unbolted and opened the door that led to the basement. He didn't have far to go. On the stairway landing was

Paul Garland's brown-handled claw hammer. Herrin immediately grabbed it.

He was careful to close and rebolt the door and turn the light out as he walked toward the den, where he was to sleep. In the den his sofa-bed had been made ready and on it were two sheets of yellow legal paper covered with writing. Richard's first thought was that it was a note from Bonnie, perhaps a message that she had changed her mind and wanted only Richard. But as he read, he realized it was not from Bonnie. It was from Mrs. Garland.

> *Dear Rick,*
> *As I told Bonnie before you came, I would be pleased to have you as our guest but for her sake, I want you to leave by* Thurs. *night. As you are aware, this is a difficult but crucial time for her. In order to reenter Yale in the fall, she needs an A in summer school. If you have her best interest at heart, you will recognize that she needs to be able to focus and concentrate on summer school without distractions. . . .*
> *Whatever happens and whatever your relationship will be, it can wait six weeks. Therefore, as I said to her, please* do not call *while she is in summer school. . . . If you are sincere that you care deeply about her, you will see this too. . . . This will be the third time that her academic career is at a crisis. The first two times you were not helpful to her. Please be helpful this time.*
> *Good luck with your thesis.*
>
> *Sincerely,*
> *Joan Garland*

Herrin lay the note back on the bed. He resented Mrs. Garland saying that he was of no help to Bonnie, that he had contributed to her crises. He was convinced that they had rejected him from the beginning and were now trying to blame him for Bonnie's problems. Richard never understood why Bonnie's parents disliked him, just as he never saw the gulf widen between himself and Bonnie until it was too late.

Herrin turned his attention away from the note and searched through his plastic flight bag. There he found his suicide rope and a yellow towel. He could use the towel to wrap the hammer. Bonnie's parents, her two brothers, and her grandfather were all in the house. Asleep, Herrin hoped. But if anyone wandered out into the hall and saw the towel in his hand, he could say he was on his way to the bathroom.

Safely upstairs without incident, Herrin stopped outside Bonnie's bedroom and set the hammer, towel, and rope on a box in the hall. He entered her room and walked toward the bed, leaning cautiously over Bonnie to make sure she was sound asleep. He didn't want her to know, or to feel any pain as she died. Bonnie lay quietly under the sheet, unaware that the man who had been her first and deepest love was planning to kill her.

Herrin returned to the hall and retrieved the hammer. He took off the towel and set the hammer under Bonnie's bed. Standing over her, he again made sure that Bonnie was asleep. A lifelong accumulation of humiliation and anger now assumed control of his body. It had followed him silently from one affront to the next. From the chaos left by his father's abandonment, to the embarrassment of eczema and bedwetting, to the swap-meet work which he hated but never rebelled against. He had buried it when he was overwhelmed at Yale. With women it had been one defeat after another. They were his ideal, his only hope for manhood, and they had rejected him, even deceived him.

Bonnie had injured him more than any other woman could. As she slept now under the thin summer sheet, her soft loving body taunted him. The thought of another man holding Bonnie's nude body, making love to her, was too much for his confused mind to bear. There was no choice but to end this last humiliation.

Herrin bent down, picked up the hammer in both hands, then raised it in an arc over his head. With an exploding swiftness, he swung the hammer down, smashing it into Bonnie Garland's left temple. The force of the blow turned the sleeping young woman onto her back with a sudden jerk. Bonnie's eyes turned up and rolled back into her head in a deathly white stare. Through her red hair Herrin could see the blue mark where the hammer had collapsed her skull. Blood was beginning to trickle from Bonnie's ear.

She began to make a raspy gurgling noise. It frightened Herrin, who now feared that Bonnie might be conscious and aware that he was her attacker. He reached down with his left hand and lifted Bonnie's head off the pillow, as he might have done to wake her from a peaceful sleep after making love.

"Bonnie?" He called her name. "Bonnie? Bonnie?"

There was no response, but the noise from deep in her throat continued, her eyes fixed vacantly to the top of her head. Herrin put her head back down on the pillow and lifted the hammer again in both his hands. This time he brought it down hard on her forehead, splitting her skull wide open and spraying blood in Herrin's face, onto his bare chest, his pants, onto the walls, even to the top of the ceiling over her bed.

Richard wanted Bonnie's death to be swift, complete. He raised the hammer up and once again slammed it violently against her head. But she continued to rasp for breath. Herrin panicked at the thought that she was still alive. Could he cut off the source of the air that was making those terrifying gasps? He lifted the hammer and smashed it against her neck, but the sounds of dying life continued to taunt him.

Stop her heart, Herrin's raging mind told him. He brought the hammer down fiercely on her chest, the lovely bosom that had once sustained him. The repeated blows had now fractured her skull in three places, lacerated her thyroid gland, and smashed her larynx, the source of her brilliant soprano voice. But Herrin was not sure he had completed his deathly work.

The hammer was now covered with wet blood and too slippery for him to grasp firmly. He set it on the bed beside Bonnie's naked, limp body. The sheets were stained red. The one that had been covering Bonnie had been almost tossed aside in the violence of the hammer blows. He now had only one deadly instrument left. Herrin clenched his bloodstained hands around the neck he had once caressed, and squeezed with the two-hundred-pound power concentrated in his fingers.

Bonnie's lifeless body continued to make the struggling noises that seemed to grow louder and louder. Finally, exhausted and frightened that someone in the house would hear her dying gasps, Herrin loosened his stranglehold around Bonnie's neck and rose from the bed. The blood was dripping onto the floor at his feet. As he looked down, he was startled by the image of the blood seeping into the family room below and awakening Bonnie's grandfather.

Herrin left the hammer on the bed, grabbed the car keys off the night table and ran frantically from the house, the sound of Bonnie's death gurgle still pounding in his ears.

CHAPTER SIX

The Death of Bonnie Garland

IT WAS SHORTLY after two in the morning when Richard Herrin drove away from the house in the Garlands' Chevy Impala, his mind locked on suicide. More than four hours later, he had abandoned the notion of killing himself and was knocking on the door of the rectory of St. Mary's Catholic Church in the small upstate New York town of Coxsackie, telling Father Paul Tartaglia of his crime.

Neither Tartaglia nor Police Chief Ronald Rea, who had rushed to the rectory as soon as he got the call, could believe Richard Herrin's incredible story. The unusual nature of the case was compounded when Rea had called the Garland home to check on the crime only to have a woman reply with a good natured "hello." If someone had been killed in that home, it was obviously not known to its residents. Rea called the Scarsdale Police and asked them to check Herrin's story.

The Scarsdale dispatcher took Rea's call seriously. Six policemen in three cars, almost eight percent of

Scarsdale's entire police force and one quarter of its vehicle pool, were immediately detailed to the Garland home. Lieutenant Jack Donovan, Sergeant Anthony Filancia, Patrolmen Philip Porcelli, Jack Breslin and Richard Motko, and Detective Robert Rizzo all arrived within minutes of one another, none knowing what to expect.

They gathered quickly outside the still house that bright Thursday morning in July. Filancia filled Motko in. Chief Rea had called from the upstate town of Coxsackie to say he had someone in custody who claimed to have killed Bonnie Garland at this address. Donovan told Porcelli about the call. But as Donovan looked around, it appeared that no one was home. There was no sign of activity inside, no cars in the driveway. The house seemed deserted. The officers split up to look for an unlocked door or window as Rizzo pushed the front door bell.

It was now just a few minutes before eight. Inside the house, for the second time in less than fifteen minutes, Joan Garland was roused from bed. Now the front door bell was ringing insistently. By the time Mrs. Garland had gone downstairs her father had already opened the door. When Bonnie's mother arrived she looked out on a porchful of policemen.

"I think you have the wrong house," she said, taken somewhat aback. "We didn't call the police."

A swarthy middle-aged man politely answered. "Mrs. Garland, I'm Detective Robert Rizzo of the Scarsdale Police Department. May we come in for a moment, please?" It was Rizzo's way of saying that he was at the right house. Mrs. Garland invited him into the entryway, curious to learn why all these policemen were at the door.

"Do you know a Richard Herrin?" Rizzo asked deliberately.

"Yes." Joan Garland was perplexed.

"Do you have a daughter named Bonnie?"

"Yes."

"Do you know where Richard Herrin is now?" Rizzo

felt as if he were walking a tightrope. But he had no choice. His information was thirdhand. He didn't want to sound an alarm if it wasn't necessary.

Joan Garland now realized that the police had not mistaken her home for another. "Yes," she replied quickly. "He should be in the guest room."

"Would you mind checking the room, ma'am?"

Leaving Rizzo and his colleagues standing at the front of the door, she hurried to the first floor study, as if willing to follow Rizzo's clues one at a time. Her suspicion that something might be wrong grew to anxiety when she looked in the room. There was no Richard Herrin. His bed was unused and the note which she had left on it the night before still sat on the unwrinkled sheets. She rushed back to the policemen.

"He's not there," she exclaimed.

"When was the last time you saw him?" asked Rizzo.

"He was in my daughter's room about nine last night."

"Would you mind going to see if he's there?" Before Rizzo had finished his question Joan Garland had already turned and was running up the front stairway calling her daughter's name.

Rizzo and two of the other officers followed, but they stopped a few steps above the first landing, not wanting to overstep the bounds of propriety. The police stood their ground as Mrs. Garland entered Bonnie's room just above them and a dozen feet ahead.

In the next instant they knew. All bounds of propriety burst with Joan Garland's shriek. "Oh my God! Oh my God! Her head is full of blood! What has he done to her?"

The screams shot through Rizzo.

"At first I thought she was crying," Joan Garland later recalled, straining to hold back tears. "She was lying on her back. There was blood all over, and her breath was coming like she was sobbing. I called her twice. She was completely naked and uncovered. I thought she had been beaten."

Rizzo charged up the stairs, running into Mrs. Garland as she ran from the room. "What did he do to her!" she gasped again. Rizzo grabbed Mrs. Garland and quickly passed her to the man behind him.

"I ran into the room and I saw a female lying on the bed," Rizzo recounted. "I ran directly up to her, and all I remember seeing was the big gaping hole in this girl's head."

After more than six hours of lying unconscious in a pool of her own blood, Bonnie Garland was alive. Joan Garland was still screaming in the hall. Lieutenant Donovan, who had been right behind Rizzo, shouted down to Porcelli to get the stretcher. Porcelli was back in a few minutes and running up the stairs. He set the stretcher down in the hall, and started to open a bedroom door—"Not in here," someone yelled—before he finally rushed into Bonnie's bedroom.

In nine years as a Scarsdale policeman Patrolman Philip Porcelli had never seen as gruesome a scene. "She was lying on her back, her eyes were fixed straight up above," recalled the veteran police officer. "She was breathing very laboredly. It sounded as if she had either some kind of mucous or blood in her throat. However, she was breathing. There was a gash on the left side of her head, approximately over the ear and slightly to the rear, approximately half to three quarters of an inch wide. It appeared to be right into the skull itself. In addition, right on her forehead, just to the left of the center, there was one—one round mark that looked—that appeared to be right into the skull also. That is the best way I could describe it, as if you hit a very soft piece of wood with a hammer very hard."

Before he could move her, Porcelli had to remove the claw hammer that was on the bed beside Bonnie, on her left side, near her neck. He scanned the floor quickly, picked up a yellow towel that was lying at the foot of the bed and, with two fingers and the towel he picked it up close to the head of the hammer and laid it down on the couch alongside the bed. Then he rolled up the bedding on either side of Bonnie and with the help of another officer carried her down the two or three steps onto the waiting stretcher.

It had all happened quickly. The peace of the Garland home had been shattered forever.

Patrick Garland was now emerging from his bedroom. He had heard the doorbell ringing earlier, but thought it was the maid. Then, moments later it seemed that the house was exploding outside his door. "I heard a lot of footsteps and a lot of noise, commotion, and then I heard my mother screaming, and then I heard somebody trying to get into my bedroom, and I said, 'No, not in here,' and then I got up and got out of my room. . . . There were a lot of men running up the stairs to my sister's room, and my mother was still screaming."

Patrick was riveted in place in the hall until he saw his sister on the stretcher. "They were carrying her down the stairs, and she was gasping for air. She was making large, loud gasps, very hoarsey. . . . ," Patrick later recalled. "Her hair was all dark. It was a deep red. It was kind of gooey-looking and—her face was kind of a pale blue."

Patrick watched as they carried his sister down the stairs. He followed her out the front door and across the lawn to the police wagon which sped Bonnie Garland towards the White Plains Hospital.

IN COXSACKIE Richard Herrin sat mute in an old wooden chair in the small room that was the entire Police Headquarters. Until the phone rang, Rea was still suspicious of Herrin's story. "The description of the murder was totally beyond my belief," the Chief remembered later. "I couldn't believe a man could do that. Especially the man that was sitting in front of me. He was quiet, very soft-spoken, very gentle. I had him pegged not guilty for a while. I really did. He had to convince me that he did it."

But when he picked up the phone, Rea received the

confirmation that he needed. It came first with the Scarsdale Police's report that they had found Bonnie Garland brutally beaten, and then through Richard Herrin's own explosive protest that she couldn't be alive.

"For a moment I was a little scared," Rea remembered. "I knew he was handcuffed to the chair, but I didn't know if he was going to snap on me. I mean, suddenly he was screaming that she had to be dead because her head split open like a watermelon and the hammer stuck in her head and he had to pull it out. When he started to shout that kind of thing, it really got to me. I mean, Jesus Christ! He said *the hammer stuck in her head!* Okay? It stuck in her head. *He had to pull the damn thing out!* Hey. You leave a scene like that and you figure that person's dead. . . ."

When he settled Richard down, Rea called Pat Sinclaire, the village's stenographer, to confirm that she was coming to work that day. "Ronnie said he had something important and I had to take a statement, but he didn't say what," Mrs. Sinclaire recounted. "Ronnie was an excitable person anyway. So I really didn't think too much of his call. I just got dressed and went to work."

But when she arrived that Thursday morning Mrs. Sinclaire was shocked by the gravity of her assignment. She picked up her steno pad and walked into Rea's office, where she was introduced to Richard Herrin. "He seemed to be a nice-looking kind of college guy," she remembered. "He was sitting in the chair with a blanket over his shoulders. He didn't have a shirt on. He had his legs folded up under him Indian style. He didn't look all that clean and his hair was kind of long. But he looked like an average college kid who was maybe hitchhiking for a little while. He was very polite when Ronnie introduced me. He sure didn't look like he'd just killed someone a couple of hours before. But then, what do you look like when you kill somebody a couple of hours before?"

Mrs. Sinclaire pulled up a chair next to Herrin and explained that she hadn't done a lot of shorthand since leaving New York. She asked if he would please not talk too fast. Herrin said sure.

"I didn't have time to *think* about what he was saying. I was taking it down, and inside it was like 'Oh my God!' It was such a gruesome story. And what really surprised me was that he was so calm. He was slow. He didn't stumble. He didn't falter. He didn't stutter. I was shocked at the placidness he displayed when he was giving me that statement."

Herrin stared at the floor as he spoke, looking up occasionally at Mrs. Sinclaire to make sure she was keeping up with him. His confession would later be used by the District Attorney's office to claim that Richard Herrin had planned the killing of Bonnie Garland. Not only that it was brutal, but that it was a premeditated act.

I arrived at Bonnie Garland's house at approximately 8:00 P.M. on Monday evening [Herrin here confuses the day; it was actually Tuesday.] The purpose of my visit was to meet and straighten out our relationship which was temporarily on the rocks. I wanted to see her face to face to hear in her own words what she had told me in a letter. My actions were precipitated by the fact that she wanted to begin dating others, sleeping with others and yet wanted me to remain part of her life. Wednesday evening after having been assured that it was what she wanted, knowing that I couldn't have her exclusively, knowing that I didn't want to share her, and knowing that I didn't want to live without her, I entertained the thought of killing her in her sleep. We were in her room. I was going to stay the night in her room. She went to sleep first and I told her I would join her when I was sleepy. Once she was asleep I began thinking of how I would carry out my plan which at that time included suicide. I went downstairs to a kitchen closet, took a hammer from the closet, wrapped it in a yellow towel and left it outside her room in the hall. I went into her room to make sure she was still asleep and went back out to the hall and got the hammer. Placed the towel and hammer under the bed and made sure again she was still asleep. I took the hammer and struck her on the head at least three times. I may have struck her in the chest, may have tried strangling, but I was too weak. I was dressed only in my pants. I grabbed the car keys, left the house through the rear entrance, got in the car and drove to Coxsackie where I turned myself in to Chief Rea. The crime occurred at approximately 2:00 A.M., give or take an hour.

It took fifteen minutes for Herrin to finish his account. Pat Sinclaire got up and left the room quickly. At her own desk, she proceeded to transcribe her notes.

"Even when I brought the typed statement back in, and he read it over, he wasn't at all upset, didn't break down crying," Mrs. Sinclaire recalled. "Well, I'm sure he was upset, but it's just that he didn't act it. Maybe he was in shock or something."

It surprised Mrs. Sinclaire even more when Herrin picked up an error in her typed transcript. "There's a portion of the statement where he says, 'I didn't want to live without her.' Well, I had written 'leave.' But he picked it right up, and he said, 'This should be "live."' So we crossed it out and wrote over it 'live' and he initialed it. This really surprised me. I mean, he knew exactly what he had said."

Richard Herrin seemed also to know exactly what he had done. But did he really know? His fate would ultimately turn on that epistemological riddle.

JUST AS RICHARD HERRIN was finishing correcting his statement, Bonnie Garland was being rushed into a White Plains Hospital operating room in what neurosurgeon Dr. Herbert Oestreich called "very marked extremus." Dr. Oestreich, who had been in the emergency room as Bonnie was brought in shortly after 8:30, knew immediately how critical her condition was. She was unconscious and suffering from a depressed skull fracture with intracerebral hematoma, brain contusion, and brain laceration. Aside from the multiple injuries to the head and neck, of more immediate concern was the profuse bleeding and the absence of blood pressure or a palpable pulse.

"Very quickly, we took her to the operating room," recalled Dr. Oestreich, who had been a White Plains neurosurgeon for almost twenty years and knew the Garlands. "We tried to control the bleeding. As we gave her blood, she began to bleed again, and we tried to take out what clot there was within the brain and what broken fragments had been driven into the brain. We tried to clean up this controlled bleeding."

There was another complication as the anesthesiologist tried to place a tube in her throat in preparation for surgery. It was obvious that there had been some injury to the neck because of the black-and-blue marks, or ecchymosis, that were observable in the middle of the neck on either side. But as the tube was being placed in Bonnie's trachea, the surgery team discovered more internal hemorrhaging.

What Bonnie Garland's chances of survival were at this time, Dr. Oestreich didn't even want to guess. "It's like this," the surgeon later explained. "I'm going to save them. And if I don't save them, then they didn't have a chance to survive."

By 9:30 A.M. with the bleeding now under control, Bonnie was ready for surgery. For the operation Dr. Oestreich was assisted by Dr. Arthur Lerner and Dr. Lawrence Kadish, two other prominent White Plains surgeons. They worked on Bonnie for three hours. When the complex surgery was finished, they felt there was some measure of hope. Her condition was still very critical, but it had at least stabilized. She was wheeled into the intensive care unit where, still unconscious, her vital signs were monitored continuously. Outside her door her parents kept constant vigil.

RICHARD HERRIN was keeping his own agitated vigil in Coxsackie. "Every time the phone would ring," remembers Chief Rea, "he would jump. He thought it was Scarsdale calling with news about Bonnie. He was pretty nervous about it. He was hoping that she was dead. He was hoping she would die, he really was. He said he didn't want her to suffer."

Rea watched Herrin closely. When he saw his head drop to his chest in exhausted sleep, the chief retrieved an old pillow and told him to put his head down on his desk. He cleared away some of the clutter: his bronzed name-plate, the photo of his wife, stacks of reports and papers, and an ashtray of a man holding a sign that read "sex relieves tension." Herrin placed his head down on the desk. "He maybe had two half-hour naps the whole day. Not much. He'd whimper a little bit in his sleep," Rea recalls.

Richard Herrin was Coxsackie's biggest crime suspect ever. Rea pulled his rarely-used forensic science kit off the shelf and took scrapings from Herrin's fingernails and blood samples from his chest, and carefully put them in small plasticine envelopes which he dated and identified. He recorded Richard James Herrin in the "Unattended Death" file because there was no homicide category in Coxsackie.

At 11:45 that morning Rea wrote in his daybook that the Scarsdale Police "asked me to hold Richard J. Herrin, as they were getting a warrant for Assault 1st and Attempted Murder."

Sitting on the biggest crime in his life, Rea guarded Herrin jealously. "I sealed off that office," he recounted later with professional pride. "I wouldn't even allow the secretaries to come in. Nobody was going to get him. The State Police heard that I had somebody in there for a big crime. And the state troopers, they want all that shit. They called and said, 'Wouldn't it be better if we housed him up here?' And I said, 'No. He's safe right where he is.' "

Since Rea had no temporary lockup, Herrin stayed handcuffed in the chair next to Rea's desk. "Richard sat in the chair all day. He didn't get up once. Not once. And I was right there with him the whole day," Rea continued. "He'd sleep off and on and we'd talk. I asked him, 'How many times did you try to kill yourself?' And he would tell me that he was thinking about it from the time he left the house. . . . I asked him why he did what he did and he said because he couldn't live with the thought that she was going to sleep with other men. He was telling me about Yale and I thought, 'This guy must be influential or something. He is going to Yale.' Christ, I figured, smart guy, rich family, that kind of shit. I didn't know then that he was Hispanic or anything. He seemed to talk about everything easily. Very relaxed."

At about four o'clock, Donna Rea, the Chief's wife, brought some meatball sandwiches to the station, Herrin's first food all day. "He said, 'Tell your wife thanks for the sandwiches, they were delicious.' He was always very polite."

At 4:30 Detective Rizzo arrived with Detective Richard Freda from Scarsdale with a warrant for Richard Herrin's arrest. "I met them out back and told them that everything was fine, under control, and all he needs is a little understanding right now," Rea recounted. "I was worried about that. 'Cause I didn't know these cops from Adam. They could be typical New York City cops as far as I was concerned, and I didn't know how they were going to treat him. I mean they just came from the crime scene. And I was afraid their first reaction would be 'okay, you scum bag.' I didn't know if I was going to have a couple of irate hot dogs coming up here. You gotta picture what could be going through these detectives' minds. After doing a whole day at the crime scene. If I was a detective and I was doing that, I think I'd want to grab the guy a little bit, you know. Look at what this guy did to this girl.''

But as soon as Rea met Freda and Rizzo, he knew he didn't have to worry. ''They were very professional. In fact, when Freda stuck his hand out and shook hands with Richard I knew it was okay. And I told Richard, 'I want you to know they're not going to abuse you, they're not going to hurt you.' Because he was a little worried about what was going to happen next. Earlier he had wanted to know if they were going to hurt him.''

By six o'clock Freda and Rizzo were ready to leave. Herrin climbed into the back seat of the Scarsdale police car. Both hands were handcuffed to the metal grille between the front and back seats. He was still bare-chested and barefoot, but the temperature was in the high eighties that day, warm and sunny.

Rizzo and Freda drove straight south along the New York State Thruway, arriving in Scarsdale shortly after eight o'clock. Richard Herrin was silent most of the drive. He cried some of the time, slept some of the time. At police headquarters the detectives took him through the back door and up to the second floor detectives' room, where he was booked, fingerprinted, and his picture taken. They asked if he wanted a lawyer and he said no. They asked if he wanted his parents notified and he said no. They asked no questions about what he did to Bonnie Garland, only had him write an affirmation of the "voluntary statement" he had given Rea earlier that day.

Using the same uneven spacing between words that he used to compose his last note to Bonnie, he wrote, "I Richard J. Herrin have read the above statement and recognize it as one I made to Chief Ronald Rea of the Coxsackie Police Dept. It is an accurate and true statement made of my own free will. . . . I am writing this statement in the presence of Det. Sgt. Richard Freda and Det. Robert Rizzo of the Scarsdale Police Dept. at their headquarters. I have not been coerced into writing this statement nor have I been promised anything as a result. Richard James Herrin. 7-7-77. 9:15 P.M.''

• • •

As RICHARD finished signing his name to his admission of the crime, at the White Plains Hospital the machines monitoring Bonnie Garland's vital signs indicated an abrupt change in her condition. "She became worse," recalled Dr. Oestreich, who had been close to Bonnie the entire day, "and we knew there were problems." Dr. Oestreich and his colleagues suspected that there might be more internal bleeding and a failure of her blood to clot properly. "We felt that this was probably attributable to the fact that she had been without blood pressure for so long a period of time," he later stated.

Bonnie was rushed back to the operating room for emergency surgery. As soon as the doctors opened the sutured head wounds, their suspicions were confirmed: There was bleeding. Suddenly, Bonnie's heart began beating with irregularity. "Again," remarked Dr. Oestreich, "we felt that was attributable to the lack of blood pressure for an extended period of time. Despite a variety of measures, her heart ceased beating."

Bonnie Garland died at 10:38 P.M., more than twenty hours after her lover had smashed a hammer into her skull while she slept.

Richard Herrin, pride of East Los Angeles, high school valedictorian, graduate of Yale University, was charged with murder.

CHAPTER SEVEN

Tears for a Killer

IN WASHINGTON, D.C., the morning after Bonnie's death, Paul Bardack left his work as an editor at the American University Law Review in order to write a long-delayed letter to his friend Richard Herrin. His mother had forwarded a letter from Richard to him a couple of weeks before, but between work and law school studies he had no chance to respond. It wasn't going to be a long letter; Paul just wanted to tell his old buddy how elated he was that Herrin was coming to Washington for graduate school. They would be back together again as they had been at Yale.

As Bardack started to write, his mother phoned him. Strange coincidence, he thought. She was asking him about Richard Herrin. "And then she asked, 'Wasn't he dating Bonnie Garland?' " Paul recalled. "I said, 'Yes, that's his girlfriend.' For a moment I figured that they were killed in a car accident or something. Then my mother said, 'Oh my God, he killed her! That's what the *Daily News* says.'

"I just started shaking. I couldn't believe it. I believed my mother had said it, but I knew that Rich was not a violent person at all." Bardack hung up the phone, still trembling. He composed himself and called his mother back. When he learned where Richard was being held, Paul made plans to visit the Westchester County jail.

In East Los Angeles, biology teacher Ben Wadsworth was working in his cramped office at Lincoln High School when a colleague walked in. "Wasn't there a Richard Herrin here as a student?" he asked. Yes, Wadsworth had known him well. "I just heard that he killed somebody back East," the other teacher blurted out. Wadsworth didn't even blink. "Must be a different Rich Herrin," he replied, going back to his work.

At an airport in the Midwest Bonnie Garland's new boyfriend, Jim Lawrence, was changing planes on his way to see his dying grandmother. He stopped to browse at a newsstand. Lawrence hadn't spoken to Bonnie since the previous Monday, in Scarsdale, when he had wished her well in her difficult task of extricating herself from Richard Herrin. He had thought about calling her a number of times since, but had decided against it; he didn't want to inflame the situation if Herrin were in the room.

Lawrence moved toward the newspapers and, by habit, picked up *The New York Times*. His heart stopped. On the front page, side by side, were photos of Bonnie and Richard. The headline was inconceivable, a blur that refused to register on his mind: "Yale Senior Slain in Scarsdale; Boyfriend Surrenders to Priest."

"It happened like that to a lot of people," said Laura Kidd, a Glee Club colleague of Bonnie's who had come to work Saturday morning to find a short message: "Your mother says to buy *The New York Times*."

THE HAMMER BLOWS that ended Bonnie Garland's life precipitated a wave of disbelief and sadness that spread quickly across the country to family and friends of Bonnie and Richard. "I had trouble sleeping for a week," recalled a Yale woman who knew them both. "I couldn't help identifying with Bonnie; I felt so much grief. But what Rich did was so beyond my comprehension that I had trouble being angry with him. The anger seemed small in comparison with the confusion, the sorrow, the pain.''

Had Richard and Bonnie not been, as the *Times* headlined, ''unlikely figures in a murder case,'' then Bonnie's killing would not have been front page news and a source of so much bewildered grief. There had never been a killing in which both perpetrator and victim were Yale students. Such a tragic event was not supposed to happen in serene suburban Scarsdale, New York, where there had never been a civilian homicide in the town's history. In the long months that followed, tragedy turned to acrimony as people struggled to make sense of what had happened.

On Sunday afternoon, three days after the killing, mourners crowded into the Scarsdale Congregational Church for Bonnie Garland's funeral service. The chapel across the street from the Scarsdale Village Hall where Richard Herrin would soon be brought in handcuffs for his first court appearance, was banked with red roses and white chrysanthemums. Bonnie's body lay in an open casket. ''They laid her out in her Glee Club outfit, the long black skirt and the white blouse,'' remembered Bruce Peabody, one of almost thirty Yale Glee Club members who had traveled to Scarsdale to sing at the service. ''For us that was really the last way we'd seen her. It was really wrenching emotionally to know that just the week before we had been singing together in Norway.''

It had been just the week before that Bonnie's parents had felt renewed. Their daughter had a new boyfriend and any wounds of adolescent rebellion seemed to be healing. ''She came home bubbling, gloriously happy over this trip,'' Joan Garland told a reporter just before the funeral. ''It had been an enormous source of personal joy to her, a triumph.''

The peace of Scarsdale had been shattered by Richard Herrin's attack, and the community registered outrage against her killer. ''Bonnie's death has created a storm of feelings in those who knew her best and loved her most,'' Reverend Gary Brown told the mourners at Bonnie's funeral. ''Some of the most powerful feelings may be those of bitterness and hatred. Those awful feelings are undeniable. I maintain that expressing them is healthy and necessary. . . . In this terrible situation *especially*, we must speak the unspeakable and ugly thoughts, born of frustration, helplessness, and rage. The weeping and the curses and the fury are all right.''

But the friends of Richard Herrin could not feel enmity toward a man they considered truly generous and kind. In New Haven, Sister Ramona Pena at More House Chapel read the newspaper account of the killing, then immediately sent a telegram to the Westchester County Jail. ''Rich, I'm thinking about you. I'm praying for you. I love you.''

It was the message that launched a crusade. With Bonnie Garland barely laid to rest, friends of Richard Herrin initiated a campaign of support for the killer unprecedented in the history of Westchester crime. The operation would shock Scarsdale almost as much as the killing. Joan and Paul Garland would come to see it as ''the second assault'' on their lives. It would transform Bonnie Garland's killing into a modern metaphor for what some saw as a debasement of justice and morality, but what others viewed as a sublime trial of the highest principles of Christian integrity.

WITHIN DAYS of the killing Sister Ramona, the first woman chaplain at More House, had met with A. T. Wall, Herrin's former Yale roommate, and Herrin's mother, Linda Ugarte. Mrs. Ugarte had immediately flown east from Los Angeles and was staying with Ramona to plan strategy. It would prove to be an able trio. With the help of Wall's connections at Yale Law School, where he was a student, they gathered a list of prominent criminal lawyers. Before the week was over they had retained the services of a leading New York City trial attorney, Jack Litman, for a fee well below his normal stipend. ''It was an obvious human tragedy,'' recalled Litman of his first reaction to the case. "The young man was in trouble and was supported by some very good people. I decided to take the case."

And the support grew each day. Attorney Litman, Sister Ramona, Wall, Linda Ugarte and Father Peter Fagan, another associate chaplain at More House, were able to construct a defense apparatus capable of tapping both the intellectual resources and prestige of Yale and the energy of the religiously zealous.

Given the bloody circumstances of Herrin's crime and his family's poverty, the likelihood that he would be released from jail prior to his trial was slim. By legal criteria Herrin was a poor candidate for bail. His character, reputation, habits and mental condition were known to the court only by virtue of Bonnie Garland's death. He was unemployed; he had no ties to the community; and though he had no criminal record, the weight of the evidence against him was overwhelming. Even if a bail request were granted, the chances were that money required to obtain release—usually between $50,000 and $100,000 on murder charges—would not be available to this son of the Los Angeles ghetto.

What Richard Herrin had in his favor was the dogged determination of his attorney and his friends in the Yale community. On July 13, six days after the killing, A. T. Wall sent out a nationwide appeal to friends, relatives, former classmates and professors of Herrin's. In the first two sentences of his letter, Wall set the tone which would echo through all the controversial efforts on Herrin's behalf.

"The terrible events described in the enclosed articles are most likely not news to you," he wrote. "While we are left only to mourn Bonnie's tragic death, it is important that having lost one life, we do what we can to salvage another." It was that sentiment, to save the remaining member of the ill-fated couple, that would infuriate so many people. It was an appeal that wrapped Herrin in the robes of tragic anti-hero.

The response to Wall's letter was immediate and overwhelming. If Herrin had no roots in Westchester County, the mail that landed on the desk of Acting

Supreme Court Justice John Walsh proved that he had strong connections everywhere else. There were impressive letterheads in abundance. They reflected institutions seldom seen in a criminal court on behalf of an indicted murderer. The Congress of the United States. The University of Southern California School of Medicine. The American University Law Review. The Rhode Island Hospital Trust National Bank. The Scripps Institution of Oceanography. The City of Los Angeles. Most numerous were those stamped Yale University: the Yale Peabody Museum of Natural History, the Yale Department of Geology and Geophysics, the Yale Office of Undergraduate Admission, the More House Catholic Center at Yale.

Most of the letters made it clear that Richard Herrin, though an accused killer, was reaping the rewards of a Yale education. The Director of Yale University's Minority Admissions Office, Consuelo Gayton, wrote Judge Walsh that she knew "many students who went to Rich because he would listen, encourage, console, or help them out of loneliness or homesickness by simply being *there*."

Karl Waage, the head of the university's prestigious Peabody Museum and Yale's Bateman Professor of Geology, confided to Judge Walsh in his letter that "this is a tragedy I have been unable to comprehend. . . . Unless he has suffered irreparable psychological damage, those elements of good character and dependability he displayed day after day during three years together must still be a part of him."

Even the Associate Dean of Yale College, Martin Griffin, wrote in Herrin's behalf. He told Walsh that "obviously I write this letter as a private person and not as an employee of the university." The letter was brief and to the point, but emphatically sympathetic. "I would like to state my belief," said Griffin, "that if he were released on bail he would discharge reliably and conscientiously any conditions that you would impose on him."

One letter, from East Los Angeles, was laced with grammatical errors and composed in faltering prose.

"Dear Judge Walsh my name is Manuel Ugarte and I'm Richard Herrin step father. I believe that a boy that I have raised and brought up since he was 4 years old and has been more than a son to me, more like a friend; can not be capable of a crime of this sort: Well not aware of what he was doing." "I'm not much of a writer," wrote Sigfrido Chavez, Herrin's best friend in high school, "but if I were there in person I would probably convince you of Richard's honesty."

Several of the letters strongly implied that Richard Herrin, Yalie and devout Catholic, should be immune to the institutions and procedures of the American criminal justice system. One friend of Herrin's told Judge Walsh that "This man is not a criminal. I suspect that no punishment which the criminal justice system can dispense can add to the remorse which he must feel in the face of his own knowledge and that of his God." It was a paradigm of both liberal Christianity and anarchy. Richard Herrin would punish himself.

Cumulatively the letters made it sound as if Richard Herrin were a commendable candidate for high office, not someone seeking to be let out on bail from a murder charge. It was support based on a belief that Richard Herrin was a good person: that his act was a temporary and fleeting aberration of character; that he need not be punished so much as consoled. It presumed that Herrin was not so much the willful perpetrator of the crime as he was its fellow victim.

The Herrin defense group meanwhile was seeking a place of residence for Herrin that would fulfill the law's requirements that he have ties to the community once he was out on bail. The ideal solution, suggested by Jack Litman, would be to house Herrin in a religious institution. Sister Ramona, Father Peter Fagan and Father Richard Russell, the senior More House chaplain, immediately tapped the diverse resources of the Church. Within days Father Fagan had secured an offer of lodging for Herrin with the *Fratres Scholarum Christianarum*, an order of unordained Catholic clergy with a longer history of service than Yale University. The community of fourteen Christian Brothers resided in

Albany where they operated, appropriately, a residential treatment center for young boys in trouble with the law.

The Brothers did not know Herrin but they agreed to visit. Brothers Thomas Gavin and Robert McCann drove the hundred miles from Albany to Valhalla, the small town where the Westchester County Jail is located. They interviewed Herrin for an hour and took a favorable report back to their twelve comrades.

"We were able to come to a common decision," the Brothers wrote to Judge Walsh the next day. "Should the court release Richard on bail, the Brothers have agreed to take him in to live with us. . . . There is a rhythm to our lives that we see as a help to Richard at this time in his life. . . ."

The letter proved crucial. On July 28, Judge Walsh agreed to release Richard Herrin into the custody of the Christian Brothers. "This is the most impressive bail application I have ever seen," Walsh concluded. It was Herrin's first legal victory.

Even the $50,000 which Walsh had set as bail took only a few days to locate despite Herrin's own meager resources. Family and friends from Los Angeles together could scrape up only a little more than $11,000. Once again the Yale Catholic community came to the fore. One member of the More House congregation, Dr. Marie Brown, a Yale pediatric cardiologist, had been following the story in the papers and had noticed Linda Ugarte at church. She had never met Richard Herrin until she was taken to see him at the Westchester jail. "He seemed close to suicide," she remembered. "I felt I could avert that. Tragedy compounded makes no sense." Brown immediately put up her $55,000 Bethany, Connecticut, home as collateral.

On August 11, at the same hearing in which he was indicted on a charge of murder, Richard Herrin was released on bail.

JOAN AND PAUL GARLAND and their friends were stunned. The support for the man who had killed their daughter seemed unconscionable at best, dangerous at worst. "That a person who has committed and confessed to a brutal killing of a defenseless person in her sleep in the middle of the night," an outraged Paul Garland told a reporter, "and who is released back into society with no psychiatric evaluations and with no one therefore having any idea how dangerous he is to himself or to other people—I cannot conceive that Bonnie or any other person of any common sense or good conscience would want that for a moment."

In the modern equation of crime there is apparently more to do for the living criminal than for the dead victim or her survivors. The well-orchestrated defense campaign was providing Richard Herrin with more sympathy than that given to the Garland family. But it was sympathy founded on premises that the Garlands could not countenance. Their daughter was barely in her grave and people were calling for the rehabilitation of Richard Herrin.

Father Richard Russell, the soft-spoken elder chaplain of More House, tried to explain to the Garlands why he and his colleagues were working on Richard Herrin's behalf. "I believe that all involved, including myself, are working from a Christian concern over a brother who has fallen," he wrote. While the priest sympathized with the Garlands' "pain and agony," he stressed that "my conflict between [that sympathy] and my own Christian response is indeed intense. For to err is human; to forgive, divine. I hope that you do not feel that pledging ourselves to that path is presumptuous."

But what Father Russell believed to be a Christian duty, Paul Garland considered "reckless behavior." In frustration, the Garlands wrote a complaint to the Chancellor of the Archdiocese of New York. "Tremendous efforts by persons affiliated with the Catholic Church have succeeded in obtaining extraordinary favorable treatment for the confessed killer of our daughter," they stated. "But for such intervention by them, Herrin would be in a secure place (prison), without the possibilities now available to him to escape, to commit suicide, or to inflict further violence upon others, perhaps including our family.''

The Garlands were convinced that the Church had thoughtlessly given its support to a man who had just destroyed their daughter and their peace. But others pointed out that the Yale Catholic community did not represent the general Catholic attitude toward the killing, on the part of either the clergy or the laity.

Reverend Monsignor Joseph T. O'Keefe, Chancellor of the New York Archdiocese, answered a letter that the Garlands had sent to Terence Cardinal Cooke. In his response, O'Keefe emphasized the separation between the official attitudes of the Church hierarchy and the conscience of its members. ''I think you realize that those involved are involved as individual citizens, not as spokespersons for any church,'' O'Keefe wrote Paul Garland. ''If, in questions asked . . . in your letter, the world 'Church' were changed to 'Citizens,' the issue might be clearer.''

HERRIN'S FREEDOM became a source of constant fear to the Garland family, who were concerned that he was still the same unstable person who had brutally killed their daughter. Because of what Herrin had done, several of the Garlands had started treatment in psychotherapy. Paul Garland, who normally traveled many thousands of miles a year on business, was afraid to leave his family alone for a single night as long as Richard Herrin was free and living only one hundred miles away. His teenage daughter, Cathryn, was afraid to be left alone in the house.

''I wish you could guarantee me that he will not come back to do further harm to my remaining children or to my husband or me,'' Joan Garland wrote to Judge Walsh. ''I wish that my heart did not jump now when I hear a creak in the house at night. I wish my thirteen-year-old daughter was not afraid to go to sleep because she is afraid she will be murdered in her bed.''

Was Richard Herrin dangerous? Or was he now stable? Could he be trusted not to kill himself or someone else? Was he the Richard Herrin of the bail support letters? Or was he the Richard Herrin of the bloody claw hammer?

Ironically, in their letters of support to Judge Walsh, many of Richard Herrin's friends worried about their friend's mental and emotional state. "To think that this gentle, soft-spoken intelligent man could commit so horrendous a crime can only mean that he had indeed gone mad," concluded one friend.

Was Richard Herrin still mad?

THE DAY AFTER the killing, Richard Herrin had been summoned into the office of Dr. Harvey Lothringer, a psychiatrist in the Westchester County Jail's Forensic Psychiatric Unit in Valhalla. Lothringer had been told by the prison's admitting officers that Herrin had tried to commit suicide after leaving the scene of the crime. Herrin repeated his story to the psychiatrist who then ordered him transferred to the Forensic Unit, prescribing "suicidal precautions" and 25 mg. of Librium.

In his records Lothringer wrote: "Mental Status— Depressed, anxious, with suicidal ideation active. No signs or symptoms of major psychosis."

During the five weeks prior to his release on bail, Herrin was housed in the psychiatric ward of the prison. The unit was newly constructed, and with its brightly painted walls, air conditioning, and trained-staff, it was an oasis compared with the main facility. In jail for the first time in his life, Herrin was spared the inconveniences and dangers of prison. From the day following Bonnie's death until August 12, 1977, when Sister Ramona drove him up to Albany freed on bail, he was kept under almost round-the-clock psychiatric surveillance.

Was he mad?

"Much smiling," the Superintendent of Admissions noted in the records on Herrin's first day in the unit. "Easy going, inappropriate manner and affect—no connection to feelings. States he is very hard to get angry—almost never is. Quickly becomes extraordinarily close with inmates assigned to watch him because of potential suicide. Much blocking re: facts of his own life.''

Another staffer later that day wrote in the log: "Patient is in good physical condition. His mood is depressed, trying to force himself to smile. Admits he was thinking of killing himself yesterday but decided against it.'' A third observed remarked that Herrin "seems to have made friends with inmate C——. Spent time playing ping-pong. Watched T.V. and movie. No suicidal problems. This P.M. is aware that he can have medication if needed.''

As the days progressed, it was becoming clear that the meaning of Richard Herrin's mental state was as ambiguous in the abstract as it was in real life. If he were "smiling" and "easy going," if he played ping-pong and watched television, did that suggest that he was back to normal? Or, because it was only two days since he had smashed his girlfriend's head in with a hammer, was it "inappropriate manner and affect," and a sign of madness? Since Bonnie Garland had often told him that he was "not in touch with his emotions," did the fact that a psychiatric social worker observed that inmate Herrin had "no connection to feelings" mean that he was back to normal? Or did it mean that he was insane?

When Paul Bardack arrived at the Westchester County Jail, soon after Herrin's arrest, he met a Richard Herrin who seemed painfully aware of his emotions and overwhelmed by remorse. "Rich came into the booth,'' Bardack later recounted. "At first, he didn't know it was me. He saw me and started to run away. Then he looked at me and started crying. It was a few minutes before either of us could say anything. It was so awkward. He was perspiring. I think he was wearing the same slacks as on the night of the killing. He said, 'I'm such an animal. I don't deserve people like you to come here and see me.' He said he was in the basement room and he got consumed by the devil. He said, 'I did the act and the life was taken.'

"He said that afterward he tried to kill himself by driving over a cliff or ramming the car into a tree. He said the Lord had led him to a church. I told him to shave and get some clothes and lose weight; I said appearance means a lot in court. Somewhere in the conversation I said something to the effect, 'We've been friends in good times and we can be friends in bad times and there can be good times again.' He cried at that. If the guard had told him, 'No, we don't go this way; we're taking you that way and we're going to hang you,' he would have gone. He even said, 'I don't deserve to live.' "

The days would pass without major incident. Herrin never took any major medication and never attempted suicide.

FROM THE PSYCHIATRIC forensic unit of the Westchester County Jail on Friday, August 12, Richard Herrin moved into a quiet residential neighborhood in Albany where fourteen Christian Brothers welcomed him into a comfortable, intensely spiritual community.

Inside the two-story, red brick house Herrin stepped into a religious haven. Each of the Brothers had a private room along a carpeted hallway. They shared a living room which doubled as a chapel, a television room and a dining hall which opened onto an interior courtyard. Richard Herrin was given his own room on the second floor and was accepted unequivocly by his new guardians.

If Herrin had hoped that he would be safe from publicity at the Christian Brothers, his expectations were shattered on his first morning in Albany. He awoke to the newspaper headline, "Extra Security KO'd for Accused Killer." The paper announced that the man "who had confessed to the claw-hammer murder of his Scarsdale girlfriend" had arrived at the Christian Brothers. "He will not be confined to the brothers' residence," it added ominously. Asked by the paper why no extra security was planned, Brother Thomas Gavin said, "Our security is God."

As much as the Brothers tried to protect Herrin from publicity, his notoriety continued. The District Attorney's office in Westchester would twice try to have his bail revoked. Until his trial began the following May, the Garlands would not cease in their efforts to secure the reincarceration of their daughter's killer.

To pursue every legal option, Joan and Paul Garland hired a veteran Westchester trial lawyer, State Senator Joseph Pisani, as their counsel. Pisani soon took his clients' crusade as his own. At the second bail hearing, on September 7, Pisani was able to present to Judge Walsh a small bundle of letters from the Scarsdale community expressing its outrage at the release of Herrin. But the judge would make only a minor concession, blocking Herrin from entering the County of Westchester while on bail. The Garlands listened quietly from their seats as Judge Walsh announced the new limitation of Herrin's freedom.

"Lip service" was Pisani's characterization of the Judge's ruling. Pisani ridiculed it, believing that if Herrin were bent on further damage to the Garland family, a court order would do little to restrain him.

"The court totally ignored the Garlands' plea and let Herrin go up to Albany and stay in some nonsecure place where all he had to do was some night take a car, drive back, and do it again," Pisani pointed out. "To my way of thinking, that was one of the cruelest things the law could do to a family that had been terrorized to the point the Garlands had been. They spent night and day worrying. And in addition to that Herrin's lawyer kept saying that they may try the insanity defense, planting seeds in the minds of everyone that perhaps this guy was crazy. If that was the case, what was he doing out of jail?"

What particularly incensed Pisani, who is himself a Catholic, was how protectively the clergy surrounded Herrin the day of the hearing. "I walk into the courthouse with the Garlands," he recounted. "The Garlands are standing by themselves, outside the courtroom, having just lost their daughter in such a terrible way. They're standing there and I'm with them. And there is the defendant just a few yards away, surrounded by members of the clergy in their clerical garb. You've got to understand the dynamics of the situation. The parents of a murdered girl standing here, and the defendant right there with the priests and brothers and nuns all around him. And they are fawning over him, joking and smiling, *trying to lift his spirits!*

"What misplaced sympathy, what misplaced acts of charity. If anyone needed charity and sympathy and consolation, it was the Garlands. I think the judge made a mistake in setting bail."

The next day Pisani wrote an angry letter to the Catholic Bishop of Hartford, Connecticut, in whose jurisdiction More House rested. He objected to "the Church being used in this most unfortunate and indeed scandalous way." The Bishop's response was brief and objective. "This is not a matter in which a bishop can lay down the law one way or another for his priests."

Paul Garland also continued his petitions to the Catholic hierarchy, requesting that the Church stop the clergy's support for Herrin. Garland had asked for a meeting with Cardinal Cooke and a date had been set for Saturday, February 18, 1978, at 11:00 A.M. But the meeting never took place. Garland had requested the presence of two attorneys representing him. O'Keefe responded that such an arrangement would be "not helpful" because it would require the Archdiocese to have its own attorneys at the meeting, which would turn it into a legal situation. The meeting was cancelled when Paul Garland informed the Archdiocese that he had plane reservations for a family vacation on February 18 and would not be able to attend.

Everywhere the Garlands and their friends turned, the response was the same, even at secular Yale. The Garlands believed the university improperly allowed its faculty and students to use the school's name in their support of Herrin, misleading people into believing that the killer had official school backing. It was doubly distressing to Paul Garland because Yale was not only Bonnie's alma mater, but his own as well.

"My expectation from the Yale community was that it would cry out against this brutal act and demand justice be done," Garland wrote in a letter to the Yale Corporation. "What has happened, incredibly, is largely to the contrary. Yale people, past and present, have rushed to the aid and support of the killer, in an organized and systematic manner, and have succeeded in clothing him with the aura of Yale sponsorship and support. . . . Those who have stepped forward seem to have been able to block out the horrible crime involved and to write the type of letters which a candidate for a job or college might receive. Surely a murder is an occasion for moral outrage and not for attestations of the fine character of a confessed killer.''

In the letter, Garland announced that he was terminating all his relationships with the university. The one exception was the Bonnie Garland Music Fund which Garland had established in his daughter's name to help other students further their singing careers. Even there the thought of Richard Herrin tormented him. He wrote: ''Throughout the rest of my life, I will hear the Yale voices raised in praise of the killer and the silence of those who might have protested.''

THE GARLANDS and Pisani decided to put Herrin under surveillance. In the fall of 1977, Pisani hired a private investigator and sent him to Albany. The detective discovered that Herrin was living as if nothing had happened. He was working at a gift shop a couple of blocks from the Brothers' residence, taking anthropology classes and playing interscholastic rugby at the State University of New York just a few miles away. Wanting to avoid publicity, Herrin had lied. He had enrolled in the easy-access program at SUNY using the pseudonym of Richard James and an address that was not his Christian Brothers' residence.

When the news reached the local press, SUNY was flooded with calls. The administration informed Herrin that he had to leave. ''He was walking the streets,'' Pisani later recounted. ''A man accused of this terrible murder, who might have been insane. He was sitting in the classrooms at night with other women. People not knowing who he was. Doing it under an assumed name and at taxpayer's expense. With the comfort and cooperation of the people with whom he was living. I thought that was disgraceful. I was outraged."

Pisani did some more investigating. He found out as he told Assistant District Attorney William Fredreck, that "on August 15th, subsequent to the incident, Yale University, at the request of the defendant, sent out transcripts of his academic record to SUNY Albany. I reasonably expect that he had made a very 'quick' adjustment from his alleged temporary insanity and anticipated fully to attend school in Albany awaiting trial. I certainly think this has relevance in terms of the cold-blooded nature of this defendant."

Herrin, according to the Christian Brothers, was devastated by the publicity and his subsequent dismissal from school. None of the Brothers understood the reason for the uproar. "We thought of Richard as a good, honest person," remembered Brother Thomas Gavin of the incident. "There was no reason to be afraid of him. Using a different name to register we thought of as simply a way of going to school without his being harassed or ostracized."

That Richard Herrin was a good person who had committed one irrational act was a belief that his supporters cultivated throughout the ten months that he was free awaiting trial. "His mood was very positive," recalled a woman for whom Herrin worked part-time. "He was cheerful and open." He was playing the guitar at the Christian Brothers' Mass, just as he had played at St. Thomas More at Yale. He helped out in the Brothers' kitchen, just as he had bused dishes at the Yale Commons as a freshman. He was living as a free man.

It was as a free man that he drove with Brother Thomas to White Plains, New York, in late May of 1978, and entered the courtroom to stand trial for the murder of Bonnie Garland.

CHAPTER EIGHT

The Trial

FOR MOST OF THE PEOPLE crowded onto the wooden benches in Room 1200 of the Westchester County Courthouse in White Plains, New York, this was the first look at the man accused of committing the most vicious crime in Scarsdale's history. But as Judge Richard J. Daronco, his voice crisp in the hushed room, read the second degree murder charge to the 150 prospective jurors, Richard Herrin seemed miscast as an indicted murderer.

The young man seated at the defense table bore little resemblance to the front-page photographs that appeared the day after the killing, news pictures reminiscent of the crazed brutality of Charles Manson. They had shown a wild-looking man with full beard, oily long black hair over his ears and down his forehead. He stood with hands manacled in front of a shirtless and flabby belly. In a macabre way, the cold printed image of a half-naked killer was reassuring. The bludgeoning death of Bonnie Garland seemed more comprehensible when accompanied by such a portrait.

But on this morning of May 15, 1978, the person of Richard Herrin had assumed a new quality. With his dark blue suit, striped tie, trimmed black hair and face free of stubble, Herrin looked more the Yale graduate than the killer. The flaccid bulges of July, 1977 were now hidden by his dress and his appearance was enhanced by the trappings of civility.

The courtroom was the largest in the modern twenty-story judicial headquarters of Westchester County. Situated twelve floors above the suburban town of White Plains, its formality masked the strong emotions surrounding the case. The judge, in his black robes, the vestment color for ancient wakes, sat front and center on a raised bench. In front of him, at the right side of the room was the long rectangular table of the prosecutor butting against a low rail running almost the width of the court. On the left, was the identically-shaped table of the defense, where Richard Herrin sat flanked by his lawyer, a law partner of Litman's, a law student assistant, and a sociologist.

The reporters and sketch artists sat in the seats reserved for them in the first row. Behind them were Herrin's friends and family. As if following the protocol common to weddings, they had chosen to be on the left side of the aisle, the same side as the defendant. Herrin's mother, Linda Ugarte sat ashen-faced beside her constant companion, Sister Ramona Pena. The Hispanic nun from the Catholic chapel at Yale, her short hair streaked with grey, was the model of the modern female cleric. She had given up the nun's habit for skirt and blazer ensembles. For Herrin, Ramona had been part of the trinity of special women in his life.

Next to Ramona and Linda Ugarte sat Father Peter Fagan, the bearded young priest from Yale, now dressed in clerical black. The three had been Herrin's unfailing allies. They were a constant reminder to the court of Richard Herrin's human credentials.

"Ladies and gentlemen, what happened in the early morning hours of July 7, 1977, is an absolute tragedy. If any of us could turn back the clock, we would.'' Defense attorney Jack Litman began his opening remarks to the unselected jury panel with a deliberateness that hushed the audience. With his deep, resonant voice, well-tailored suit and tan, horn-rimmed glasses, Herrin's chief counsel made an imposing presence in the courtroom.

Slim and of medium height, the thirty-four year old brown-haired defense attorney paced slowly in front of the jury box where the first panel of prospective jurors was seated. He was sophisticated and articulate, but behind the smooth demeanor was a seasoned attorney: a six-year veteran of the turbulent Manhattan District Attorney's office, where he rose to become the Deputy Chief of the Homicide Bureau. During his subsequent three years in private practice as a criminal defense lawyer Litman had never lost a homicide case.

He spoke clearly, but so quietly that the prospective jurors had to strain forward to hear. ''We have a young girl with a beautiful life who is no longer with us,'' he said. ''We have bereaved and grieving parents who would give anything to turn the clock back. We have a young man sitting over there who is beside himself with grief. And if he could turn back the clock, he would. But we can't, ladies and gentlemen. And the trial of this case is not about what we can do to turn back the clock, but to determine why it was that Richard Herrin took the life of the woman he loved more than anything in the world.''

Jack Litman knew that to clear his client of murder he would have to find a jury willing to believe that the death of Bonnie Garland was a tragedy for everyone concerned, including Richard Herrin. On every level, from the minutiae of legal technicalities to the details of body language, Litman knew that he had to put as much distance between the violent Richard Herrin of July 7, 1977, and the ''young man sitting over there who is beside himself with grief.''

It was to be more than a rhetorical trick. Changed social values and new laws had made it possible for a

trial court to weigh not only *who* killed Bonnie Garland
but *why*. It was now judicially proper to pass judgment
on the complexities of Richard Herrin's character as
well as his acts on one specific night.

In an earlier era the facts would have quickly sealed
Richard Herrin's fate. Prosecutor William Fredreck, a
husky, aggressive 32-year-old Deputy Chief of the Westchester District Attorney's Trial Bureau, was more convinced of Herrin's guilt than that of any of the other
two dozen homicide suspects he had tried in six years.
At the prosecution's table a few feet to the right of the
defendant's Fredreck sat by himself. He was as different
in courtroom technique from Litman as in his opinion
about Herrin's guilt and as uncomplicated in his approach to law as he was matter-of-fact in the courtroom.

"Are any of you going to be disappointed," he asked
the veniremen after Litman had concluded, "if this
turns out to be a pretty clear-cut case of premeditated
murder?"

Fredreck knew exactly what the law said: "A person
is guilty of murder in the second degree when with intent
to cause the death of another, he causes the death of
such person." And he could recite from memory the
statement that Herrin had given Coxsackie Police Chief
Ronald Rea only a few hours after fleeing the Garland
house: "I entertained the thought of killing her in
her sleep. . . . Once she was asleep I began thinking of
how I would carry out my plan." The statement was
Fredreck's "smoking gun." It was proof that Herrin *intended* to kill Bonnie Garland, the state of mind required for a murder conviction.

"If there is presentation of evidence of premeditation, of planning, will you consider that?" Fredreck
asked the prospective jurors. The question was part of
his uncomplicated strategy: He could lose the case only
if the jury ignored the facts.

Even Litman knew that if a vote were taken, most of
the 150 Westchester citizens in the courtroom would
have responded to Fredreck's question with a hearty

"yea." Litman had already commissioned a telephone survey in Westchester. "Sixty percent of the people," he later explained, "said that from what they had read, Richard was dead guilty and what's this trial all about anyway."

But what the trial ultimately proved to be about was human nature and the place of psychiatry in a court of law.

NOT LONG AFTER Litman agreed to represent Herrin, he put the prosecution on notice that he would set out to prove that a murder is not always a murder.

Litman gave the first sign of his determination less than three weeks after the killing. On July 26, 1977, he submitted a detailed brief to the court asking that Herrin be granted bail. At about the same time, he arranged for two psychiatrists to interview Herrin at the county jail. Litman was already making the legal system's complexity work for his client. While submitting the three-score letters testifying to Herrin's unimpeachable character he was simultaneously preparing to argue that Herrin was insane when he killed Bonnie Garland.

But Litman did not immediately reveal his strategy. On August 25, when Judge Isaac Rubin formally asked Herrin how he pleaded, Litman spoke for Herrin. With Joan and Paul Garland looking on, Litman simply stated, "Not guilty." He then waited a full month and a half, two weeks beyond the deadline, to file his "Notice of Defense of Mental Disease or Defect."

The prosecution had already lost three valuable months after the killing. From a psychiatric point of view, the more time that passes between the claimed moment of insanity and the later professional examination, the more difficult it is to determine the validity of the claim. Although the insanity plea gave the prosecution's psychiatrists the right to interview Herrin, Litman filed a motion objecting to the examination. He eventually managed to keep the District Attorney's psychiatrists away from his client until January, 1978, six months after the crime and the supposed period of insanity.

Few legal maneuvers were left unused by Herrin's counselor. On October 10, the same day as he presented the insanity plea, Litman filed an "omnibus motion" that sent the prosecution back to the law books. He argued that the indictment against Herrin should be dismissed because the grand jury had been improperly instructed. Evidence obtained from Herrin's Fort Worth house, Litman argued, should be suppressed because it was seized without a search warrant. The statements Herrin made to Chief Rea and Father Tartaglia in Coxsackie should also be suppressed, he claimed, because they were made involuntarily.

By the time the D.A. had responded and Litman had answered the response, three weeks had passed. Though Litman would eventually lose on all counts, such measures served to delay the trial and to put still more distance between Herrin and the hammer.

In the meantime, Litman's men initiated a countrywide canvass, interviewing a hundred of Herrin's friends and family members, piecing together a story of his life to substantiate their claim that the only explanation for his killing the woman he loved was an inexplicable loss of reason.

The Garlands were becoming concerned that justice would not be done. "We see this motion," Joan Garland complained, "as the beginning of a long series of legal maneuvers that will prolong this trial; will delay it and prolong our agony and the agony of my children. . . . We will never be able, it seems, in the near future, to lay this thing to rest."

Even though Paul Garland was an experienced lawyer, the killing of his daughter was a crime against "the People of the State of New York," which had taken the prosecution out of the family's hands. The Garlands and Pisani eventually resigned themselves to working through the D. A.'s office, but did not desert the battle.

"Mr. Garland is a very intelligent man," remembered prosecutor Fredreck, "a very strong man. He wasn't going to sit down and play possum for anyone. At the beginning of the case he was very skeptical of the District Attorney's office. He wanted to do everything he could to make sure the case was handled right.''

Garland, with the help of Pisani, who has sponsored legislation to abolish the insanity defense, kept in constant contact with Fredreck. They discussed strategy, offered advice. As a public prosecutor, Fredreck had to be careful to avoid being influenced by private citizens, even the parents of the victim. He was willing to keep the Garlands informed, but when they offered to put their financial resources at the D. A.'s disposal, Fredreck refused.

Garland had shown Fredreck a list of ten leading psychiatrists, including the president of the American Psychiatric Association. ''I was familiar with most of the names on the list and assured them that I was going to get the best. They were concerned that the budget of our office was not what it should be. But I told them in no uncertain terms that there was no way our office could accept as much as a nickel from them.''

Garland also asked what he could do to help with the investigation of the case. ''I said, 'Nothing,' '' Fredreck recalled. ''He said, 'I have to do something.' 'You do what you have to do,' I told him. 'I can't stop you; but don't interfere with me.' ''

What Garland did, in February of 1978, was hire the Wackenhut Corporation, a private investigative firm. Its detectives fanned out across the country, but they were either frustrated in their attempts to interview Herrin's friends or found that he was much the same person described in his bail application.

After ninety-eight hours of investigation, Wackenhut closed the book on Richard Herrin. It had cost Paul Garland almost $2,300 and did little to aid the prosecution. For the Garlands, it only added to their frustration. ''I've handled about thirty murder cases,'' Fredreck later commented, ''and have never seen a family react as strongly as the Garland family did. But it didn't surprise me. In fact, the reverse surprises me:

That more families who have lost a loved one don't take the offensive. Most families sit back and accept the fact that there's nothing they can do about it. . . . But as far as what the Garlands did in this case—the loss of their daughter—God bless them. More people should do it.''

Much of the Garlands' frustration stemmed from the nature of Herrin's legal defense. Prosecutor Fredreck got a taste of it before the trial began, when on a crisp winter day he walked out of the Westchester County Jail in discussion with a psychiatrist, Dr. John Train. Train had just interviewed an indicted cop-killer whom Fredreck was about to prosecute, and was explaining that he could find no justification for the defendant's claim of mental or emotional disturbance.

"If you think this guy wasn't emotionally disturbed," Fredreck announced, "you won't believe the next one I'm going to give you. It's really a bunch of baloney."

Train, whose psychiatric practice frequently involved testifying in courts of law, occasionally for Fredreck, asked which case he was talking about.

"The guy's a Yale graduate. He killed his girlfriend because she jilted him. He's got no history of mental problems. Compared with the fellow you just examined, it's a piece of cake."

The psychiatrist surprised Fredreck with his response. "Herrin?"

"Yes," replied the prosecutor quizzically. "How'd you know?"

"Because I've already been retained by his defense attorney."

Unlike the "whodunits" of the past, there seemed no way to predict how a mental disturbance case would go. There was also no way to predict which psychiatrist would be an advocate for which side, even if all the "facts" were in hand. It appeared that one man's "baloney" was another's insanity.

BEFORE ENTERING the wood-paneled courtroom on the morning of May 15, 1978, Jack Litman had given a nervous Richard Herrin some instructions. "Richard, I want you to look them in the eye," he told his twenty-four-year-old client. "They" were the more than one hundred prospective jurors who would be called into the jury box to answer queries from both attorneys and the judge. "If you can't make eye contact, if anyone refuses to look at you or seems to be afraid of you, let me know about it."

Jack Litman knew that if Herrin were to be adjudged innocent of murder, he would first have to become a human being in the eyes of his judges. It was important to know which of the prospective jurors was capable of seeing Herrin as something other than a killer. Did a man stare at him with intensity? Did a woman quickly avert her eyes to avoid his?

In the trial process, it is always important to gauge the jury. But the "voir dire," as the interrogation of prospective jurors is called, is the only time that an attorney can actually do anything decisive about it. Litman had asked his law partner, Herman Kaufman, and his law student assistant, Russell Gioiella, to watch prospective jurors' reactions to him, to Herrin, to a particular question. Jay Schulman, a sociologist who had aided the defense at the Attica and Wounded Knee trials, was also part of Herrin's team, surveying the two rows of veniremen for telltale expressions of compassion or hatred.

Litman, who is blind in his right eye, wanted to make sure he didn't miss anything. "I have terrible vision," he explained, "and I can't quite see all twelve people when I'm talking to the one at the end. If someone at the other end is saying, 'What is this guy talking about?' I want to know about it. So it's important to have someone else with you in the courtroom."

It would take almost three days of tedious questioning before the first juror was accepted, and ten days before the full complement of twelve jurors and four alternates was chosen. From an unprecedented group of five hundred Westchester residents, only 150 passed the initial screening. They were the ones who claimed to have no opinion on the case and for whom a long trial would pose no hardship.

Bill Fredreck was searching for dispassionate, independent-minded jurors who would not be afraid to disagree with an expert witness. There would be a good deal of psychiatric testimony, much of it conflicting, and Fredreck wanted jurors who would use "common sense" to make up their own minds.

To each potential male juror, Fredreck posed the same question. "Did you ever have a girl break up with you?" One man answered, "Sure." "Did you kill her?" the burly Fredreck asked bluntly. "No," the man responded. This was the type of response he sought.

Jack Litman's approach to jury selection was different. He wanted "virgin" jurors, people who had never served before. "Once a juror knows how to say 'guilty' it becomes easier to say it the second time around," Litman explained. He wanted "humanity" in his jurors, people who would be able to empathize with what Richard Herrin was feeling when Bonnie Garland wanted to break off their relationship. "There is no dispute that Richard Herrin struck Bonnie Garland in the head with a hammer," the auburn-haired attorney told the veniremen. "Where the issue is in this case— and it is a very serious issue—is what was going on in Richard Herrin's head at the time."

On the second day of jury selection Litman surprised the court. He announced that he would not only claim that his client had a mental disease when he killed Bonnie Garland, but that Herrin was also suffering from "extreme emotional disturbance." Though each plea was increasingly common, the two were rarely used together. The insanity defense meant that Herrin either didn't know, or didn't appreciate, what he was doing and was therefore not criminally responsible. The extreme emotional disturbance defense admits criminal responsibility but claims that Herrin was suffering from such severe stress that it should be considered a mitigating factor. By law, if a jury accepted such a defense, Herrin's murder charge would be dropped and a charge of first degree manslaughter would be levied. Litman, the master strategist, had just placed another obstacle before the prosecution.

Litman knew that during the trial he would be describing a young man who appeared to be perfectly normal, yet he would argue that Herrin had "snapped" under the pressure of losing his lover. Litman wanted jurors who could appreciate the power of emotions. He sought jurors who knew that even seemingly placid, unassertive people carried strong feelings deep within them.

"Have you ever been in the army, sir?" Litman asked one man at the far end of the jury box. The man, nearing fifty, said yes. "Did you ever see someone with shell shock or battle fatigue?" Again, yes. "Tell me about it." Litman was as anxious for the other people to hear the man's answer as he was to hear it himself.

"Oh, yes. I remember in a battle once this guy who snapped."

"What kind of guy was he before that?" Litman prodded gently.

"He was the last guy I thought would go."

"Why was that?" the attorney asked, offering a subtle hint. "Because he seemed well put-together?"

The man was now shaking his head in confident affirmation. "You're absolutely right. You can never tell."

The jury selection was also influenced by outside factors including publicity about the case. There had been considerable newspaper coverage of the killing, a fact Litman used, unsuccessfully, to try to have the trial moved out of Westchester County.

Though it was Litman who complained about the publicity, Bill Fredreck was not happy with the press exposure either. Many of the jury candidates had read a *New York Times Magazine* article about the case, and they admitted that they might not be able to put it out of their minds, which was grounds for automatic dismissal from the panel. "When I pick a jury," Fredreck later explained, "especially in a case like this, one that will involve so much psychiatric testimony, I want intelligent people. And it happens that the more intelligent people read *The New York Times*. I lost a nice pool of jurors because of that article.''

Tedious as it was, the jury selection was the trench battle that could determine the war. By the time Patricia Policriti was sworn in as the first juror, and therefore as forelady, three days had passed, more than four hundred of the original five hundred prospects had been dismissed. Policriti was only twenty-five years old and had never before served on a jury. She had been born and raised in nearby Harrison and was a graduate of Iona College in New Rochelle with a degree in sociology.

The next day, the fourth of jury selection, was the most productive. Juror number two was Pasquale Toglia, a sixty-three-year-old heating mechanic and native of New Rochelle with two daughters and two sons in their twenties. Milton Nelson, sixty, a pharmaceutical salesman, was chosen as juror three. Juror number four, William Doyle, was a hard-driving insurance broker in his mid-thirties.

Juror five, Domenic Sarno, was Jack Litman's favorite from the beginning. Sarno was a grey-haired, spectacled man of seventy-two whom, because of his age, either attorney could have dismissed without using a challenge. Litman was attracted to him because of what he called his ''soul.'' One of Sarno's favorite activities was traveling. When Litman asked him what he liked about traveling—''the places?''—the elderly man responded, ''Oh, no, forget the places. I like to meet the people.'' Sarno sat in the second row of the jury box, exactly in the center. Seated in front of him, Jennie DeMilto, a vivacious thirty-four-year-old secretary, was sworn in as juror number six. Jennie's boyfriend was a policeman, which Fredreck considered a good omen. He would later learn that omens are not always valid.

On Friday, the fifth day, only Lorraine Kwasnica found a permanent seat in the jury box. Kwasnica was twenty-eight and a marketing administrator with the phone company in Yonkers. The eighth juror was Anneliese von Gruenberg, a middle-aged German-born woman. For von Gruenberg, who still spoke with a soft accent, taking a seat in an American jury box was "a whole new experience." Litman had a feeling she would be good for his case.

The seventh day passed without a juror being chosen. On Wednesday, the eighth day, Fredreck and Litman agreed on a factory worker, Patrick Kelly, and a teacher, Daniel Cardinale. Litman had his reservations about Cardinale, a forty-eight-year-old man with a teenage daughter, but he hoped Cardinale's work with emotionally disturbed children would make him sensitive to Herrin's problems. As events would prove, Litman's reservations were well-founded.

Patrick Kelly, juror number ten, was seated in the first row just in front of Cardinale. Only twenty-five, he had graduated with a teaching degree but had settled for a place on the assembly line. Kelly would be another one of Litman's virgin jurors. He paid no attention to murder stories in newspapers or on television and had never before heard of either Bonnie Garland or Richard Herrin. Soft-spoken and good-natured, Kelly seemed the kind of person who would take the case as it came. It was a possibility both lawyers welcomed.

By Thursday, the ninth day, the final selection was made. Bill Fredreck had used all but three of his twenty challenges, and Jack Litman had only one left. Richard Pfeifer, who was sitting in juror chair number eleven, had expressed no obvious biases. Litman was like a coach trying to decide when to use his last time-out.

"Pfeifer was probably the worst choice I had on the jury," Litman later recalled. "He was a fundamentalist. He did say some nice things, like he met his wife on campus and understood what it was like, but he was obviously a very religious man. People who are very, very religious take killing very, very badly. There it is in the Ten Commandments: 'Thou shalt not kill.' It doesn't say, 'Thou shalt not kill *unless* you're suffering from extreme emotional disturbance.' But I had only one challenge left, so the question was do you take him or do you dismiss him and get stuck with whomever is next." Litman let Pfeifer stay, but he was right about fundamentalism and killing.

As it turned out, Litman liked the next person. Frank McDermott was a forty-five-year-old executive who had once worked on Wall Street. Though he was a first-time juror, as Litman preferred, McDermott seemed to be the unpretentious, plainspoken type that Fredreck wanted. McDermott also had three young daughters, a fact that Pisani, the Garlands' attorney, had urged Fredreck to consider. Frank McDermott was seated and, except for choosing the four alternates, the jury was now complete.

After more than sixty hours of questioning, Fredreck and Litman had selected a cross section of Westchester County. The jury was made up of eight men and four women ranging in age from twenty-five to seventy-two, in education from high school to a college degree. Some were married and had children, including daughters; others had brothers and sisters but no spouse. Some were professionals, others blue-collar. There were Catholics and Protestants, but no Jews and no one from Scarsdale, the Garlands' home town.

"A lot of it is sixth sense," Jack Litman later explained about the jury-picking process. "And most of it is hocus-pocus. And in the end you can only do the best you can. The most important thing is that after you select the jury, you forget about it. There's not too much you can do about it after that point."

THE NEXT WEDNESDAY, shortly after ten in the morning, Court Clerk Millie Marolla stood beside her chair in the front of a filled-to-capacity courtroom to announce the beginning of the first murder trial ever to involve Yale students as both suspect and victim. "The People against Richard Herrin," she said as Judge Daronco settled into his chair. "Are the People ready?"

"The People are ready, Your Honor," replied prosecutor Fredreck from his table on the right side of the room.

"Defendant ready?" asked Marolla, standing only a few feet from Jack Litman, his assistant Russ Gioiella, and Herrin.

"The Defense is ready, sir," Litman answered for his client. Whether Richard Herrin, dressed in the same blue suit he had worn on the opening day of jury selection, went to jail for twenty-five years, or less than one year, now depended on Jack Litman. Should Litman lose, it was also possible that the Yale graduate from the Los Angeles barrio could spend the rest of his life behind bars.

Daronco, at forty-six already the senior-ranking county judge, gave some brief instructions to the jury, then turned the floor over to the prosecution. William Fredreck, looking like a linebacker in a three-piece suit, sauntered to the lectern in front of the jury box to make his opening statement.

"May it please the Court, Your Honor, Madam Forelady, ladies and gentlemen of the jury," Fredreck began. Though he had graduated from law school only six years before, Fredreck had worked his way to the second-in-command position at the Trial Bureau, prosecuting killers, dope-dealers, car thieves and rapists by putting in numberless hours of overtime that never showed in his modest salary. For most of May, while working full time on the Herrin case, he had not been home for dinner. "Twenty-seven days," his wife complained. After hundreds of hours of preparation, he was convinced that Richard Herrin was both sane and guilty of murder.

"As far as I'm concerned, it is an open and clear-cut case," Fredreck said, running his eyes along the two rows of jurors, "and it is going to take a very short time for me to complete it. . . . The evidence in this case, ladies and gentlemen, will show you that this defendant, Richard Herrin, was, in fact, criminally responsible for his actions and is accountable under the laws of our state; and that he intentionally killed Bonnie Garland.

Not in an emotional outburst or an extreme emotional disturbance. . . . But rather, the evidence in this case, I submit to you at the outset, is going to show that this killing was premeditated; it was planned; it was cold; it was calculated.''

The words chilled Herrin's friends and family, huddled together in the second row. On the opposite side of the aisle were the friends and family of Bonnie Garland. Mrs. Garland's sister, Agnes Vanek, the Reverend Roger Johnson, minister at the Scarsdale Congregational Church, and Sol Friedman, a retired lawyer and neighbor of the Garlands, were there to take news of the proceedings back to Bonnie's parents.

"Let me caution you at the outset," the brown-haired, mustached prosecutor told the jurors, "that the time we are concerned with here is the early morning hours of July 7th, 1977. The place we are concerned with is the bedroom of Bonnie Garland."

The young prosecutor pressed on with a no-nonsense style as he paced the courtroom. Whenever he could, he warned the jurors that his opponent, Jack Litman, would be trying *his* case with sleight-of-hand and not with reason. "I don't prove the charges to you by asking questions ad nauseam in jury selection," said Fredreck, taking a swipe at a successful Litman tactic. "I don't prove these charges to you by subliminally advertising over a period of two weeks. But I intend to prove these charges to you by calling witnesses to the witness stand to testify under oath."

Fredreck had enough experience with the insanity and extreme emotional disturbance pleas to know how complicated trials of the mind could become. A few years before, he had taken a criminal law course at New York University from Jack Litman. Now he was facing his former teacher, who he knew was capable of masterfully complicating what Fredreck saw as a simple case. The young D. A. was warning the jurors of his mentor's strategy in advance. "I'm anticipating that there might be some character evidence produced by the defense on behalf of the defendant," he continued. "At the outset,

I want to ask you to keep your minds open and look at the relevant and material issues here and not to be sidetracked; not to allow any smoke screens to divert your attention from the issues.

"Did Richard Herrin intend to kill Bonnie Garland at a time when he was criminally responsible? That is the issue. . . . And I don't care what Herrin's friends say in this case, unless they were there.

"The second thing I want to caution you about is what Mr. Litman mentioned . . . ad nauseam in the jury selection process, that he intends to call psychiatrists. Well, they weren't there, either." Fredreck, born and bred in Brooklyn as one of six children, was a man who called the shots as he saw them. "I'm just asking you people," he told the jurors, most of whom had never been closer to a trial than a Perry Mason television show, "to make sure that any psychiatrist's opinion is supported by the credible evidence in this case. I ask you to use your common sense in evaluating the testimony and the opinions given by any psychiatrist, and if it doesn't match with your common sense, use your right as a juror to reject it." Fredreck paused. The crowd was silent.

"Ladies and gentlemen, I am about to present evidence of premeditated murder and nothing can change that. Nothing reduces that to manslaughter. Not the fact that Mr. Herrin has able counsel, not the fact that he is a Yale graduate, and not the fact that he has some friends—perhaps clergy—who will come forward in his behalf."

Behind Fredreck, Richard Herrin sat at the defense table absorbing the attack. The dozens of hours spent reliving the events of his life with his attorney and psychiatrists had not prepared him for the harshness of center stage.

Fredreck had his back to the defendant as he sketched the portrait of the murder. He skipped over the story of Richard and Bonnie's two-year romance as if it were a footnote. In less than two minutes he had arrived at Bonnie's Glee Club tour of Europe the month before her death. It was then, Fredreck told the jurors, that she "realized that her social life in New Haven had been restricted" and wrote to Herrin that she wanted to see other people.

"Mr. Litman used the word 'rejection' over and over again during the jury selection process," Fredreck went on. "There was no rejection. A twenty-year-old girl who dated but one man said to this man who *supposedly* loved her, 'I want to see others. I want to spread my wings. Stand by me, Richard. I still love you.'" For Fredreck, the case was almost that elemental: Bonnie Garland, not unlike many other women, wanted a new boyfriend. Richard Herrin didn't like the idea so, unlike most spurned lovers, he killed her.

He flew to New York two days after he got the news, Fredreck continued, "to get her back exclusively." When he failed, there was only one eyewitness to what happened next. It was Herrin himself, and the prosecutor slowed his pace to let the jury know the import of that testimony. "*In the defendant's own words,* 'I entertained the thought of killing her in her sleep. Once she was asleep, I began thinking of how I would carry out my plan.' Ladies and gentlemen, listen carefully to what the defendant's psychiatrists have to say about *that*."

Firm in his belief that the only issue was what happened in Bonnie's bedroom early that Thursday morning, Fredreck proceeded to describe what Herrin did after he had hatched his "plan." It was a quick, synoptic account, but Fredreck pointedly broke the action three times with a single phrase. With that phrase, he hoped to show Herrin's sanity and the critical time-lag between Herrin's forming his intent to kill and his first hammer blow.

Herrin went downstairs and found the hammer, Fredreck explained, "*but he didn't go up and kill Bonnie!*" Instead he went to his own room and picked up a towel to hide the hammer in before returning to her bedroom, "*but he didn't go in and kill Bonnie!*" Then he set the hammer and towel down, went into her room to make sure she still slept, *then* retrieved the hammer and walked back into the room. *"But he didn't kill Bonnie then!"* Fredreck repeated the phrase, draining the last ounce of premeditative calculation out of Herrin's movements. He finally told the jurors that Herrin "took the hammer out of the towel and hit her in the head three or four times."

Fredreck once more appealed to the jury "not to be misled by immaterial or irrelevant matters," thanked them and sat down.

Jack Litman was pleased. The lean, gritty speech by his former student had taken less than fifteen minutes. In Litman's estimation it was a strategic *faux pas*. His own case, in style and substance was designed to exploit Fredreck's straightforward approach. As soon as Litman stepped up to the lectern, he demonstrated his contrasting strategy with a small personal touch.

"May it please the court, Judge Daronco, Mr. Herrin, Mr. Gioiella, Mr. Fredreck, Miss Policriti, ladies and gentlemen of the jury," Litman began. His first objective was, as he later put it, to "engage the souls" of the jurors. He immediately proceeded to flatter them as "independent and intelligent people, who have sophistication and common sense." As the attorney for a man who had confessed to killing a young woman, he could ill afford the approach that he believed the prosecution had mistakenly taken: lecturing, cautioning the jurors as if mistrustful of their abilities to render a proper decision.

Litman was letting the jury know that they were the most important people in the room. "No one, ladies and gentlemen, can judge the decision you make. You are completely sovereign in your determination of the facts of this case. . . . And when you make that decision, I think the evidence will show, despite what Mr. Fredreck calls a clear and open-and-shut case, that it will be among the most difficult decisions you will ever have to make."

Litman moved slowly along the line of jurors, modulating his voice between tones of conversational comraderie and persuasive oration. He was a courtroom chameleon who prided himself on knowing everything he could know about his client, his case, his opponent, the law, and his audience. He adjusted his voice, his gestures, his strategy to only one end: the exoneration of his client.

He could just as easily, as he did after the Herrin trial, win acquittal for a police officer who had allegedly shot two unarmed Hispanics, one in the back, as he could successfully defend a New Jersey man who was charged with killing a cop. For Litman, if there was a secret to being a good defense lawyer, it was "dominating a courtroom and preparing your head off." A person had to be "a little bit of an actor" and at the same time "proceed sort of like a director," fitting all the pieces together, Litman believed.

Litman's first brush with courtroom drama had come in high school when he played the role made famous by Lee J. Cobb of the obdurate juror who kept voting "guilty" in *Twelve Angry Men*. Litman's performance was so successful that his classmates wrote in his yearbook, "Guilty or not guilty?" At Cornell University Litman had majored in theoretical mathematics and French literature, but in his senior year he changed his mind. The catalyst was his senior thesis about French novelist Georges Simenon, creator of Inspector Maigret.

"I read about ninety of his novels," Litman recalled, "and became very interested in Maigret as a detective who solves the crime but who is more intrigued by the person who commits the crime than in solving it. You know on the third page who did it. The interesting thing is the relationship he develops with the person he catches."

Litman decided to apply to law school and become a criminal defense attorney. The only school he applied to accepted him: Harvard, where Litman took every course in criminal law available. Combining his Harvard-gained skills and his innate curiosity about people, Litman had come to this point in his career to defend Richard Herrin, the man whom everyone knew had killed Bonnie Garland. Like Inspector Maigret, Litman was more intrigued by Herrin's person than by his specific act of violence. It was that curiosity that he had both to explore and to communicate to the jury.

"My point of view," Litman later explained, "was that this case was a very difficult human matter, a very complex, sad, tragic affair and I wanted the jurors to see the sadness, the tragedy, and the human aspect of it, and forget about the obvious, which was that he hit her with a hammer while she was sleeping."

In Richard Herrin, Litman had what even prosecutor Fredreck would later call "the perfect client." He was not a hardened criminal; he was a Yale graduate. Like a magnet, the dichotomy between Yale and Murder attracted curiosity as strong as if the case were a classic "whodunit."

"Even if it weren't a legal issue, the jurors are going to want to know why Richard did what he did," Litman said later. "They are going to say, 'Hey, that fellow over there doesn't look like a criminal. Why did he do it?' They want to know. . . . I think the prosecutor tried to deny that to them. And to deny jurors their human curiosity and their human involvement is a terrific mistake."

For the next hour and fifteen minutes Jack Litman avoided that mistake. He recounted a tale which at its end had some of the jurors—and Richard Herrin himself—moved to tears.

"AS YOU HEAR the evidence, I urge you to ask yourself, with common sense and reason, why this tragedy occurred," Litman intoned as he looked from Patricia Policriti on his left to Frank McDermott on his right. "Why was it that Richard Herrin took the life of the woman he loved? Ask yourselves whether what Richard Herrin did for weeks before the early morning of the seventh day of the seventh month of 1977 were the acts of a rational, sane person, or were the acts, as the evidence will show—and not just from psychiatrists—of irrationality, the work of an unfeeling, robotlike machine.

"Ask yourselves . . . how else it was that he took, in such a brutal fashion, the life of the one person he was totally devoted to for three years; the person he was to marry, the person he was to live his life with, the person he was totally dependent upon."

The answers, Litman told the jurors, were to be found in part in a flaw in Richard Herrin's personality, one which goes undetected until intense stress is applied. "Then the normal machinery of the mind, like the normal machinery of the body, simply breaks down."

The defect, said Litman, was what psychiatrists call a borderline personality. "But the label is not important, ladies and gentlemen," he continued. "What is, as the testimony will show, is that Richard Herrin had an overdependency on external sources. And specifically, on relationships with women. An overdependency that was necessary to provide him with any sort of identity, with self-esteem, with a sense of worth."

Like the R. D. Laing of the courtroom, Jack Litman used the jargon and substance of elementary psychology to seduce an intrigued jury, leading them through the intricacies of the human psyche. Herrin's dependency, the attorney explained, was like the symbiotic relationship between a mother and her baby, a relationship that all of us have experienced. "The mother is happy rearing the baby, and the baby does not conceive its existence outside of the mother. Most of us, however, outgrow this extreme dependency. We develop a feeling of self-esteem, of self-worth, of self-identity that is somewhat apart from other people and somewhat apart from the environment. We can stand on our own two feet in terms of our esteem.

"But Richard Herrin could not. Early on he developed an intense fear of abandonment by his loved ones. He was unconsciously unable to distinguish between himself and the object of his love upon whom he came to rely to such a dependent extent."

As Litman spoke, the jurors followed his movements around the small courtroom area that he was pacing out as his territory. It ranged from the edge of the prosecutor's table, in front of Domenic Sarno, toward the end of the jury box where Richard Pfeifer sat, a few feet from the first public row, where reporters were busily writing in their notepads. Behind Pfeifer, Frank McDermott was impressed with Litman's ability to express himself.

"You will also hear that Richard Herrin, not wanting to be rejected and wanting to be accepted by his loved ones, *for his entire life* totally suppressed any hostility or any anger," Litman explained. "You will hear from many people that he never was able to express it in the normal channels that all of us have, of losing our temper, of striking out in words. He was *unable* to do that."

Herrin's childhood was marred, Litman explained, by the violence and drunkenness of a father who abandoned him and his mother when Richard was two; it was scarred further when a new man, his stepfather, appeared and captured the love of his mother upon which he had relied for emotional sustenance. Richard had to turn to school, where he excelled, "to gain the self-esteem and feeling of self-worth which is necessary to him."

He did so well that he gained admission to Yale, but once there quickly found he couldn't compete and once again turned elsewhere "to obtain from others his needed sense of self-worth." He turned to religious activities, to the Mexican-American student group, and most importantly "to intense relationships with women to allay his concerns, to put off his fears of his poor performance." Just the year before he met Bonnie, Litman confided to the jurors, Richard had a relationship with a woman that was "a definite precursor, a definite foreshadowing of his situation with Bonnie."

Behind Jack Litman, Richard Herrin was motionless and impassive. He no longer tried to make eye contact with anyone. Most spectators saw only a blue-suited back and the profile of an expressionless face. His secret life was now public gossip. To a roomful of strangers his attorney was revealing details he had previously kept hidden from everyone.

Twenty minutes had passed, but Jack Litman had only begun. At the prosecution's table a few feet from where Litman was pacing, Bill Fredreck shifted grumpily in his seat, hoping to communicate his frustration to the jurors. Litman was weaving an interesting yarn, but as far as he was concerned it had nothing to do with Herrin's guilt or innocence.

But it was as if Fredreck's opening statement had left a void in the room, and Litman was now filling it. The prosecutor wanted to separate Richard Herrin's brutal act from his past, but he had done it by omitting his history. Fredreck left that terrain open to Litman, whose account of Bonnie Garland and Richard Herrin's romance began to take on a life of its own. It became more powerful as Litman chronicled each event with the same irresistible theme, as if it were a Gregorian chant in which the individual words eventually seemed to merge.

"You will hear . . ." Litman repeated the phrase over and over. "You will hear" that the relationship "was not just a college romance"; that Richard Herrin "officially proposed marriage"; that Richard Herrin and Bonnie Garland spent two weeks alone together in Washington, D.C., "where all they did is stayed and looked at each other"; that Bonnie Garland and Richard Herrin's mother "had the *exact same birthday*." He continued the story of their fatal romance, pausing at the point when Bonnie went on her European Glee Club tour in the spring of 1977. "As sure as that clock strikes 12:00 every day," Litman said pointing to the white-faced institutional clock at the rear of the courtroom, "Richard Herrin would write a letter so that the letter would arrive in each and every city that Bonnie Garland would be in on the tour."

The self-assured defense attorney then walked to the lectern that he had so far avoided as if it were an unnecessary prop, and picked up a small stack of papers. "Here, for example, is a letter he wrote to her at the beginning of the tour."

Litman had now engaged his listeners. He had made Richard and Bonnie's love part of the courtroom atmosphere, potent by the knowledge of inevitable tragedy.

" 'Hello Sunshine! I was at the art museum yesterday. I came across a picture that reminded me of you very much. When I read the label and found out it was the "Birth of Venus," I got goosebumps all over. Now I understand a little bit more about classical beauty, because that is you.' " Litman read from the postcard though he knew the words by heart.

One by one he read Herrin's increasingly desperate letters, with a voice masterfully modulated to impart each touch of passion. " 'I love you, Bonnie. I moved into the Devery's house yesterday and it's the loneliest place I've ever lived in. There's nobody around and nothing to do. I've been thinking about you all day, babe. I've been thinking about you all day every day, babe. I've never missed you so much. I've never yearned for you like I do now. . . .' "

Between the reading of each letter, Litman reminded the jurors that Bonnie still hadn't written Richard. " 'It's tearing my guts out,' " he read. " 'I have never, never been so sad and lonely.' " But Richard kept writing, said Litman, "failing to see the handwriting on the wall," until he wrote the last letter to Bonnie only two weeks before killing her. " 'My love is waiting for you, with open arms and open heart. Come soon and fill my life with your love, warmth and happiness.' "

Litman put the letters down and moved on, but not without noting that several of the jurors were brushing tears from their eyes. Behind Litman, Court Clerk Millie Marolla saw the tears on the cheeks of Richard Herrin. Instinctively she reached into her purse for a handkerchief which she handed over the small rail to the defendant. Despite his many conversations with Litman, it was the first time Herrin had heard the story laid out, as his attorney had said, "like a mosaic."

For another forty minutes, Litman kept up his searing chronology of events. The account was as full of emotional drama as Fredreck's narrative had been lean. Step by step, the audience was led to see Richard Herrin walking "unconsciously" toward his psychological "no exit" until, as Litman told the jurors, "there will come a point, ladies and gentlemen, when you try to follow what is going on in Richard Herrin's mind . . . and you simply will not be able to follow it anymore."

Standing in front of juror Domenic Sarno, Litman looked up and down the rows of panelists. "Because none of you," he continued, "have ever gotten to that state that psychiatrists call psychosis . . . when all of a sudden, the emotion that is within you is totally depressed. . . . What they call a dissociated state. What his psychiatrists call a depersonalized state. And the only alternative to his irrational mind at that time . . . was to kill her and to kill himself. Without feeling, without appreciation of the enormity of what he was doing. And he went about doing it as one goes about doing a routine household task."

Bill Fredreck leaned back, shaking his head. "Schmaltz," he thought, hoping the jurors would read his mind. Litman was turning the facts upside down. Herrin's actions just before the killing had just been characterized by Litman as a "routine household task." Instead of considering it the cool behavior of a calculating killer, the defense attorney had cleverly termed it the "robotlike" action of insanity. Fredreck listened in admiration of his former teacher's dramatic technique.

"Ladies and gentlemen, consider two things when you think about the state of rationality of his mind," Litman continued. "He is killing somebody, bludgeoning someone with a hammer, brutally and violently taking someone's life. And at the same time, he has a thought that he doesn't want her to suffer, doesn't want her to wake up. Ask yourself if there is any sane, rational mind that could not put those two thoughts together and appreciate the horror and the enormity of what was being done?"

"Schmaltz" or not, by the time Jack Litman finished his hour-and-a-half opening statement he had flooded the courtroom with the essence of human tragedy. He had overwhelmed the prosecutor's attempt to bar emotion from the trial.

There was no better confirmation than the tears. Though Judge Daronco had already instructed those involved in the case to "leave sympathy and prejudice outside this courtroom," there was no way to outlaw crying. When the jury had left the room for a short recess, Daronco did take note of the emotionally-charged atmosphere by scolding Court Clerk Marolla for handing Herrin the tissue. There was little else he could do to defuse an atmosphere which the defense attorney had so ably charged.

The legal battle lines were now clearly drawn. The opening statements made it apparent that this was to be a trial of simplicity versus complexity, the actions of a man on a given night versus his psychodynamics over an entire lifetime. It was to pit the old concepts of justice against the new psychiatric criteria; the tradition of "equality before the law" would struggle against the revolutionary modern belief that before the law each and every person is a psychological and emotional exception.

It was not a trial to determine who killed Bonnie Garland. It was the weighing of "hammer killing" and "confessions" against "dissociations" and "psychoses." Whether Room 1200 of the Westchester County Courthouse would be the courtroom of Sherlock Holmes and Perry Mason or of Dostoyevsky and Freud would depend on whether the jury decided to put Richard Herrin on trial, or instead, to judge his unconscious mind.

TEN MINUTES into the testimony of Fredreck's first witness, Jack Litman rose to his feet to register an objection. It was the first of many objections in what one juror later called "a real jack-in-the-box trial." On the witness stand, only a few feet from jury forewoman Pat Policriti, a gangly, nineteen-year-old Patrick Garland had to be coaxed to move closer to the microphone. Patrick had been the last person to see Richard Herrin and his sister together.

To prove that Herrin was both sane and free of any emotional disturbance, Fredreck had Patrick tell the jurors that he had seen Herrin at seven o'clock on the night of the killing, and that he did not look or sound other than normal. For Fredreck it was more evidence of Herrin's guilt.

Litman seemed unconcerned with the testimony until Fredreck asked Patrick to describe what he had seen the next morning after he heard his mother scream. The defense attorney was convinced that he had to block the prosecution from influencing the jury with graphic images of Bonnie's killing. Litman knew that his client's freedom depended upon focusing the trial on Herrin's psyche instead of Bonnie's battered body.

"Objection, Your Honor." Litman rose to his feet.

Daronco overruled him, but Litman asked for permission to approach the bench.

"If there is going to be testimony that elicits a body being brought downstairs," the defense attorney told Daronco, "I don't see the relevance of it." Litman feigned ignorance about what might be coming next, but in fact, his long opening statement, with its portrait of a gifted, sensitive, but flawed young man, was constructed to deflect just such material.

It was relevant, Fredreck explained to the judge as he joined Litman at the bench, because Bonnie's serious injuries demonstrated Herrin's *intent* to kill. Judge Daronco immediately agreed with the prosecutor.

"Judge," Litman shot back, "if I may be heard for a second. Your Honor, I thought we have been talking about no sympathy or prejudice going into this trial. We conceded that he intended to kill her. That is not an issue in this case."

"He still has a right to prove it," Daronco replied.

"I concede it!" Litman was beginning to raise his

voice. "What is happening is that you're allowing in proof that is monumental. What happens when he saw his sister? He is going to have an M.E. [Medical Examiner] testify on top of that."

Daronco was nonplused. "Yes," he said.

"How many witnesses?" pressed Litman. "We concede the issue."

"We understand," Daronco replied, using the plural as if speaking for the prosecutor as well. "The intent is a very—"

"I concede it, Judge," Litman interrupted.

"Intent is an issue in this case."

"It is *not* an issue!"

Daronco had had enough. "Objection overruled. You have an exception," he told Litman, and directed Fredreck to continue his questioning.

But the prosecutor didn't get far. In the next few minutes, as Patrick Garland in a barely audible voice tried to describe his sister being carried down the stairs, Herrin's lawyer was on his feet a half-dozen times. His objections were of no help in changing Daronco's rulings, but when it came to questions of blood and gurgling noises and gory details the jury would at least know that the defense attorney represented the voice of discretion.

If Litman couldn't keep Bonnie Garland's condition from the jurors, he would try to show that Herrin was not the animal the bloody images implied. When he cross-examined Patrick Garland later that afternoon, he sought to have the prosecution's own witness do that for him.

"Now, you said you got along well with Richard, is that right?" Litman asked. He was following a cardinal rule of courtroom inquisitors never to ask a question unless you know the answer.

"Yes," Patrick replied in a low voice.

"Played backgammon together?"

"Yes."

"And you said you went bowling together?"

"Yes."

Like spectators, the jurors watched the exchange between Litman, standing at the far end of the jury box, and Bonnie Garland's brother, fidgeting in the witness chair at the other end.

"Do you remember that Christmas of '76, when Bonnie and Richard went to get boots for you, as their Christmas gift?"

"Yes. I was with them."

With his quiet responses, the sandy-haired brother of Bonnie Garland, because he had every reason to hate Richard Herrin, lent credibility to Herrin's case. Under Fredreck's earlier questioning, Patrick Garland had told the jurors about the phone conversation he had with Herrin on July 4, three days before the killing.

As Fredreck saw it, the point was that just three days before the crime, at a time when his attorney argued that Herrin was descending toward a massive mental breakdown, Herrin easily carried on a normal conversation about the Los Angeles Rams, the Oakland Raiders, and Pink Floyd.

But later in the day, Jack Litman asked Patrick about that same conversation, seeking to turn it to Herrin's benefit.

"And you came back, and you told Richard on the phone that she was asleep?" the lawyer asked.

"Yes. Sleeping."

"Sleeping?" Litman gave his voice a slight touch of bemusement. Patrick had already explained that it was about 5:30 in the afternoon. But Litman wanted the point made again.

"Right." said Patrick.

"Richard didn't then hang up right away, did he?"

"No."

"He asked you a few more times if he could speak to Bonnie, didn't he?"

"Not that I recall."

"But you do remember going back and asking about—"

"I went on my own."

Litman took the cue from Patrick's interruption.

"Why did you go on your own?" he asked.

"Because I really thought—" Patrick hesitated, revealing the confusion of a younger brother mediating between his sister and her boyfriend. "I didn't know what was going on, and I figured that she should talk to him now."

For Jack Litman the point was not Herrin's state of mind but Patrick's. The defense attorney was trying to show that Bonnie's brother was fond enough of Herrin to go back to his sister a number of times—"on his own"—to intercede on his behalf.

BILL FREDRECK was beginning to experience the judicial "double-bind effect" inherent in psychiatric cases. In his opening statement, he had promised to prove that Bonnie Garland's death was a cold, premeditated killing. But as the prosecutor began introducing his witnesses, Jack Litman was slowly driving a wedge between the killing and the killer.

If they testified to the gruesomeness of the act, he conceded it. If they testified that Herrin had admitted bludgeoning Bonnie Garland, Litman led them to describe how Herrin had winced, had cried, that he was distraught, that he was remorseful, anything but the cold-blooded killer that Fredreck suggested. Litman was setting the crucial emotional foundation for what would later become a powerful psychiatric case.

When Father Paul Tartaglia took the stand as the prosecution's second witness, he immediately displayed an attitude that would prompt even Bill Fredreck to admit that "turning himself in to the priest was the smartest move Richard Herrin ever made."

The night before, Fredreck had had a scare when he met Tartaglia for dinner. "All of a sudden I thought I was going to be in trouble," recalled the D.A. "We talked for two or three hours and at the end he said to me, 'Bill, I'm glad I had this opportunity to sit down with you, because I'm very sympathetic to Herrin. And I was going to go into court tomorrow and testify from my heart, and not my head. But now I'm convinced that the state is not attempting to railroad the kid. You're giving him a fair shot.'

"I drove the priest to his hotel after we ate and he said, 'I've got to call Jack Litman.' And I said 'Why?' He said, 'Because I told him I'd call him when I got in.' And I went home that night thinking to myself, 'Boy, am I glad I talked to him.' Had I just said to him, 'Father Tartaglia, I'll see you in court tomorrow morning,' he might have dropped a bomb on me."

At the beginning of his testimony Fredreck let the priest make a short statement defending his decision to take the witness stand. "It seems that the communications media use terminology that sometimes makes us very uncomfortable," Father Tartaglia began, "and I feel that when this young man came to me, he did not come in the capacity of penitent." In his Roman collar and quiet, earnest voice, Tartaglia, who that day was celebrating the twentieth anniversary of his ordination, resonated sincerity. He also displayed sympathy for Richard Herrin.

"When the boy left me," he continued, uninterrupted, "I did not know what his religious affiliation was. It had never come up. And to that extent, I'd like to state the fact that he did not come to me in my capacity as a confessor. Otherwise, I would not be here and would not be able to give any testimony . . . I think the young man needed a friend, and that is why he, perhaps, saw the church—I don't know for sure—and figured that the rectory was right next door, and that he needed someone to talk to."

"Did you let him into the rectory, Father?" asked the prosecutor.

"Surely."

"What happened?"

"Well, on the way in, I said to him, 'What happened? What is the trouble?' And he said, 'I killed my girlfriend.' "

Had it been a traditional murder case, the admission would have been ample reason to close the ledger on

Richard Herrin. But as the priest continued, he sounded as if he were a witness for the defense rather than the prosecution. "And we got into conversation, and I—I started to understand, you know, that we were—that I was really in the midst of a very tragic situation. Because the boy did come through, you know, with sincerity."

That "sincerity" became Fredreck's dilemma. A few minutes later he attempted to get Tartaglia to lay the foundation for refuting Herrin's psychiatric pleas by describing his normal behavior in the rectory. But the testimony carried little weight compared with the overall impression of the sincere, tragic figure the priest was portraying.

"Father, when he spoke with you, was he candid?" asked the D.A.

"Very much so," answered Tartaglia.

"Did he speak to you *productively*, Father?"

"I would say productively, yes. There was no point at which I asked him something where I got an incoherent answer. There is no point when that happened."

"He always spoke *coherently* to you, Father?"

"Yes."

Uncharacteristically, Litman had not raised a single objection during the prosecutor's examination of Father Tartaglia. His client could scarcely have begged for a more credible and more compassionate eyewitness.

"Were you apprehensive for your safety at all, sir?" Litman asked when he cross-examined the priest.

"Not one bit," the priest replied.

Later Litman asked, "Father, what did he do before he left the rectory? What did you say the last thing he did before he left the rectory was?"

"As I said, in a sense of relief, he put his arms around me."

"And embraced you?"

"Embraced me, expressing his gratitude and relief."

"Did he appear to be concocting a story, sir?"

"No," the priest replied matter-of-factly. "I have no reason to believe that."

Litman walked back across the court room and sat down, satisfied. The prosecution's witness had strengthened the defense with his sincere appraisal of Herrin as a fellow victim of the tragedy.

Herrin's lawyer knew how well the point had been made when Fredreck got up for a "redirect."

"Father Tartaglia," Fredreck asked, "would you say, sir, you feel a lot of compassion for Richard Herrin?"

The priest didn't hesitate. "Absolutely," he said.

JACK LITMAN would not have a sympathetic prosecution witness the next day when Joan Garland stepped into the witness box.

No sooner was Mrs. Garland sworn in than the defense attorney was on his feet calling for a meeting with Fredreck and Daronco at the side bar.

"Your Honor, we have already had testimony from two police officers yesterday about Bonnie's condition when she was found on the morning of July 7th," Litman began, making no effort to hide his frustration. "We've just had descriptive testimony from a doctor who operated on Bonnie. . . . For [Joan Garland] to testify—and even as a human being—to put her through going up to the room once again and seeing her daughter in bed, in a pool of blood—I really fail to see, Judge, how it can possibly further an issue in this case, and I would appeal to the Court's discretion to limit the testimony."

Litman refused to let the issue rest. It was the third time he had badgered Daronco about the relevance of Bonnie Garland's condition. At one point the day before he had testily asked the judge, "Is there any dispute her daughter is dead?"

Fredreck was shaking his head. "I have to smile a little bit when Mr. Litman talks about putting Mrs. Garland through something, when the only reason we are here is because of conceded acts of his client."

"Oh, come off it, Mr. Fredreck, please," Litman

shot back. "We're talking about how to conduct a trial!"

The prosecutor placated Litman somewhat, but then conceded that he was going to call one more witness after Joan Garland, a police detective, "who found a lot of evidence in that room."

"The fact he found evidence doesn't mean he has to go into blood." Litman would not give in.

"Well, you know," said Daronco with understated calm, "when you have a killing, there is going to be blood."

The judge then told the attorneys to resume the trial.

As he would do during Joan Garland's entire two hours on the witness stand, Richard Herrin had kept his eyes conspicuously averted from Bonnie's mother.

"You have to lean forward, Mrs. Garland," Judge Daronco was saying. "Speak right into the microphone."

Joan Garland followed the judge's directions, moving forward in her chair to find a comfortable position.

"Do you know the defendant in this case, Richard Herrin?" asked Bill Fredreck.

Instinctively, Joan Garland looked at Herrin, just twenty feet away, his head now lowered before the question. "Yes, I know him."

"How long a period of time, Mrs. Garland, have you known Richard Herrin for?"

"I first met him in March of '75—he came to our house on spring vacation."

"Did he come there with Bonnie, ma'am?"

"Yes, he did."

"Was Richard Herrin Bonnie's boyfriend?"

"Yes, he was."

"Before Herrin became Bonnie's boyfriend, ma'am, did Bonnie have another boyfriend?"

"No, she didn't."

For prosecutor Bill Fredreck, Joan Garland represented the only witness capable of portraying Richard Herrin as something other than the devoted, gentle friend and lover of Bonnie Garland that Litman had described in his opening statement.

"Mr. Garland never liked Richard Herrin," Fredreck recalled later. "Never liked the guy and, unfortunately, the proof of the pudding was the death of his daughter. . . . When I first met him, he referred to Herrin all the time as 'the killer.' He never called him by name; just 'the killer.' "

There were other hints, from other sources, that punctured Litman's story of an ideal young man and an ideal relationship. The night before Mrs. Garland's testimony, Fredreck had received an anonymous phone call at home from a woman who said she was a student at Yale. "She told me that she had been a friend of Bonnie and Richard's," Fredreck explained. "She also told me that Herrin wasn't the great guy the newspapers were portraying him as. He was sort of a male chauvinist with Bonnie. If she wanted to go to the Commons by herself, she had to seek his approval. That kind of thing." They talked for twenty minutes and the D.A. had decided that she "sounded like a rational, reasonable person. But she wouldn't give me her name, come hell or high water."

Though he might have used such witnesses, Fredreck didn't seek them out. As far as he was concerned he was prosecuting a killing, not a romance. "I was aware of it, of course; of their relationship. But I was trying something that happened in July of 1977, not 1974 or 1975."

Consistent with his theory, Fredreck's questioning of Mrs. Garland immediately brought her to the week preceding the killing. Unlike Father Tartaglia, whose testimony was filled with emotional footnotes, Joan Garland spoke in a surprisingly unbiased manner. Only when she began to recount her Sunday morning discussion with Herrin did her opinions emerge.

"He said that all through the last semester he had to pry out of her who she was going out with," Bonnie's mother said. Later, Herrin told her that "he had thought that if he came up, that he could claim her again or reclaim her—which made me think it sounded like a lost package."

"All right," said Fredreck, glancing up from his notes on the lectern. "Now, Mrs. Garland, based on the conversations that you've had with the defendant on July third, the short greeting, any other conversation you may have had on July fifth, 1977, and the conversation of one P.M. on July sixth and six-thirty P.M. July sixth, did the defendant *talk* or *appear* or *act any differently than any other time*?"

The question was of crucial importance to Fredreck's obligation to prove Herrin's sanity and rebut his defense of extreme emotional disturbance.

"No," was Mrs. Garland's unequivocal response to the question. "He seemed just the same as always. Very quiet, never laughed."

There were some trial observers who described Mrs. Garland's witness stand demeanor as "unemotional," as if to demand of Bonnie Garland's mother public grief as a measure of love. Others called it "self-controlled." "She cried her eyes out many a day in my office," recalled Bill Fredreck. "I think on the stand she realized she was in a court of law."

The courtroom quieted as Joan Garland, with muted sobs, remembered that morning when the Scarsdale police came to her door and asked if her daughter and Richard Herrin were there. "I went running into the study and the bed was there un—you know, just sheets. And I went running upstairs, calling Bonnie. I opened the door of her room, and at first I thought she was crying. She was lying on her back. There was blood all over, and her breath was coming like she was sobbing."

Richard Herrin, his eyes still tightly closed, winced. His face was red and tears rolled down his cheek.

"I called her twice. She was lying on her back with her arms at her sides. She was completely naked and uncovered. I thought she had been beaten. I said, 'Oh' twice."

The newspapers had their copy for the next day's headlines: "Jury in Slaying of Bonnie Garland Hears Details of Her Fatal Injuries"; "Bonnie's Mother Describes Her Death, Herrin Weeps"; "Bonnie's Mom:

'Blood All Over' "; "How Ma Found Body of Coed, Beaten and Bloody."

It was the explosive material that Litman knew would do the most to hurt his client. When he got up to cross-examine Joan Garland, he proceeded as delicately as if approaching an undetonated bomb. He needed to lead the jury away from Herrin's hammer blows and back to the concealed emotional causes.

Litman knew that the romance of Bonnie and Richard was essential to his case. It established Herrin in human terms as a boyfriend and lover and set the background for his alleged breakdown. Joan Garland was by no means a pliant witness and she made sure Litman would have to work for his romance. Even that resistance the defense attorney tried to turn to his client's advantage.

"Do you remember Bonnie ever discussing with you anything about potential wedding plans she had with Richard?" Litman wanted the jury to know that Bonnie was as serious about Richard as he was about her.

But Joan Garland replied quickly and firmly, "Never."

"Were you aware that Richard is a Roman Catholic?" Litman approached it from another direction.

"I didn't know until after the crime," replied Mrs. Garland.

"Don't you remember having a discussion with Bonnie at home," he pressed softly, "when she mentioned to you whether it would be all right for a Roman Catholic to marry a Protestant? Do you remember such a discussion?"

"Never," Joan Garland again asserted. "He never even went to Mass at Christmas when he was with us, and my daughter did."

That bit of information the defense attorney did not need. Because he hadn't asked for it, he succeeded in having Judge Daronco strike it from the record. Theoretically, it was also struck from the jurors' minds.

Litman kept prodding with his marriage questions. He showed Mrs. Garland a letter Bonnie had written to

Herrin telling him about a discussion she had with her parents about interdenominational marriages.

"That is your daughter's handwriting, madam?" Litman was turning a subtle screw.

"She asked if a Catholic could marry a Protestant in a Catholic ceremony nowadays and we said yes," explained Joan Garland after reading the letter. "There is no particular reason to remember that. I thought if we had that discussion—and I presume we did, since she said so—we thought we were talking about philosophical matters."

If the jurors still believed that the Garlands' discussion was only philosophical, Litman pushed a bit farther. "To your knowledge," he asked, "at the time that you had this discussion, is it fair to say that your daughter and Richard were romantically involved?"

"Yes, they were."

The point had been made: Bonnie Garland loved Richard Herrin. The relationship was not just Richard Herrin's obsession.

When Jack Litman completed his cross examination, Bill Fredreck had no further questions. The prosecutor was far more pleased with Mrs. Garland's responses than he had been with Father Tartaglia's the day before. Whether the jury expected more tears from the mother of the slain girl, Fredreck did not know. He could only hope that he could persuade them to stay focused on the "sheer brutality" of Herrin's act.

To keep the killing clearly in mind for the jury, the prosecutor next called on Dr. Stephen Gootblatt to relate the clinical findings of Bonnie's autopsy.

"The cause of death," reported Gootblatt, "was contusions, abrasions, and lacerations of the scalp, fractures of the skull, with intermeningial hemorrhage, and lacerations of the brain, contusions of the neck, with fracture of the thyroid cartilage and laceration of the thyroid gland, hemorrhage, and shock. . . . My opinion is that there were at least three separate blunt force injuries to the head, and one—at least one—to the neck."

Richard Herrin listened intently as Dr. Gootblatt

spoke, paling at the description of the act that his defense attorney was claiming he had committed without a trace of emotion.

As COURT ADJOURNED each day, Herrin was confronted with the flash of strobes and the whirr of motor-driven cameras as he stepped out into the courthouse's underground garage. So far, he assiduously followed his attorney's instructions to talk to no reporters, but the photographers, who were barred from the courthouse, bothered him.

This Thursday, after Joan Garland's graphic testimony, he especially wanted privacy. He delayed leaving the building for two hours, hoping the media would tire of the wait. But photographers from *Newsweek*, the *New York Post* and the *New Haven Register* had patiently staked out the garage. They were ready when Herrin emerged arm in arm with his mother, accompanied by Sister Ramona and Brother Thomas of the Christian Brothers. Herrin and Brother Thomas were going to a Christian Brothers' house in the Bronx; Herrin's mother and Sister Ramona to More House at Yale. The *Post* photographer's flash malfunctioned, but Gene Gorlick of the *Register* snapped the most controversial of the trial's photos as the four were getting into their cars.

Gorlick moved in close just as Herrin, with one arm over his mother's shoulder, planted a kiss on the nun's lips. The moment was frozen. The next day it stretched a half-foot across the New Haven paper's front page above the headline, "Bonnie's Mother Describes Her Death; Herrin Weeps." Ramona later complained to the paper that she received hate mail because of the picture.

As HE HAD PROMISED the jury, Fredreck completed his case quickly. He called only three more witnesses on Friday before resting. The first of those was inconsequential to the murder charge and was disposed of handily by Jack Litman. An investigator with the D.A.'s office told the court that the Garlands' 1974 Impala, which Herrin was accused of stealing, was worth $2,800, a value in excess of the $1,500 required for the grand larceny charge to stick. "Is it fair to say," Litman asked early on in his brief cross-examination, "that you have never examined the car in question?"

"No, I have not," replied the investigator.

When Fredreck called Detective Robert Rizzo, one of the Scarsdale police officers who went to the Garland home on the morning of July 7, Litman was on his feet. "Do you want to hear [Mrs. Garland's] shrieks one more time, Judge?" he complained at the side bar. A few minutes later Fredreck sought to introduce as evidence eight photographs that Rizzo had taken of Bonnie's bedroom.

"Yes," the officer said, describing one of them, "that is after I pulled the bed out, that's the portion of Bonnie's brain."

Litman was quickly up again at the sidebar of the bench. "You don't advance the cause of justice," complained Herrin's counsel, by now repeating himself like a tape-recorded message, "by overwhelming people's passions and emotions with gory photographs, not when it is not in issue."

However fruitless these constant objections, it was important to Litman that the jury know he was making them. "I objected a lot because I wanted the jury to understand that I thought the prosecution was deliberately trying to prejudice them." Litman wanted not only to dominate the courtroom, but as the defense attorney for a confessed killer, he ironically sought to become "the moral force" during the trial.

By contrast, Bill Fredreck had no choice but to ignore certain sensitivities about blood and shrieks in order to show how brutal Herrin had been.

When he called Coxsackie Police Chief Ronald Rea to the stand as his last witness, Fredreck kept his questions strictly tied to the issues of Herrin's intent to kill and his mental and emotional state. Presumably Rea, who spent eight hours with Herrin on the day of the killing, was the best witness of Herrin's behavior.

As he did with Father Tartaglia, the prosecutor asked the chief a set of questions designed to show that Herrin was acting and speaking normally at the time of his arrest. Rea substantiated Herrin's seemingly normal behavior.

It was left to Jack Litman to exploit those eight telling hours in Coxsackie. Litman wanted to use Chief Rea to show that there was much more to Herrin's confession than the twenty-three lines he dictated to Rea's stenographer that morning. He asked about everything from how Herrin was sitting in his chair to what his reaction was when Rea told him that Bonnie's larynx was smashed. "He was pretty shocked," said the Chief. "She was a good singer and he started getting emotional about it."

Litman elicited from Rea that Herrin had told him that he had been romantically involved with Bonnie Garland for two and a half years, that when Bonnie went to sleep the night of July 6, Herrin began to leaf through a magazine, and it was only then that "the notion came to him that he had to kill her and kill himself."

The prosecutor bounded up for redirect and went after Litman's subtly phrased question to Rea. The defense attorney had asked whether Herrin told him that "the notion came" that he "had to kill." If there were any single phrase on which the outcome of the trial could turn, it was that. The difference between Herrin's written statement that "I entertained the thought" of killing and Herrin's supposed comment to Rea that "the notion came to me" was the difference between being in control of his actions and acting like the robotlike machine portrayed by Litman.

"Chief, did the defendant use the word 'notion' to you at all that day that you recall?"

"Well, when Mr. Litman phrased the question to me, I believe Richard said, 'I thought about killing her.' *He* said 'notion.' I don't recall him saying 'notion.' ''

Judge Daronco was confused. ''When you say, 'he said ''notion,'' ' who are you referring to?''

''Richard Herrin,'' replied Rea, but he too was confused.

''Did he use that word?'' asked Daronco.

''I don't believe he did, Your Honor,'' replied Rea, finally straightening the record. ''Notion'' was Litman's word, not Herrin's.

It appeared to be a defeat for the defense attorney, but Litman quickly evened the score when he rose for the recross.

''In fact, Chief,'' he began immediately, ''when he told you that he was—that Bonnie was sleeping and he was going through the magazine, he said to you, didn't he, sir, that it hit him, that he had to kill her and kill himself? Isn't that what he said, Chief?''

''Basically, yes,'' replied Rea, who was not one to split hairs.

''Thank you, sir—''

''Not exactly like that,'' the Chief continued. ''He didn't say that exactly, no. He just said, 'It came to me.' ''

'' 'It came to me'?'' repeated Litman, content that he had preserved the notion of unconscious motivation. ''Thank you very much, sir.''

CHIEF REA stepped off the witness stand a little after 12:30 Friday afternoon. He was the last of prosecutor Fredreck's ten witnesses. But it was Jack Litman who had the last strategic victory in the brief two-day People's case.

After the Assistant D.A. read the jurors a number of documents marked as evidence, including Herrin's ''voluntary statement'' about the killing, he rested his case. But Jack Litman was soon demanding the floor. The defense attorney reminded Judge Daronco that he had also given permission for Litman to read certain ''documents'' to the jury.

Daronco could not easily forget since Litman had engaged the Judge in a heated argument the day before claiming the right to introduce into evidence a number of letters written by Herrin. Fredreck objected and Daronco sustained, telling the defense attorney to wait his turn and introduce them when Herrin testified. But Litman, who could be as sharp with judges as he could be gentle with jurors, would not accept the ruling.

"Forgive me one second," he retorted. "Maybe I'm in a different world. We are trying the case. We know what the issue is; we've laid a foundation for the introductions of these letters."

"Objection sustained," repeated Daronco.

"They indicate the defendant's state of mind," Litman persisted as the judge started to move back toward the bench. "Let me talk for a minute if I may. You're allowing him to bring in conversations—"

"We are into the People's case," the judge interrupted.

"I don't care where we are," the attorney snapped. "As long as I lay a sufficient foundation, I don't care if we are in the middle of a busman's holiday."

Losing his patience, Daronco sustained the objection for the third time. "You have an exception to the Court's ruling," he told Litman. "All right," he addressed Fredreck, "call your next witness."

A half-hour later, however, Daronco surprised everyone. He had had "an opportunity to reflect," and had reversed his earlier ruling. Litman could read his documents to the jury.

It was a tactical coup of consequence. It meant the defense would have the last word in the prosecution's own case. And a long word it would be, timed perfectly to launch Litman dramatically into round two. For fifteen minutes, Litman read six letters from Herrin to Bonnie spanning the crucial six weeks between Bonnie's Glee Club departure and her return to Scarsdale a week before her death.

The letters would show, Litman contended, a jumble of hidden emotions that would eventually explode on

July 7. Standing directly in front of the jury box, the defense attorney was reading a letter Herrin had written to Bonnie on May eighth. "I'll be in L.A. from June seventeenth to June twenty-sixth (two weekends and one week)," he quoted Herrin. "I promise you, Bonnie, that I'll be sweating my—" —Litman shrugged his shoulders— "off trying to write my thesis. I want to have lots of time to spend with you when you come down."

The silent shrug of the shoulders had been a deliberate Litman ploy. "While I was doing it," recalled the attorney, "I said to myself, 'You know, maybe I can bait this guy.' And sure enough, in fifteen seconds Fredreck was up."

"Judge, for the record," the prosecutor announced, "the word that Mr. Litman did not read was 'I'll be sweating my balls off.' "

It was as if a unicorn had bolted into the courtroom, stopped, and raced back out. Half the jurors' faces registered the surprise. Litman immediately noted it, saying, "Thank you, Mr. Fredreck," seeming to dismiss it. But "the balls issue" would never go away. One woman member of the jury would approach Fredreck after the trial to say she had been "furious" with him the whole time for using the word in court.

"Hey," says Fredreck, recalling the episode. "I said 'balls' and she's upset with me when this guy hit a girl on the head four times with a *hammer? She's upset with me for saying 'balls'?* . . . I don't like getting up in front of a jury and using foul language, but Jack was making this guy sound like a choirboy. I said to myself, 'I can't allow this to happen. They're getting the wrong impression.' And when I heard that it didn't go over too well with some of the jurors, I had to laugh to myself: Here we are, talking about a girl being bludgeoned to death, and they're upset with foul language. *And I didn't even write the letter. Herrin did!*"

Litman believed that Fredreck had committed an error. "What Fredreck did made it sound as if he were crass and I was humane," he later explained. "In little ways like that he allowed me to become the moral force in the courtroom. And he just became the force of law and order. And you know, you can play the law-and-order game when you have a bad person sitting over there who appears to be very bad, and has done this kind of thing before, who's a predator on society. But I don't think anyone viewed Richard that way.''

HOW THE JURORS ''viewed'' Richard Herrin was, in the end, what would determine the outcome of the trial. Where the battle between Bill Fredreck and Jack Litman was fought was on the question of *how broad that view should be*, how much of Richard Herrin should the jury be allowed to see.

''This was a case that on the surface appeared very facile and very straightforward,'' Litman later explained, ''but the more you scratched the surface, the more you realized how complex it was. The human complexity and the legal nuances made it a very extraordinary case.''

Litman would make ''complexity'' Richard Herrin's most formidable courtroom ally. Because of two New York State laws he was able to bring all twenty-four years of Herrin's life into the courtroom and make them all relevant to guilt and innocence. New York State Penal Law 30.05 was the first of these laws. Amended just ten years before Herrin killed Bonnie Garland, it represented the latest refinement of the century-old insanity defense, which had become a jungle of legal nuances.

''A person is not criminally responsible for conduct,'' it stated in deceptively straightforward language, ''if at the time of such conduct, as a result of mental disease or defect, he lacks substantial capacity to know or appreciate either the nature and consequence of such conduct or that such conduct was wrong.'' According to the American Psychiatric Association there were dozens of mental disorders ranging from ''profound mental retardation'' to ''schizophrenia'' to ''inadequate per-

sonality." The fact that Richard Herrin *claimed* to have
any one of these mental diseases, or defects, allowed his
attorney to introduce any evidence which would substantiate that claim.

The insanity plea had been coming under increasing
scrutiny from legislators and a skeptical public. In February of 1978, three months before the trial, the New
York State Department of Mental Hygiene released a
lengthy report recommending drastic changes in the use
of the insanity plea. Among its criticisms were "poor
statutory definitions, vagueness, uneven application,
lack of understanding by juries and the public, and
superficial and incomplete psychiatric testimony."

There had been a dramatic rise in the number of
people declared innocent for reasons of insanity. In the
eleven years from 1965 to 1976, according to the study,
insanity acquittals had increased from 53 in the first six
years to 225 in the next five years. Half of these acquittals involved murder charges. The average length of
confinement for those found not guilty of murder by
reason of insanity was less than a year, only 238 days. If
the formula were to hold in Richard Herrin's case, it
would mean that if found insane, he would be free eight
months after the trial.

Even more disconcerting was the conclusion that
among those who had successfully used the insanity
defense were some "individuals who are neither medically psychotic nor legally insane." They had no previous psychiatric or criminal records and some fell into
what the study called the "I-can-feel-sorry-for-you"
category. The pattern of acquittal seemed to have been
fashioned for killers such as Richard Herrin.

The second law in Litman's defense arsenal was
barely ten years old. It was equally important in "inject-
ing complexity" into the trial, as Litman put it. Penal
Law 125.25 was actually the second degree murder
statute under which Herrin was indicted. But one subdivision offered the defendant an opportunity to trade
murder for the lesser charge of manslaughter. He had to
prove that when he committed the crime he "acted

under the influence of extreme emotional disturbance for which there was a reasonable explanation or excuse, the reasonableness of which is to be determined from the viewpoint of a person in the defendant's situation, under the circumstances as the defendant believed them to be.''

Litman had already offered to plead guilty if the District Attorney would give Herrin a manslaughter conviction under the extreme emotional disturbance clause. Westchester District Attorney Carl Vergari refused to plea-bargain for many reasons, the most important of which was that manslaughter could mean less than a year behind bars. With life imprisonment on the line, Jack Litman would apply his courtroom prowess to the task of exploiting the open-endedness of extreme emotional disturbance.

It would take almost four days and fourteen witnesses for Litman to present the jurors with Herrin's defense, and it took two more days for his psychiatrists to analyze that defense. The people testifying on behalf of Herrin came with impressive credentials. In addition to Herrin's own mother and the mother of a friend, there was the chaplain of Yale University's Catholic community, and several Yale University students who had gone on to become accomplished citizens. Herrin himself would testify for a day and a half.

Through Litman, the witnesses drew a portrait of Herrin's life. It was intricately crafted, but designed to leave only one impression with the jurors: That when he killed Bonnie Garland, Herrin had to be either mentally disturbed or emotionally out of control.

The prosecutor was occasionally successful in blocking testimony. When Litman asked Albert Macchioni, Herrin's freshman counselor at Yale, to describe a 1972 incident in which Herrin prevented a fight between Anglo and Chicano students, Fredreck objected and Daronco sustained. Litman protested unsuccessfully.

But despite such an occasional prosecution victory, Litman was winning the war of attrition. Gradually the jurors learned that Richard Herrin was kind, gentle, peaceable, unaggressive, religious, always helpful, and never angry. They learned that he always stuck by his friends, that he never had a bad word to say about anyone, that he played his guitar every Sunday at the More House Chapel at Yale. Litman approached Herrin's history from every angle. If blocked by Fredreck in one direction, he came at it from another.

When the prosecutor prevented Ellen Wertheimer, a Yale classmate and Law School student, from answering Litman's request to "describe him as a person," Litman, like a sailboat headed upwind, tacked. "Ever see Richard Herrin angry?"

"No."

"Ever see him express hostility?"

"No, never."

"Was he a competitive individual?"

"No, he wasn't at all."

"Sophisticated?"

"No. I—very naive person. He always really took people at their own valuations of themselves and never —never thought bad things about anybody."

"Never thought *what* about anyone?"

"Bad things."

"Was he a loyal person?"

"Extremely. He would do anything for his friends."

"Did you observe this over two years' time, during your time at Yale?"

"Yes. People would ask for help, and he would always give it. Help moving or, you know, help with anything."

Fredreck's primary strategy was to deflect this barrage of praise from Herrin's friends. He had to remind the jurors that the issue was not Richard Herrin at Yale, but Richard Herrin in Bonnie Garland's bedroom that night in July of 1977.

From each of Herrin's friends, Fredreck elicited an admission that he or she had not seen or talked with Herrin for several months prior to the killing. At the same time, he implied, that the man the jury was looking at was only a cut-to-order defendant, made up especially for the trial. "When you last saw the defendant, Mrs. Watson," he asked one of Herrin's Texas Christian University classmates, "in June of 1977, did he appear to you then as he does today?"

"His mustache is gone, his beard is gone . . . he's lost a little weight, and he's got a suit on."

Yet even these questions ran the risk of fueling one of the defense's primary arguments. Of course Richard Herrin was different. To Litman, the killing of Bonnie Garland was a complete character aberration for the model young man from East Los Angeles.

LITMAN HAD DEVELOPED another strategy, one that was sensitive and had to be carried out gingerly lest it backfire on the defense. Prosecutor Fredreck had not brought in any evidence that would show that Bonnie had any love interest, or sexual partner, other than Richard Herrin. Fredreck felt that it was of no advantage to this case and it spared Bonnie's bereaved parents further grief.

But Litman had other concerns. He was defending Herrin. If Bonnie's sex life at Yale with other men could be used to his client's advantage, he would use it. Litman wanted the jurors to know that Bonnie Garland was not just the naive 17-year-old whom the prosecution had depicted, an innocent who had been manipulated by the older, more sophisticated Yalie.

With his witnesses, Litman attempted to show that Bonnie was actually more sophisticated than Herrin, and thus help reverse the manipulator/manipulated roles. He led Ellen Wertheimer to tell the jurors that Herrin was "a very naive person." Then a few minutes later she added that Bonnie Garland was "a world traveler and handled herself very well with other people." Was she more sophisticated than Richard? Litman asked. "I think so," said Wertheimer.

It was in the middle of the testimony of Bonnie's roommate, Elaine Moss, that Litman's strategy was revealed. "Now, directing your attention to the spring semester, what happened then?'' he asked, referring to 1977.

"One night in February," Elaine replied, "a fellow came over to the room and ended up spending the night with Bonnie; and ended up spending most of the nights for the next couple of weeks in the room with Bonnie. Until I—"

"Your Honor, this is completely incompetent and irrelevant," Fredreck shouted.

"Excuse me, Mr. Fredreck," Litman snapped.

"Just a moment, just a moment, gentlemen," Daronco interrupted, trying to prevent verbal mayhem in open court. "Side bar."

When the two attorneys arrived at the bench, Litman quickly explained to the judge that that was all Moss was going to say about the incident. "That somebody slept in the room with Bonnie?" asked Daronco. "Is she going to identify the individual?"

"She's not going to identify the individual," said Litman. "And there is no reason to sully his reputation, the same fellow that was on the boat."

After a heated interchange in which Litman told Fredreck, "Keep your voice down," Fredreck angrily answered: "And I think it is an assassination of the deceased's character by defense counsel."

"Judge, if I can talk, please?" said Litman, turning then to Fredreck. "Can I talk?"

"Yes, you may," nodded Daronco.

"Thank you very much. First of all, I think that comment by Mr. Fredreck is totally inappropriate and so outrageous. From what we have, we have Bonnie, this young girl that this big Svengali fellow over here twisted around his finger—with the mother coming in and testifying how she was a little girl and now she is a big adult—I don't think—"

"The comment made—" Daronco interjected.

"I haven't finished, Judge. That is number one. Number two, the testimony will show that Richard Herrin was aware, in part, of what was going on, and what he was aware of, in part, is part of the reason for what happened to his psychological state of mind, and it is very important."

Daronco was unpersuaded. He told the attorneys to get back to their places and ordered Moss's testimony stricken from the record. "The jury will disregard it."

The next day, the *New York Post* headline read: "Bonnie Was Sleeping With Someone Else." The testimony may have been stricken from the record, but Litman's point had found its mark. He may not have sought to sully Bonnie's reputation, but he definitely wanted the jurors to, as he later remarked, "appreciate it as a moral question." He wanted them to know who the sexually sophisticated party to the relationship was.

"Here's Richard, sitting down in Texas, as monogamous as the day is long," Litman explained later. "He's monogamous and she's out there flirting around . . . Not that it means that if you're screwing around with other people, you don't love Richard any more or any less because most people can appreciate that that's not true either. But clearly, if you're being monogamous, you know that it's all for Bonnie. And when Bonnie writes the same letters, which are therefore somewhat deceiving, the jury gets the impression that the morality is more on his side than it is on hers. That's all. . . . The greatest thing was when the prosecutor tried to object. Because then it looked like he was trying to hide something from them."

JUST AFTER LUNCH, Jack Litman advised Daronco and Fredreck that he was going to call Herrin's mother to the stand. He hoped to get the early life of Richard Herrin into the court record. The prosecutor told Daronco that if the psychiatrists thought that Herrin's childhood was important to their evaluations, then he would not object.

"I think my opinion is that in a general way," Daronco told the attorneys, "the mother can testify generally about her son's background, where he was born, how he grew up. But to go into specific details about how many candles he lif—"

"How many acts of violence by his father against him?" asked Litman.

"Specifics, no," Judge Daronco replied. "I don't think that would—"

"Well then, Judge," Litman retorted imperiously. "We may as well take the whole science—or whatever psychiatry is—and throw it out the window, because we are not going to have a fair trial."

The "science-or-whatever-psychiatry-is" approach to insanity was an avenue designed to appeal to the jury as much as popular psychology and psychiatry appealed to many Americans in books, films, magazines and newspapers. Was there, in fact, a science of "extreme emotional disturbance"? Was there a measure of emotions other than the emotions of the jurors? How could these eight men and four women judge Richard Herrin's emotions unless they could feel them in the courtroom? Litman was asking. Though sympathy was precluded from the courtroom, the law did not rule out empathy.

There could have been no more empathetic witness than Linda Ugarte. The short, plump, bronze-skinned, sad-eyed mother of Richard Herrin was the last person to step into the box on day four. In a quiet voice only slightly inflected with Spanish, she spoke like a person incapable of telling a lie, a woman of earthy sincerity.

When Jack Litman asked her to "tell us a little bit about Richard's very early childhood," Mrs. Ugarte didn't describe it as either harsh or happy. "After Richard was born I had a miscarriage because my husband was always drinking and the bills were never paid, and so we moved from one house to another house, and then I got pregnant again and I had a full-term baby. But I lost him when he was five weeks old."

"What kind of neighborhood is Lincoln Heights?" Litman asked Herrin's mother.

It was "where the Mexican people live," she said.

Litman then asked, "Were you aware of any emotional problems [Richard] had?"

"No, I wasn't," Linda Ugarte responded innocently. She was still unversed in the idiom of modern society in which most children are considered to have some emotional problems.

"Let me ask you this," the defense attorney said helpfully. "Did he have any problems with bedwetting of any sort?"

"Yes, he did. When he was about four years old until he was about twelve or thirteen years old he wetted the bed."

She seemed uninhibited about revealing the truth as she recalled it. When he was four, Mrs. Ugarte recounted, Richard would "break out with this rash on his little legs and on his feet," and when he went to school he "had to buy him these high stockings, which they call them knee stockings, which only girls wore, and he had to put on little sandals—he couldn't wear no shoes."

Linda Ugarte fit Jack Litman's ideal of a powerful witness, "a very hard-working, salt-of-the-earth kind of human being." In the courtroom, she and the Harvard-educated lawyer made a potent combination. They were both on the same side and both emoted a human force. At one point Litman, self-described courtroom chameleon, even picked up Linda Ugarte's nickname for her son. "When Ricky was a child . . ." he began.

The attorney took Linda Ugarte through her son's life: the drunken father who abandoned them, life in a neighborhood without playmates, ceaseless work in the swap meets, Mass every Sunday, never angry or upset, all kinds of awards in high school, Yale, the "real pretty little bracelet" waiting for the woman he would marry. Mother and son wrote and telephoned each other all the time, and Richard had told her about Diane. "He was hurt by this girl, because Richard never liked people to lie to him, and he never liked to lie to people."

When he met Bonnie, "he said he didn't want to get hurt like he had been before. So, he was going to be very, very careful with the relationship." Mrs. Ugarte told the jury that she had met Bonnie for the first time at her son's Yale graduation.

"Did you—" Litman started to ask.

"She was a fine woman, was—she was a warm,

beautiful girl. I just loved her." After describing their emotional parting in Los Angeles, Mrs. Ugarte stopped and began to weep, unable to continue.

Daronco called for a recess and excused the jury from the courtroom. When they came back, Jack Litman asked, "That is the last time you saw her?"

"With tears in her eyes," said Herrin's mother, "kissing me on the cheek."

The jurors had heard from Linda Ugarte that she loved Bonnie Garland. Bonnie was welcomed into the Chicano family's home. Richard was not so warmly welcomed in the Garland home. Joan Garland didn't cry when she told the jurors of her daughter's death; Linda Ugarte wept as she described the last time she saw Bonnie. "She really loved that girl," Litman recalled, "and that was an important thing for the jury to see."

ON TUESDAY, June 6, the fifth day of the trial, a groomed Richard Herrin, dressed in the same navy-blue suit, walked slowly to the witness stand in the crowded courtroom with a slight stoop. The defendant slid quietly into the chair and awaited his lawyer's first question.

Ignoring his usual "thank you, Your Honor" or "good morning" salutation, Litman began the questioning. He was careful to address his client with the appellation of ultimate respect: "Sir."

"Mr. Herrin, how old are you, sir?"

"I'm twenty-four years old," replied Herrin softly.

"On July the seventh in the early morning of 1977, did you strike Bonnie Garland repeatedly with a hammer, sir?"

"Yes, I did."

"Why did you do it?"

"I don't know."

"Did you love Bonnie Garland, sir?"

"I did, very deeply," Herrin spoke in a hushed voice. "She was part of my life."

"In your prior twenty-three years up to that point,

had you ever struck anybody so much as with a fist?"

"No, I never did."

It was as if Litman had shot the courtroom with adrenalin. With five quick questions he came to the heart of his entire case. Richard Herrin was young, he had never been violent in his life, he loved Bonnie Garland deeply, he bludgeoned her to death but he had no idea why.

It was Herrin's first public utterance since the crime. Even his pleas of "not guilty" had been spoken by Jack Litman. There could have been no more dramatic courtroom opening for the long-awaited protagonist than an admission that he had killed Bonnie Garland. It immediately cleared the air of any lingering doubts about *what* Herrin did and left Litman free to unravel slowly the complexity of *why*.

Jack Litman would give the jurors almost two full days to get acquainted with Herrin. "I usually don't like to have my client testify because I feel I can do a better job telling the jury what happened," the attorney explained later. "But Richard is a very articulate young man, very bright, and he makes, what is the most important thing, a very sincere and honest appearance."

Litman, like a good dramatist, began with the November evening of 1974 when the tragic love affair first began. Within a couple of weeks of their first meeting, Herrin told the jurors, "We began spending all of our nights together in my room," and continued to do so for the entire academic year.

"Did you become sexually intimate right away with Bonnie?" Litman asked.

"No," said Herrin.

"When was it, if you can recall, that you first had sexual intercourse with Bonnie?"

Herrin remembered that it was March 12, 1975. Litman knew the answer but he could play the role of innocent interrogator.

"By the way," Litman asked, "the letters and the cards you received from her over the years, did you keep them, sir?"

"Yes."

"Where did you keep them when you were living apart?" asked Litman.

"I kept them in a pile right next to my bed," Herrin responded.

"What for?" Litman queried.

"Well," said Herrin softly, "the times when I would be feeling lonely or sad, I would just pull some of the letters out and go through them."

Letters by the side of the bed. It was a mundane matter which could not be invented, yet it would be recognized by people with what Litman called "soul" as the nucleus of romance.

Prosecutor Fredreck remained seated only with the greatest of self-restraint. Just as Jack Litman had conceded the killing and objected to Bill Fredreck's bloody evidence, so the prosecutor conceded the romance and objected "to all these questions and answers dealing with 1975." When Herrin started talking about Diane, Fredreck was up again. "We are talking about the spring of 1974 now. The crimes charged are July of 1977! I have an objection to this testimony." But Judge Daronco overruled the prosecutor as often as he objected.

Herrin continued to testify through the afternoon. The closer he got to July, 1977, the more Litman drew from him signs of emotional turmoil and stress. Gradually, Litman built the tension as he led his client into the period when Bonnie left for Europe, where she spent six weeks without writing to her despondent lover.

Herrin then told the jurors about the "little nightmares that would pop into my head." He closed his eyes and spoke softly. "I could see Bonnie lying naked with her breasts and genital area having been mutilated with a knife. And that was associated with—with the idea that she had slept with someone while on the tour." Herrin said that he pushed those thoughts out of his head, repulsed by them. But for Jack Litman it was a resounding theme confirming the kind of "seething" emotions within Herrin's subconscious.

Finally, at 4:30, Judge Daronco suggested that Lit-

man finish his questioning the next day. Herrin had
been the only witness that day. He would be the only
one the next.

HERRIN RESUMED his place on the stand the next morning at 10:45. Litman then took the court through a
ninety minute exposition of the killing. Beginning with
the day Herrin flew to Scarsdale, Litman brought his
client to an almost minute-by-minute description of his
actions, his feelings, his thoughts on the night he killed
Bonnie Garland.

"At that time, when you left Fort Worth in the early
morning of July third, 1977, did you have any thought
at all of killing Bonnie?"

"Not at all," replied Herrin.

It was Litman's pulse-monitoring question. A few
minutes later, after Herrin had told the jurors that
Bonnie wouldn't come to the phone, Litman asked
again, "Did you have any thought of killing Bonnie?"

"No."

Later that night, Herrin explained, Bonnie called
back and they talked. She told him to come over.

"How'd you feel?" asked Litman.

"I felt great," Herrin responded. "I was back in
touch with her."

Herrin told the jury how Bonnie woke him up that
morning of July sixth with kisses and hugs, urging him
to come to Columbia with her to register. "She was in a
very good mood." But then on the drive to Manhattan,
said Herrin, Bonnie told him she still wanted "to live
life as a single girl" and "all of a sudden, my world
started falling apart again."

"Have any thought at all about killing Bonnie?" Litman had once again returned to this key question.

"No."

"Have any feelings of anger?"

"No."

They went up to Bonnie's bedroom and watched
television, said Herrin. They sat on the bed. "We were
smooching, kissing and—"

"Any thought of killing her?"

"No. She—in fact, she told me that she wanted me to spend the night with her and that I could just get up early in the morning and go back to the den."

But Bonnie decided to go to sleep before Herrin was ready, a little before midnight. Herrin turned the television off and Bonnie got into her bed.

"Where were you in the room?" asked Litman.

"I was sitting on a couch a few feet away from her."

Herrin told the jury that he was flipping through a *Sports Illustrated*, "more or less just turning the pages."

"And what happened when you were turning the pages of the *Sports Illustrated*?"

Herrin hesitated. "I kept looking over at Bonnie," he began. "Look at her and then look back at the magazine. Looked back at her, looked back at the magazine. Flip a couple of more pages and look back at Bonnie." There was almost no inflection in Herrin's short recounting. He hesitated again.

"Then what?" Litman helped.

"Sometime while I was flipping pages and looking at Bonnie, it came to me that I had to kill her and then kill myself."

The sentence seemed to jump out into the courtroom. It made no sense to kiss someone good night one moment, then decide to kill her the next. But it was the essence of Herrin's defense.

"Did you debate that in your mind?" asked Litman, knowing that he had to highlight the absurdity, even the insanity, of what Herrin had just said.

"No."

"Did you question yourself about it?"

"No."

"Did you try to analyze it?"

"Try to what?" interrupted the prosecutor.

"Analyze it," Litman repeated.

"Analyze it? Okay."

"No," said Herrin, "I didn't."

"What were you feeling at that time?" Litman continued.

"Wasn't feeling anything."

"Did you feel anger at Bonnie?"

"No."

"Resentment?"

"I didn't feel anything."

"Feel ashamed?"

"Objection, Judge," Fredreck said, trying to halt a long list of questions emphasizing Herrin's state of mental and emotional paralysis. "He said three times, 'I didn't feel anything.' "

"Yes," Daronco agreed. "Sustained."

But Herrin was now feeling something. He squinted slightly as he described his search for a weapon in the darkened Garland home. His face began to show expression as he told of his discovery of the hammer downstairs, and his final stance, hammer in hand, over a sleeping Bonnie Garland.

"What were you feeling?" Litman asked once more.

Once again Herrin murmured, "Nothing."

"What did you do?"

"I took the hammer from the towel, and I picked it up, and I hit her in the head with it. I hit her one time." Herrin closed his eyes as he spoke, now breathing heavily as if sobbing. He haltingly described how Bonnie's eyes rolled back in her head and her body jerked. He remembered the noise she was making and his picking her head up and calling her name.

"I could see that she hadn't died, she was still alive and I thought she was conscious. I thought she would be in pain. I thought she—" Herrin paused, now beginning to cry quietly. "If she was conscious, she would know that I was the one who was standing over her."

"What did you do?"

"I put her head back down, and I hit her again with the hammer. Several more times. She was still making the noise. She wasn't dead. I hit her once on the chest."

Several of the jurors turned away from Herrin. One later recalled, "I couldn't believe what he was saying. I felt like vomiting. It was so horrible." Just a few feet from her, Herrin was almost whimpering as he described groping his way out of Bonnie's bedroom and down the stairs, through the back door and into the Garland car.

"How long did you drive the car?" Litman asked.

But there was no response. Herrin opened his eyes and was now crying quietly but uncontrollably.

"All right, jurors," Judge Daronco interjected as he looked at Herrin. "We will take a short recess."

Jack Litman immediately walked to the witness stand. Sister Ramona, up from her seat, was right behind him. They led Herrin out the door behind the bench. In the hall the nun put her arms around Herrin, whose sobs could be heard in the courtroom until the door closed after him.

"I escorted Richard out of the courtroom," Litman recalled, "and he collapsed on the floor almost at the judge's feet. . . . He was really emotionally unwound, and yet he withheld his emotions until the point when he had to describe what happened, when he had to relive the incident. . . . That wasn't part of acting, it was something I knew would happen once he had to articulate it in front of the packed courtroom."

Bill Fredreck, who had sat uncharacteristically subdued during the last hour of Herrin's testimony, was perturbed. "Two of my psychiatrists had interviewed Herrin in my presence and the guy never shed a tear. He told them what happened the same as he told the jury, but he never shed a tear. . . . I'm not saying that Herrin didn't feel bad about killing the girl he loved. Of course he did. . . . But I think he overplayed it to the jury. The words he spoke were probably the truth, but I think his demeanor was dishonest."

Litman wanted to leave the jurors with the vivid image of the incomprehensibility of Herrin's act. As he was closing his testimony, he abruptly asked Herrin, "Richard, prior to the time that you were flipping through *Sports Illustrated*, when you told us about what you've already said, did you intend to kill Bonnie?"

"No, I did not."

"Thank you. I have no further questions, your honor."

•   •   •

THE COURT WAS recessed for lunch. Bill Fredreck will never forget going down to his office on the third floor of the building to plan his strategy. His boss, Trial Bureau Chief Joe West, came in and asked his deputy, "Well, what are you going to do, Bill?"

Fredreck looked up at West. "Joe, I don't have any questions for the guy."

West was surprised. "You're not going to cross-examine him?"

As the prosecutor saw it, Herrin had already admitted everything he needed to sew the case up. "The guy was giving me everything I needed," Fredreck later explained. "It was all there, in the direct. Yeah! 'I was reading the magazine and I decided to kill her.' I decided to kill her! 'I sat there until she went to sleep. I thought about what weapon to use. I rejected a beer mug, I rejected the stocking, the razor blade.' Logical thinking! How the hell could you say this guy was insane or emotionally disturbed when he was calmly sitting there deciding what weapon to use I don't know.

"But I also had the problem that the jury was going to say, 'Why isn't the D.A. going to cross-examine Herrin after he's spent a day and a half on the stand?' So I figured I had to ask him something."

Bill Fredreck's cross examination of Herrin was as brief as Jack Litman's questioning was lengthy, as bellicose as Litman's was subdued. He asked Herrin thirty-six questions in six minutes and rarely allowed more than a one-sentence answer, usually 'yes' or 'no' or 'I did' or 'I didn't.' But the prosecutor was correct in guessing that Herrin was well versed; he avoided being trapped by Fredreck. After Herrin repeated that he had contemplated using stockings to kill Bonnie, Fredreck asked, "You chose not to use them, is that correct?"

"I continued looking around the room," said Herrin evasively.

"Sometime before you killed Bonnie," the prosecutor pushed at another point, "did you decide, sir, you couldn't live without her?''

"I knew that without her that I could not—I would not care to go on living," Herrin replied, avoiding the implication of conscious decision-making.

"And you decided that you didn't want to share her with other people before you got the hammer, is that correct?"

Once again Herrin stepped aside. "The last decision I had made concerning that Wednesday evening was that I would try to go along with her plan and that I would try to go along with—with being one of several men."

Fredreck couldn't budge Herrin away from Litman's consistent line that the killer's last willful decision was that he loved Bonnie Garland.

"Mr. Herrin," the prosecutor finally asked, "in the early morning hours of July seventh, 1977, when you walked into Bonnie's room with the hammer in your hand, did you intend to kill her?"

"Yes, I did."

"I have nothing further, Judge."

BY THE TIME the prosecution and the defense had finished it seemed that there had been two different trials. One was about a killing, the other about an ill-fated romance. Few facts were in dispute. Jack Litman agreed that Herrin had killed Bonnie Garland with a hammer. Bill Fredreck concurred that Herrin had loved her and she him.

The only "fact" about which Bill Fredreck and Jack Litman radically differed was whether Richard Herrin had a choice when he killed Bonnie Garland, or whether he was driven by some mental disease or emotional disturbance over which he had no control. And in this contemporary courtroom of Freud and psychiatry, this was the central "fact," the one that would determine Richard Herrin's guilt or innocence.

The court system assumed that no juror was capable of entering the recesses of the mind without expert guidance. John Train, M.D., psychiatrist, was called to the witness stand on Thursday, June 8, 1978, the seventh day of the trial. He was to be the first of five guides through Richard Herrin's uncharted psyche. Jack Litman, who had retained Dr. Train as one of two defense psychiatrists, wasted no time in asking for a professional diagnosis.

"Can you tell us, sir," the attorney asked in formal tones meant to emphasize the scientific nature of the activity, "whether you have an opinion which you can state with a reasonable degree of medical certainty as to what Richard Herrin's state of mind was on July the seventh, 1977, when he struck Bonnie Garland?"

Dr. Train had an opinion. It was a one-sentence psychiatric diagnosis expertly tailored to answer all the essential questions asked by the law.

"At the time that he struck Bonnie Garland," Dr. Train began, "he was suffering from a very severe mental illness, a mental disease which can be classified as 'transient situational reaction' of an adjustment problem in adult life, which produced an extreme emotional reaction, which caused him to have a significant loss of his capacity to know and appreciate that what he was doing was wrong."

If the jury believed what Dr. Train had just said, it would have to find Herrin not guilty of murder. He would be found innocent on the grounds of both mental disease or defect and extreme emotional disturbance. Litman's unusual combination of the two defenses, which Bill Fredreck called "having your cake and eating it too," found perfect expression in Dr. Train's formulation. The problem was getting the jury to understand and accept it.

What exactly, asked Litman, is a "transient situational reaction"?

"In psychiatric classification," Dr. Train replied, "we apply this term to individuals who appear to be relatively normal, in that they have no history of being in mental hospitals, they have no history of attending psychiatrists. And they seem to be getting along quite well except that they are relatively unstable. . . . In people such as this, when they are exposed to an overwhelming external stress or situation, they do not have any psychological room to maneuver. . . . These individuals in this transient situational reaction enter a state of extreme emotional reaction which eventually would overpower whatever behavioral control they have and lead to a behavior that will be irrational, out of control, partly impulsive.''

The defense attorney then asked for examples of transient situational reaction. One example, replied Dr. Train, could be found in combat situations in which a soldier exposed to the stress of battle is trying to control his emotions. ''He suddenly has a lack of control and there is an outburst of emotion which sometimes has led to great acts of heroism, only an individual didn't realize what he was doing until it was all over,'' Dr. Train told the court.

As another example, Dr. Train cited a situation which suited Richard Herrin perfectly. It is a phenomenon which occurs in people ''who love each other,'' Train explained. ''When one suddenly finds that the other is unfaithful, there is suddenly this outburst of rage at this kind of unfaithfulness, giving rise to a violent action. This also would fall into that category.''

Dr. Train had just converted the age-old ''crime of passion'' into a mental illness. The murder excused in Italian serio-comedies about unfaithful wives had now been Americanized in psychiatric terms. This subtle transposition would be Bill Fredreck's Achilles' heel. While the prosecutor had been arguing that ''being rejected by your girlfriend is no reason to kill,'' Dr. Train had taken it one step further. If one suffered from a vague mental disease known as ''transient situational reaction,'' then the violent killing of one's lover was apparently not murder.

As Dr. Train continued his testimony it appeared that he was saying that the killing was not only the result of a mental illness but actual proof of that illness's existence. ''The emotions can simmer unconsciously . . . and then inexplicably give rise to a sudden thought,'' Dr. Train explained. ''And then the thought is acted upon . . . a volcanic outburst of this seething emotion that's become pent-up in his unconscious. And when it occurs, we can recognize how much tension, pressure, emotional stress it was by the intensity of the outburst.''

There could be no transient situational reaction *unless and until* there was an extreme emotional outburst. The killing proved the illness. The crime had become its own psychological justification.

What Fredreck had called the "sheer brutality" of the attack had become, in Dr. Train's analysis, further proof of the depth of Herrin's emotional disturbance. The bloody descriptions and gory photographs of a dying Bonnie Garland that Fredreck had used to impress the jury had suddenly been converted into evidence for the defense.

DR. TRAIN then told the jurors how Herrin first developed the ailment that he believed had claimed Bonnie Garland's life. He began by taking them back to Herrin's childhood.

Train's data had come from nine hours of interviews with Herrin and a total of forty hours spent studying the case. He had concluded that the root of Herrin's problem could be traced to an unstable childhood background. Herrin had been born out of wedlock and his biological father was an alcoholic who provided him with no ego nourishment and then disappeared. When Herrin was four, "a very tender period in the development of a child," according to Train, his mother found another man. Richard was just entering "the Oedipal situation of life" as his mother was "turning away from him for another man. This had an effect totally unconscious in his development," Dr. Train explained.

"To further interfere with the wholesome development," Train continued, "there was the fact that his mother had to work," so he was "never able to have the free spontaneous kind of play that children have in the streets." The result, Train testified, was that Richard learned "a pattern of defense against the anxiety of this insecurity." One defense mechanism was to be "the model good boy."

For Herrin, this posture guaranteed that he would be

liked and loved. In return, Dr. Train explained to a hushed courtroom, Richard learned to control feelings that would not be acceptable. "The only emotions that he expresses are those that he knows will impress people positively," the psychiatrist pointed out.

Dr. Train continued his explanation of the illness which masqueraded as the "model" personality. "Not being able to develop a sense of identity from his own accomplishments any more, he's now depending upon the love of others, the attention of others to make him feel that he is worthy." Again Train used childhood as an analogy. "Now, this is the exact dependency that a child has on a parent to have a sense of worth."

Over the next half hour, the defense psychiatrist explained the dynamics of this total dependency. When he finally received her "Dear John" letter from Europe at the end of June, 1977, Herrin was "fighting for his psychological life." By the night of July 6, Herrin had been "totally shattered" psychologically. "He is dissociated emotionally, he is seething underneath, out of his consciousness." And that is when, "it suddenly intrudes upon his consciousness" that he will kill her.

"Is it a cold, calculating, planned murder, Doctor?" Litman asked.

"A cold, calculating kind of murder can only occur in a cold killer," replied Train, adding a touch of circular reasoning. "That would be criminal."

"Excuse me, Doctor," the prosecutor quickly interrupted. "I object to that, Judge."

Daronco ordered the remark stricken.

"If you mean by 'cold,' " the psychiatrist continued, "that he wasn't off the wall, raving, ranting, screaming; and you mean by 'cold' that there was no display of emotion, then it *appears* to be cold. But that is not actually what is going on in the human mind. There can be no display of emotion, but underneath you can have a torrent of emotions repressed."

Litman knew this was one of the most difficult concepts to communicate to a jury. Dr. Train was saying there could be an extreme emotional disturbance without any sign of emotion. But it had been the theme of all of Train's testimony, and it was a popular theme that many laymen had learned from the media, even in school. From his early childhood, Herrin had learned to "repress" his emotions. The emotions were there, but they were hidden in his subconscious.

"Is that what was happening to Richard Herrin?" asked the defense attorney.

"Absolutely," said Train.

The psychiatrist had been in the witness box for two and a half hours before Bill Fredreck had his chance to try to impeach the psychiatrist's opinions. In a way, Fredreck had set the psychiatrist up for this four months earlier when Dr. Train was testifying in another murder trial, but that time for the prosecution.

"Did you ever have occasion to examine a man, Doctor," the prosecutor asked, "who stabbed another man one hundred and thirty-five times?"

"I think so," replied the psychiatrist slowly.

"In that case, Doctor, you wrote a report that he was not suffering from an extreme emotional disturbance?"

"I don't recall," Train said.

Fredreck approached the witness with the transcript from that trial in hand. He reminded Train that he had testified then that "in an extreme emotional disturbance, the individual is not going to be able to remember details."

Fredreck now sought to destroy the psychiatrist's thesis about Herrin's "emotional disturbance."

"After the first blow, did he tell you that her eyes rolled back?"

"Yes," said the doctor.

"Did he tell you, sir, that he recalls hearing a gurgling sound from Bonnie?"

"Yes."

"Did he tell you that her body jumped a little bit?"

"Yes."

When Fredreck continued to outline what Herrin had recalled, Train protested that Herrin was not able to remember "*all* the details" of the killing. But he finally assented.

The prosecutor's belligerent use of the psychiatrist's

earlier statements annoyed Dr. Train. "It is interesting when I testified in your behalf, you never raised that question," Train commented angrily.

"I wasn't impeaching you then, Doctor," Fredreck replied.

Jack Litman jumped to his witness's defense. "Why are you doing it now?"

Daronco tried to calm things, but Litman interrupted, "I move for a withdrawal of the jury on the Court's—"

"Just a moment," Daronco ordered. "You just wait until the Court rules on this objection before you, in a seated position, make a motion."

"Forgive me, Your Honor," the attorney apologized.

"Yes, you're forgiven. Please be seated."

JACK LITMAN'S second defense psychiatrist, Dr. Marc Rubenstein, an Assistant Clinical Professor of Psychiatry at Yale, was about twenty years younger than the white-haired Train. His presentation was shorter and had the crisp analytical touch of an academic.

Litman followed the same opening pattern that he had used with Train the day before. Rubenstein agreed that Herrin was suffering from "transient situational reaction" when he killed Bonnie Garland. But the law also required that the defendant's capacity to know and appreciate the wrongfulness was significantly impaired. Was it? Litman asked the doctor.

"Yes, I would say it was."

"Now, Doctor," Litman continued, "at the time of the attack on Bonnie Garland by Richard Herrin, was Richard Herrin aware, consciously, of emotions, sir?" The key issue here was the difference between the conscious and the unconscious.

"Essentially not," replied Rubenstein.

"Does this mean, sir," Litman pushed on, "that as a mental unit, as a psyche or whatever, that he was without emotion, sir?"

"No," said Rubenstein. "Only that he was *unaware* of it."

"Where was that emotion?" Litman was playing the role of interested observer.

"We would have to assume that at that time, they were unconscious."

"Your Honor, I object to the assumption unless it is based on a reasonable degree of medical probability." Fredreck protested. If he could eliminate the unconscious emotions, the vehicle of Herrin's vindication, his case would be won.

"Is it based on a reasonable degree of medical certainty," asked Judge Daronco, "or is it an assumption?"

"I would feel that it is based on medical certainty, because . . . of the unmistakable character of the passion expressed in the attack itself."

This was the kind of medical certainty the prosecutor could do without. Fredreck was a prosecutor who toiled in the old world of the conscious mind and conscious actions. He was the prosecutor who had made the most of the fury of Herrin's attack on Bonnie Garland. Now he was once more being frustrated by psychiatric circularity. The proof of Herrin's extreme emotional disturbance was the extreme nature of the killing. His own evidence was once again being turned against him.

Under further questioning from Litman, Rubenstein told the jurors that the night Bonnie went to bed and Herrin sat on the couch alone with his thoughts, "something happened." As the psychiatrist explained it, "He was, as best as I can tell, aware of nothing at the moment he hit her except his intent to hit her."

When Bill Fredreck rose to cross-examine Dr. Rubenstein, his immediate problem was to overcome the persuasiveness of the psychiatrist's testimony.

"Now when he hit Bonnie on the head, Doctor," Fredreck asked, "he intended to kill her, didn't he?"

"Yes, I believe he did," said Rubenstein.

"And at that point, you say that he said to you that he also planned on taking his own life?"

"That is correct."

"Okay. So that when he hit Bonnie on the head, he

knew he might very well die then?"

"Yes. That is correct."

"And he appreciated that this was wrong?"

"Well, it hinges on what we mean by 'appreciate'. I don't believe he did appreciate very well that it was wrong."

"If he didn't appreciate that the killing of Bonnie Garland was wrong, sir, why would he take his own life? Why would he *want* to take his own life?"

"Objection, Your Honor." Jack Litman was suggesting that the prosecutor was scoring points.

Daronco overruled him and Fredreck continued to follow the idea that Herrin did appreciate the wrongfulness of his act. "Did he flee from the Garland household after striking Bonnie, sir?"

"Yes, he did."

"Okay. And did he express to you, sir, a fear that the noises that Bonnie was making would wake other members of the family up?"

"Yes, he did."

"Okay. Did he express to you that, immediately after leaving the Garland household, sir, he had a concern that he might be spotted by a policeman?"

"Yes, he did."

"Okay. So, he appreciated that someone who was associated with law enforcement might be interested in him?"

"Yes."

"Objection, Your Honor." Litman again tried unsuccessfully.

The prosecutor continued to attack the defense's argument that Herrin was only acting like a robot.

As he did with Train the day before, Fredreck then led Rubenstein through the long list of details that Herrin had recalled. In concluding, the prosecutor returned to Herrin's thought of committing suicide during his drive to Coxsackie. "Do you know the one about the breaking of the teeth off the comb and pointing it at a trooper so that maybe the trooper would shoot him and kill him?

"Yes," said the psychiatrist.

"Pretty clear thinking, isn't it, Doctor?"

"In a limited sense, yes."

"Nothing further, Judge."

When Dr. Marc Rubenstein stepped out of the witness box, Jack Litman rested his case. But the trial wasn't over. The prosecution was now allowed to rebut the defense. Bill Fredreck had the first word. He would also have the last.

ON MONDAY MORNING, June 9, Fredreck summoned his own psychiatrist, the first of three he would call to the witness box. Fredreck expected them to offer the jury a different "expert opinion" about the state of Richard Herrin's mind.

Dr. A. Leonard Abrams was the Director of the Out-Patient Department at St. Vincent's Hospital in Harrison, a New York suburb. He had, by his own estimate, testified in hundreds of court cases.

At first, Dr. Abrams substantiated the prosecution's view of Richard Herrin's mental state on July 7. "He did not suffer from mental disease or defect," Abrams told the jurors. "I found no indication of psychoses. Absolutely none." Dr. Abrams told the jurors that he could find nothing to indicate that Herrin lacked "substantial ability to understand what was going on or that it was wrong."

Abrams also disagreed with the other doctors about the stress that Richard Herrin was under when he killed. "Did he suffer from an extreme, unusual, or overwhelming environmental stress?" prosecutor Fredreck asked.

"It was my opinion that he did not," Abrams replied. "He did suffer from stress, in a sense of that there was a romance that he was having a problem with. But there was not an overwhelming stress."

Fredreck asked the psychiatrist what it meant that Herrin had "made a decision" to kill Bonnie Garland and then went about the task of searching for a suitable weapon.

"That tells me that his thinking processes were going

on, that he was intact. The very fact that he remembers this is of interest, too, because it indicates, for example, there is no impairment of memory and that he was aware of what was happening or what was going on."

"What is the significance, Doctor, medically speaking, of no impairment of memory?"

"Well, if someone had impaired memory, that would indicate a psychosis, a form of psychosis."

Jack Litman then rose and began a heated cross-examination of almost forty-five minutes. Litman began chipping away at what Abrams did not know about Herrin: that he was a former bedwetter, had eczema, and had an alcoholic and violent father. Litman had Abrams admit that he had not interviewed Herrin's mother or any of his friends, and had not read any of the letters written by Herrin's friends.

"You do agree, don't you," Litman then asked, "that a complete, detailed history is necessary from a person before you can make a diagnosis or conclusion as to a person's mental state?"

"I took a complete history," the doctor protested.

Litman continued to test Abrams, but the prosecution psychiatrist refused to budge on the question of psychosis. The turnabout came when the defense attorney returned to the issue of "transient situational reaction." Litman soon had Abrams agreeing with much of his own psychiatrists' diagnosis.

"You believe, do you not, sir, that at the time that Richard Herrin struck Bonnie Garland, he was suffering from a transient situational reaction, the subdivision of which is adjustment to adult life?"

"Right. Correct."

In a few more minutes Abrams had agreed that Herrin was reacting to "an overwhelming environmental stress."

"Now," Litman asked, "the overwhelming environmental stress that you agree that he was subjected to, sir, was that his view of the possible breakup of this relationship with Bonnie Garland?"

"Right."

"Thank you, sir." The defense attorney sat down.

• • •

THE ISSUES were getting medically tangled. The expert witnesses were disagreeing about things that were supposed to be arrived at with a reasonable degree of "medical certainty." Two psychiatrists testified that Herrin was suffering from a severe mental disease they classified as "transient situational reaction." Dr. Abrams admitted that there was a transient situational reaction but said there was no mental disorder. Two doctors claimed Herrin's disturbance reached "psychotic proportions," while another repeated a dozen times that there was absolutely no psychosis. The jurors, involved in a crash course in psychiatry, were having a difficult time with the differing diagnoses.

Fredreck's next expert witness, Dr. Abraham Halpern, Chairman of the Westchester County Community Mental Health Board, professed very clear-cut opinions about Richard Herrin's mental state on July 7, 1977. Herrin suffered from no mental disease, no transient situational reaction, no extreme emotional disturbance, and he did have the capacity to know right from wrong, Halpern stated emphatically.

This was reason enough for Litman not to welcome Halpern's testimony, but the defense attorney also believed that the psychiatrist should be prevented from taking the stand. Dr. Halpern had never interviewed Richard Herrin, Litman informed the court. Litman moved for a mistrial before the doctor stepped into the courtroom. "I don't see how a doctor who has not examined this guy can get up and give his opinion," Litman had railed at Judge Daronco.

The defense attorney failed to block the testimony, but he had raised such a ruckus that Bill Fredreck had to spend almost half of his question period reviewing the psychiatrist's impressive credentials and the documents on which Halpern had based his opinion.

"I believe that an examination to determine an individual's mental state at the present time would require a direct psychiatric examination," Halpern explained. "But in the determination of the state of mind of an individual months or years before—prior to the commission of an act or during the commission of an act, or immediately after the commission of an act—a direct examination is not only not required, but practically never takes place.''

One of the reasons that Halpern had wanted to testify was to test this issue, he later explained. For years the doctor had been an advocate of abolishing the insanity defense and removing psychiatrists from the trial process completely. He hoped that if this case went to an appeals court, the question of why any psychiatrist should be allowed to testify about a person's state of mind on a given day in the past would be addressed.

"The point I'm trying to make here," Halpern now told the jury, "is that it practically never occurs that the examiner is with the individual in question just prior to the commission of an act or during an act, or immediately after that act is committed. And, therefore, it is ridiculous to think that an examination to determine the state of mind of an individual during those times can actually take place.''

Under Fredreck's questioning, Halpern spent almost fifteen minutes telling the jurors what documents he had studied to prepare for the case. In all, he said, he had put in at least thirty-six hours studying Richard Herrin.

In none of this, Halpern told the jurors, was there any evidence of a mental disease or defect. Nor was there anything to suggest that Herrin could not distinguish right from wrong. "He was not functioning under any unusual stress at that particular time,'' said Halpern.

In Dr. Halpern, Litman had his strongest adversary. Halpern proved equal to the defense attorney's verbal gymnastics, and would compromise none of his opinions. Neither would the psychiatrist be seduced into agreeing that Herrin suffered from a "transient situational reaction.''

"Can we agree on one thing, sir?'' Litman asked. "That where violence is concerned, that prior to this event Richard Herrin was a nonviolent person? Would you agree with that, sir?''

"No, sir, we cannot agree on that," Halpern replied. Halpern would not accept the opinion that Herrin's "little nightmares" in Texas were uncommon occurrences for a person of his make-up.

"Do you agree, sir, that a descriptive characteristic of a borderline personality is the occurrence of brief psychotic episodes under stress?" the attorney asked.

"I completely disagree," said Halpern. "D-I-S-A-G-R-E-E."

Dr. Halpern was willing to engage Litman and he acquitted himself admirably. But whether the jurors could follow the psychiatric debate was questionable. Litman had bet that they would not. It was also the defense attorney's strategy to portray the psychiatrist as an obstructionist whose opinions about Richard Herrin had to be suspect.

"Halpern went out on a limb for sure," Litman explained later. "And when you go out on a limb without other people backing you up, you really take a tremendous risk with a jury. . . . People are going to say, 'C'mon, his bias is so obvious that even if the rest of what he says is common sense and logic, we're going to disregard it.' "

IN THE MIDDLE of Jack Litman's cross-examination of Dr. Halpern the judge called for a recess. Sister Ramona suddenly rose from her seat to confront the prosecutor. "She came right over to me," remembered Fredreck, "and pointed her finger at me. 'You are immoral,' she said." Fredreck, who had barely met the nun, was surprised at this sudden charge.

"Sister, I beg your pardon," he said. "How so?" The nun then upbraided the prosecutor for turning over Dr. Rubenstein's notes of his interview with A. T. Wall to Dr. Halpern.

"I said something to the effect, 'Sister, you're incorrect. I don't know where you got your law degeee, but Mr. Wall was not a client of Dr. Rubenstein. The client was Richard and he waived the right to patient-doctor privilege by going with the insanity defense. And Wall's interview is not privileged.' 'It is too,' she says, 'It's privileged communications. And you're immoral for giving it to Dr. Halpern.' I said, 'Sister, speak to Mr. Litman. He gave it to me. If anyone violated a privilege it was Litman. But he didn't violate anything because there was no privilege.' "

As recess was coming to an end, Fredreck and the nun were still arguing. "I wanted to go out in the hall and have a cigarette," Fredreck recounted. "I didn't want to argue with Sister Ramona. So I said, 'Sister. I understand that you're emotionally caught up in the case. But don't talk to me about being immoral. I'm just going to ask you one question, Sister. What is the Fifth Commandment? I think you know that it's 'Thou Shalt Not Kill.' "

THE PROSECUTION'S final witness was Dr. Daniel Schwartz. If Halpern had gone out on a limb, Schwartz held fast to the main trunk of the psychiatric tree. In the process he may have inadvertently become one of the defense's best witnesses. Schwartz was the director of Forensic Psychiatry Service at the busy Kings County Hospital Center in Brooklyn and had testified hundreds of times in courtrooms. He was one of the psychiatrists called on to examine David "Son of Sam" Berkowitz, the ".44 caliber killer." A few months later he interviewed Richard Herrin.

"And what is your opinion?" the prosecutor asked his witness.

"That he was at that time undergoing some degree of a transient situational disturbance," replied Schwartz. "What we would call more specifically an adjustment reaction of adult life."

Fredreck was set back by the statement of his psychiatrist. How severely Dr. Schwartz's diagnosis weakened Fredreck's case would depend on what the jurors thought the term "transient situational reaction" actually meant. It was the key to Jack Litman's defense. He and the defense psychiatrists cited the American Psychiatric Association's *Diagnostic and Statistical Manual*, which stated that "this major category is reserved for more or less transient disorders of any severity." The *Manual* added that they "represent an acute reaction to overwhelming environmental stress." Transient situational reaction, as Litman and his expert witnesses had repeated, was thus both a mental disorder and the closest psychiatric equivalent to the legal term of "extreme emotional disturbance," the basis of a reduced charge for killing.

After Bill Fredreck had established with Dr. Schwartz that Herrin "knew and appreciated" right from wrong at the time he killed Bonnie Garland, he turned the floor over to the defense. Litman immediately returned to his favorite ubiquitous, mental disorder. "And do you adopt the terms, as we have already discussed them here in this courtroom, as transient situational reaction is defined in the *Diagnostic and Statistical Manual*, Second Edition, of the American Psychiatric Association?"

"Yes, sir."

"Now, doctor, would it be fair to say . . . that Richard Herrin was undergoing an unbearable stress in the breakup of his relationship?"

"I have always had difficulties with adjectives like 'unbearable,' " Schwartz replied. "He was undergoing a severe stress or stressful situation." Severe stress was Litman's euphemism for emotional disturbance. The prosecutor's own psychiatrist had just substantiated Litman's theory.

ON WEDNESDAY MORNING, the eleventh day of the trial, the lectern was moved directly in front of the jury box. A few minutes after 9:30, Jack Litman walked over to it to begin his final statement to the jury. He was as impeccably dressed as he had been throughout the trial. His summation was just as precisely argued. He spoke for more than two hours, his message the same as it had been throughout the trial. But this time Litman put it in the form of a question.

"Was smashing the skull of the woman who was the center of his life, without conscious motive, the action of a sane person? Or was it the irrational act of a mind so overcome with the loss of self, so overwhelmed by his stress, a mind unable to be fully aware of the enormity of the horror of what was happening?" Litman asked the jury.

Litman was appealing to the jurors' sense of curiosity. He was asking questions that had no logical answers other than the ones he had been arguing for during the last three weeks. "I suggest to you," he told the jury, "if you analyze the evidence in this case carefully, there will come a point in your analysis of Richard Herrin's state of mind when you'll be unable to follow it, unable to appreciate his mental functioning at some point on the early morning of July 7, 1977. For I suggest to you, as the evidence shows, that Richard Herrin literally went beyond the pale and crossed into a machinelike state of unfeeling destruction."

It could not be a calculated, planned murder as the prosecutor suggested, Litman told the panel. "Think of the fingerprints that Richard Herrin left all over. I had to bring that out. Mr. Fredreck didn't. His shoes that he left in the room, his socks, his shirt, his undershirt, his belt, his watch which was left on the table, his flight bag, his brush, his toothbrush, his shaving utensils, the rope, the weapon. Left right there. Everything left in the house. Ladies and gentlemen, there is no way reasonably and intelligently to view his conduct as that of a criminal planning a crime he has carefully thought out, of a criminal planning a crime that he hopes to get away with."

Once more the defense attorney took the jurors through Richard Herrin's long romance, and his depression when Bonnie suddenly stopped writing him from Europe. Litman reminded the jurors how Herrin swung madly between hope and despair during that month and a half. "It is like a piece of metal. How many times can you bend it back and forth, back and forth before it will eventually snap?'' asked Litman, twisting his hands in front of the jurors as if he were holding a piece of fatigued tin.

The defense attorney had been gradually inching the lectern to the left so that it stood between the jury and the prosecutor, preventing Fredreck from communicating his reactions to the jurors. Fredreck saw the ploy. In the middle of Litman's summation the prosecutor picked up his chair and moved it in front of the first row of spectators, in full view of the jury.

Litman reminded the jurors of what the psychiatrist had said about Richard Herrin. Whenever necessary, he scorned the prosecution's witnesses. Other times he used their comments to his advantage. ''Remember Dr. Abrams? I asked him about borderline personalities. He said 'Can't be borderline, because he's got a 130 IQ and went to Yale.' That is, you know,'' the attorney said, bending his voice toward sarcasm, ''a new thing in psychiatry. People who go to college and who have good intelligence, don't have psychological problems. You have to determine whether you will put any credence whatsoever in that type of testimony. But even on cross examination, he had to admit—because he left it out of his report—he had to admit that, yes, Richard Herrin at the time was suffering from the mental disorder of transient situational disturbance. . . . Well, now, that is four doctors who are testifying that he suffered from that mental disorder.''

And the fifth? Litman suggested that the prosecution had to get another psychiatrist because his other two had deserted him. ''They have to come in with a new one at the last minute, a replacement, and they get Dr. Halpern. On June sixth they called him for the first time. . . . Dr. Halpern, who doesn't even examine Richard Herrin. . . . Why do you think he needed someone like that? Because all the other four doctors said he was suffering from transient situational disturbance.''

Litman finished his summation with a flourish. ''We

are not looking for sympathy for Richard Herrin, for his background or his youth, or his religion, or good deeds," he told the jury. "We are not looking for it; he's not entitled to it. He is not entitled to your sympathy. But he is entitled to your impartial fairness, and he is entitled to justice. . . . And in the name of justice, good conscience, and fairness, I will ask you now, as I must, before you've had a chance to do it, to return a verdict of not guilty by reason of mental disease or defect—or at the very least a verdict of guilty of manslaughter in the first degree. Thank you very much for your attention."

The two and a half hour speech by Litman had been persuasive, and delivered with emphasis and grace. Using argument and story-telling, logic and common sense, emotion and dramatics, the defense attorney had remained faithful to the proposition that he had argued from the beginning. This case was a tragedy and Richard Herrin was one of its victims.

ASSISTANT DISTRICT ATTORNEY Bill Fredreck's summation was, in effect, a response to Litman. It was as if the overheated theater-goers were being whisked into the street during intermission. The air was cool and brisk and Fredreck intended that it be so. "I submit to you," he bluntly told the jurors, "that a verdict in this case of first degree manslaughter is a cop-out."

As the two men had differed from the beginning of the trial, so did their summations. Fredreck's closing statement to the jurors was half the length of Litman's. If Litman had seemed something of the Solon, Fredreck remained the Hammurabi, seeking a suitable punishment for the crime. "Let me talk with you people about something that we haven't spoken about in, perhaps, seven or eight days, and that is, the facts of this case," Fredreck exclaimed. "That is what you people are supposed to decide, with objectivity."

The prosecutor had no dispute with Litman's contention that Richard Herrin loved Bonnie Garland and she loved him. "But Herrin wanted her exclusively and Bonnie said, 'No, No. I am twenty years old. Let me grow. Let me spread my wings.' He didn't want to be humiliated in the eyes of his friends. Bonnie was his. You heard what he said to Mrs. Garland on July third: 'I've come here to reclaim her.' Well, he was unsuccessful. Unfortunately, he was unsuccessful. So he killed her, and then he got in the car, and he drove, and he wound up in Coxsackie, New York, and he spoke with a priest and with a police chief, and admitted his guilt to these two men."

Those were the facts, the prosecutor told the jury. "Ladies and gentlemen, based on the testimony in this case which is credible, believable, I submit to you that the defense of mental disease or defect is an insult to your intelligence."

Fredreck took on what he called "the bugaboo" of extreme emotional disturbance. He reminded the jurors that Herrin himself said he felt no emotion. "Give me emotion, ladies and gentlemen," he said. "Never mind extreme emotion and never mind an extreme emotional disturbance for which there is a reasonable explanation or excuse. This defendant, by his very words, told us he felt no emotion."

But what were some of the arguments that the defense lawyer advanced this morning? Fredreck asked the jurors. "Yes, well, to start, twenty-two times, by my count, he used the word 'rational,' seventeen times, 'normal.'

"Let me make myself perfectly clear," the District Attorney went on, his voice rising. "I'm not contending that this defendant was rational when he killed Bonnie. Rational people don't kill. Our Penal Law doesn't outlaw rational acts. It only outlaws the irrational acts. This is not the criteria here, was he rational. Take the law from the judge, not from Mr. Litman, when he defines mental disease or defect.

"Again, normal isn't the criteria, I submit. Normal people don't kill. Normal behavior is not outlawed. Normal behavior is not criminal. Were his normal mechanisms working? That is not the criteria. That is the question the defense attorney put to you, but that is not the criteria.

"No motive here? I submit to you, this defendant had the oldest motive in the world. Jealousy."

Bill Fredreck, as one trial reporter commented later, "was the picture of a morally outraged, hellfire-and-brimstone prosecutor. . . . He was the antithesis of his opponent." And he disagreed with Jack Litman on every issue.

"Mr. Litman says you can't deny the depths of their love," the prosecutor stormed. "Well, that's true as long as it was going the way the defendant wanted it to go. When Bonnie demanded her freedom, then that love changed to possessiveness and vengeance. You heard testimony that he was the big-man-on-campus in high school. Well, nobody says 'No' to number one—and that's the depth of his love."

The defense of mental instability, Fredreck warned the jury, was only "a concoction" to avoid criminal responsibility. "What he is suffering from, ladies and gentlemen, is *instant* insanity, the chief ingredient of which is fear of conviction."

THE TWO ATTORNEYS had fired their last rhetorical salvos. The following morning Judge Daronco set out to explain to the jury exactly what the law required of them in determining Richard Herrin's guilt or innocence. In his charge, he gave the eight men and four women an analysis of New York State's second degree murder statute, its extreme emotional disturbance subdivision, and the law of insanity.

He reminded them that, no matter how persuasive an attorney or an expert witness, the jurors themselves were "the sole judges of the facts within this case, as the Court is the sole judge of the law." He reminded them that they could reject an expert's opinion if they felt it was based on the wrong facts.

It was up to the prosecution, said Daronco, to prove

the defendant guilty beyond a reasonable doubt. Because of the nature of this case, it was also incumbent on the prosecution to prove Richard Herrin sane beyond a reasonable doubt.

Daronco explained that it was not the jury's responsibility to make a medical diagnosis of Herrin, only a legal determination. "It would be foolish to ask twelve laymen to make that determination when medical experts themselves disagree so on the subject." Besides, Daronco continued, even a mentally diseased person is not excused from criminal responsibility unless he also is incapable of distinguishing right from wrong. "Therefore, it is for you, the jury, to determine whether Richard Herrin, as a result of mental disease or defect, lacked substantial capacity to know and appreciate the nature and consequences of his acts, or whether such acts were wrong."

To help the jurors understand what these terms meant, Daronco offered some examples. "If a person suffering from a mental disease or defect sprays poison over the face of another and thinks it is perfume," said the judge, "such a person lacks substantial capacity to know and appreciate the physical nature of the act he is doing."

Daronco continued with his poison gas analogy. "Let us suppose the person knows or appreciates that he is using poison gas, but because of a mental disease or defect, he lacks substantial capacity to know and appreciate the consequences of his conduct, and he believes he is not spraying the poison gas on a *human being* but thinks he is spraying it over the face of vicious dog that is attacking him. In such an instance, even if he knows that he is using poison gas, he doesn't know and appreciate the consequences of such conduct."

The judge's charge gave substantial leeway to Litman's theory of extreme emotional disturbance. "The defendant's act does not necessarily have to be an immediate or spontaneous reaction to a stress or a specific incident," he explained to the jurors in language befitting a psychiatrist. "It may be that a significant mental trauma affected the defendant's mind for a substantial period of time, simmering in the unknowing and subconscious, and then inexplicably coming to the fore.''

The jurors were undoubtedly curious about why the killing took place, but motive was not a consideration in determining guilt, Daronco warned them. ''Because the killing of one human being by another is so abhorrent to us,'' said Daronco, ''we invariably, when faced with facts indicating such a killing, begin to wonder why it was done. What led one person to snuff out another's life? In other words, what was the motive? This is so common a reaction that we often hear motive discussed in connection with a killing, as if it were a necessary factor in the law of homicide. But it is not.''

For a full hour Daronco explained their duties and obligations, then gave the jurors their final charge. ''Now, the admonition that has been given to you throughout this case, not to discuss the case, is, obviously, lifted, and you are to commence your deliberations and give this case the sole attention and consideration that it deserves.''

As the court officials and spectators watched, the panel of twelve jurors rose and filed out of the courtroom to begin their deliberation on what had been transformed from a simple act of human brutality into a complex psychiatric, almost theological, debate about the inner state of one man's mind.

CHAPTER NINE

The Verdict

THE TWELVE JURORS walked down a corridor to a small sparsely furnished room reserved for their deliberation. Echoing through their minds were the more than 200,000 words of two lawyers, twenty-nine witnesses including five psychiatrists that they were now expected to condense to a single phrase of guilt or innocence.

They had been charged by the judge, but were given no procedural guidelines to follow. No one had told them *how* to make their decision, only that they were to be isolated together until they did. Nor was there a parliamentarian to show them an efficient way to reach the required unanimous verdict. They would have to improvise their way to the truth.

Richard Herrin's jurors were not even given the opportunity to choose between a simple verdict of "guilty" or "not guilty." Instead, they had left the courtroom with Judge Daronco's complex final order: "You must find the defendant guilty or not guilty, or not guilty by reason of mental disease or defect, or guilty of manslaughter in the first degree."

As a court deputy closed the door behind them, the eight men and four women were now committed to deliberate in that room until they had decided Richard Herrin's fate. Their first impulse was to try for a swift completion of the job. Not long after settling around a rectangular table barely large enough to seat all twelve, they decided to take a vote.

Patricia Policriti, the twenty-five-year-old forelady, passed out the blank pieces of paper to her eleven colleagues. Some leaned over the table and scribbled; others quietly tapped on the table. A few minutes later everyone had pushed their scraps of paper back to Policriti who tallied the votes out loud. As she read, it became clear that the only result of the first formal balloting was to banish the idea that there would be a quick verdict. Three of the jurors believed that Herrin was guilty. Three thought he was not guilty by reasons of insanity or emotional disturbance. Six had left their ballots blank.

What the vote had done was to scratch the surface of the jury's confusion. Everyone began to talk, sharing their opinions and questions about Richard Herrin's sanity. Did he know what he was doing? Did he *appreciate* that it was wrong? Why did Herrin run from the scene of the crime? Did he really try to commit suicide? Didn't he seem rational when he spoke to the priest? The discussion moved haphazardly around the table until, almost by unspoken agreement, the jurors abandoned any effort to manage a formal debate. They simply turned their chairs toward the people on either side of them and began to talk.

Though they had been together almost three weeks during the trial, the jurors still seemed a disparate group. From twenty-five-year-old Patrick Kelly to seventy-two-year-old Domenic Sarno, from Bill Doyle the insurance broker to Pasquale Toglia the elderly heating-system mechanic, from a Cardinale to a von Gruenberg and a McDermott to a Kwasnica, they appeared more the product of a random telephone-book search than of ten days of intensive voir dire. But gradually they settled into an intense but amicable routine of small group discussions through which they would try to decide whether Richard Herrin was guilty of murder.

By three o'clock that afternoon, after returning from a closely chaperoned lunch, someone suggested that the priest's testimony would help them decide on Herrin's sanity. After all, the juror reasoned, Father Tartaglia had been the first person to see Herrin after the crime. Pat Policriti passed the written request to the guard at the door who took it to Judge Daronco. Within a few minutes the jury was filing back into the courtroom where they listened patiently as the stenographer recited the lengthy examination of the priest on the opening day of the trial. Afterwards, they returned to their deliberation, more confused than ever.

No one quite understood what the law required of them. How did Herrin's mental state relate to the actual criminal charges against him? After another hour of argument about Father Tartaglia's account, the jurors decided that they needed the law of insanity and criminal responsibility explained again. Another juror suggested that they also hear Herrin's own description of the crime. Pat Policriti wrote another note to Judge Daronco: "The jury would like to hear Litman's examination of Richard Herrin from several questions before the black-and-blue mark was discussed until the time he left the house. Also, Mr. Fredreck's cross-examination of Richard Herrin."

Back in the courtroom, the jurors listened with new interest to the rereading of Judge Daronco's charge. "The law provides," the judge repeated, "that even a mentally diseased person is not excused from criminal responsibility unless, as a result of mental disease or defect, he lacks substantial capacity to know and appreciate the nature and consequences of his conduct, or that his conduct was wrong." Daronco reminded them that, as laymen, they were not expected to make a medical diagnosis of insanity. It was their job to determine whether Herrin was legally responsible for his acts.

Beverley Rogers, the court stenographer, then stood and read from Herrin's testimony. It was an almost minute-by-minute account of the killing, leaving off at the point when Herrin had begun to cry while on the stand. In the rereading, the "sanity" of Herrin's actions seemed easier to judge. Back in the deliberation room only a few jurors offered resistance to the general consensus. They had swung against the defendant on the question of insanity.

"It only took us an hour to settle the question of mental disease," recalled one woman juror. The three jurors who had previously voted that Herrin was not guilty by reason of insanity were soon won over. With a show of hands, all twelve jurors agreed that Herrin was sane. He was not "mad" when he killed Bonnie Garland.

THE JURORS rewarded themselves for their first decision by taking a break. With sheriff's deputies in front of and behind them, they marched to the nearby Scotch and Sirloin Restaurant for dinner. They were reminded not to discuss the case. It seemed an unnecessary admonition; everyone appreciated this rare opportunity *not* to discuss the trial.

It was after eight P.M. when they came back in to the jury room and the door was again closed behind them. The option for a verdict had now been reduced to the question of "extreme emotional disturbance," a decision which could also result in a "not guilty" of murder verdict. But instead of becoming easier, the decision seemed more elusive.

"No one really thought he was insane," one juror commented, "but almost everybody agreed he had problems." Few of the twelve agreed on how severe those problems were or whether they reached the proportions of "extreme." Their short-lived unanimity disappeared as the men and women again divided into small groups to thrash out the vital legal question of Herrin's emotional condition.

Most of the jurors believed the law had given them less guidance on this point than it had done with the question of insanity. How disturbed was he? They asked each other. Was the stress severe enough to interfere with his reason? Was it reasonable for someone to get so disturbed when his girlfriend broke up with him that he killed her? Was that an excuse for murder? After two hours of argument with more questions raised than answers given someone called for a vote.

For the second time that day, slips of paper were passed around, and the results were tallied by Pat Policriti. This time there were no blank ballots. Four votes were cast for murder, guilty as charged. Eight were for not guilty on the murder charge, but guilty of the lesser charge of manslaughter in the first degree. It seemed more like a straw poll than a decision. "I was pretty confused by the end of the day," admitted one juror who had leaned toward the manslaughter finding. "I'd say most people hadn't really decided yet. I think everybody just wanted to hear how everybody else felt."

The confusion soon gave way to fatigue. By ten P.M. on that first day of deliberating, as one juror later put it, "We had had it." The young forelady knocked on the door and handed the deputy a note saying that they wanted to adjourn for the night. The jurors were beginning to feel the irony of the situation: They were being locked up under guard while Richard Herrin was out free. The feeling grew as they were escorted to waiting vans and driven to a hotel whose location had not yet been told to them.

THE NEXT MORNING, soon after they had reassembled in the deliberating room, they realized that the night's sleep had done little to change anyone's mind. Once again they marched into the courtroom for guidance. Judge Daronco reread the portion of his charge dealing with the law on extreme emotional disturbance and manslaughter. "Even where the People have proven beyond a reasonable doubt that a defendant intended to cause the death of another person, and did cause her death," he explained again, "the law permits a defendant to establish as an alternative defense that he acted under the influence of an extreme emotional disturbance." Daronco reminded the jurors that the defendant had to prove this mitigating factor with "a preponderance" of evidence.

The law further required, Daronco told the anxious jurors, that the explanation for the disturbance must be reasonable. The criterion for reasonability, surprisingly, was not how they viewed the situation, but how the defendant himself saw it. "So, the question is not whether you or the average person would have reacted the way he did, or whether it was the right, legal, or logical way to react. There are no rigid guidelines that I can give you to determine this issue. You must try to place yourself in the defendant's position, as he believed it to be, and see if you can understand his claimed loss of self-control." Daronco was telling the panel that in effect, Herrin, not they, would be the standard by which his guilt or innocence would be judged.

The jurors returned to the deliberation room both clearer and more befuddled by their challenge. "Everyone could understand the law," one juror remembered, "but the problem was applying it to Herrin." For a long time they debated the question of Herrin's intent and how he felt before going to Scarsdale. Some jurors believed that Bonnie's "Dear John" letter had given him the motive to kill her. Most argued that there was no premeditation, especially since he didn't form his intent until just before he got the hammer. "Just because he was emotionally upset," one woman suggested, "doesn't mean he planned to kill her."

Another juror countered that no matter when he decided to kill, he was not so emotionally upset that he had lost control, as the defense claimed. "It doesn't make sense to do what he did because your girlfriend breaks up with you. He was acting normally during the days before he killed her. And even if there was no premeditation, he wasn't that disturbed. Sure, he was under stress, but anyone in that situation would be." Another juror listened, then replied almost plaintively, "But you have to put yourself in his shoes. Look how much in love he was. His whole life depended on Bonnie."

The discussion continued, all twelve testing the issues, arguing, but with their minds still open to other opinions. Finally, someone around the jury table called for a vote. "How many for guilty right now?" he asked, as if taking the pulse. One by one, hands went up. Richard Pfeifer, the young fundamentalist. Daniel Cardinale, the teacher of emotionally disturbed children. Milton Nelson, the pharmaceutical salesman. Pasquale Toglia raised his hand.

Finally Frank McDermott, the former Wall Street executive, signalled that he had changed his mind. He would now also have to say guilty. "It wasn't easy to understand the extreme emotional disturbance defense," McDermott later explained, "but at that point what it came down to was that I was sure that Herrin wasn't 'not guilty' but I was not really sure about manslaughter."

Five had voted for guilty, one more than on the previous vote. The four women—Jennie DeMilto, Lorraine Kwasnica, Pat Policriti, and Anneliese von Gruenberg—along with three men—Bill Doyle, Patrick Kelly, and Domenic Sarno—were still leaning to manslaughter. "It was very hard," recalled Mrs. von Gruenberg. "We all wanted to do the right thing."

The jurors decided to listen once more to the expert psychiatric testimony. Perhaps this would clear up just how "extreme" Herrin's emotional stress was. All the jurors had accepted Herrin's intense love affair as a fact. What the jurors wanted to do, as the law prescribed, was to "get into his shoes" during the week prior to the killing. It seemed the only way to decide whether, in fact, he had been "extremely" disturbed.

It took more than an hour for court stenographer Beverley Rogers to read Dr. Rubenstein's testimony to the jury. With Daronco's explanation of the manslaughter law fresh in their minds, they heard again the psychiatrist's opinion: When Bonnie told Herrin on the sixth of July, after making love to him the previous evening, that she still wanted to make love to others, he was suddenly faced with two equally "unimaginable and intolerable" alternatives. Either he would have to accept being loved along with others, or he would have to give Bonnie up entirely.

"Now, I would draw attention to the fact," the stenographer slowly repeated from Rubenstein's testimony, "that these are the only alternatives he seems to have considered at that time. That he was not able . . . to consider the kinds of things which would have passed through the mind of somebody in a stronger emotional position at that time. That is, to tell her off, blow up, get drunk, tell himself there are other fish in the ocean, go find his friends and weep on their shoulders, bury himself in his work . . ."

That was the key for many of the jurors. Why would Herrin have become so emotionally disturbed that he killed, when other people in the same situation only got mad or drunk? All afternoon they had argued it. Was it possible to be so emotionally upset that you could lose your reasoning capacity, your entire moral sense?

WHILE THE JURORS were listening to the rereading of the testimony, they had not noticed that Joan and Paul Garland had come into the courtroom. For the first time, the parents of the deceased girl were hearing detailed descriptions of their daughter's death.

"Mr. and Mrs. Garland were holding hands and I could see their knuckles turning white they were squeezing so hard," recalled a bail bondsman sitting nearby. "I've got to give him credit for his holding power, listening to how Herrin hammered his daughter to death. If it would have been me, there wouldn't have been enough guards in the courthouse to hold me down. I would have killed the bastard right there on the spot."

"Garland first appeared at the trial as the objective, international corporate lawyer," Charles Kochakian of *The New Haven Register* later wrote. "Some persons found his objectivity unnerving. On May 31st, the first day of testimony, he started a conversation with a reporter by saying, 'I am sure you know by talking with other victims of crimes. . . .' " But when Paul Garland entered the courtroom to hear the rereading of the grisly accounts of his daughter's death, he could no longer maintain such control. "By the trial's end," Kochakian remarked, "the grief of an anguished parent had broken through the objective facade."

On Thursday, the first day of jury deliberation, that grief had flared into anger. Garland had made a brief appearance in the courtroom after the jury had left but while Herrin was still seated. As Bill Fredreck later explained to Judge Daronco, "Mr. Garland, in my presence, walked into the courtroom, and in the direction of the defendant, said, 'You look like a crazy son of a bitch.' He then walked out of the courtroom with me."

The next day, as Paul Garland sat with his wife listening to the stenographer reading testimony to the jury, his anguish had broken into tears that he seemed unable to control. He heard how Herrin had told Chief Rea that his daughter's head "split open like a watermelon"; that Dr. Rubenstein had said that Herrin, while killing Bonnie Garland, had shown no more emotional concern than if he had been "carrying out an ordinary household task." Garland wept openly several times. He cried again as Beverley Rogers now read from Dr. Train's testimony as if it were happening in the present. "He brings the hammer down forcibly, finds that she's not immediately dead. . . ."

After the court stenographer finished, the jury was excused from the courtroom. Judge Daronco and Jack Litman also left, and a few members of the Catholic clergy walked to the defense table to join Herrin. Bill Fredreck was still at his table and a few reporters and courtroom buffs were preparing to leave as Paul Garland rose from his seat and walked to the first row of benches. He simply stared at his daughter's killer, standing less than a dozen feet away.

As Herrin was being embraced by his friends, Garland began to repeat, out loud, parts of the testimony that he had just heard. In a barely audible voice wavering with emotion, Paul Garland spoke of his daughter's death gurgle, and angrily told Herrin that he had been so kind to be concerned about whether Bonnie was in pain as he hit her. At that point the prosecutor turned around.

"He was repeating the testimony of Dr. Train," Fredreck recalled. "He was saying to the group, and I guess in particular to Herrin, 'then I hit her with the hammer, then her eyes rolled back.' And he was just repeating to Herrin what had happened. . . . I remember grabbing him by the arm and walking outside with him."

Paul Garland's anguish was the emotional climax of a tense trial. "This place should probably be called a hall of tragedy instead of a court of justice," commented the bail bondsman who had spent half his life wandering in and out of courtrooms and had watched the Herrin trial. "There are no winners, only losers."

THE JURY was now well into its thirtieth hour of deliberation. There was nothing to do but wait. Neither attorney was allowed to stray from the courthouse while the jurors deliberated. Every time a message was passed out of the tiny room to Judge Daronco, who was also required to wait, Litman and Fredreck were immediately summoned to the judge's chambers for consultation. At each request to hear testimony reread, whenever it might come, lawyers, reporters, friends, and court personnel all filed back into the courtroom.

While the jurors deliberated, Bill Fredreck paced all over the courthouse, nervously mooching cigarettes, returning to a smoking habit he had given up months before. The prosecutor thought it was a good sign that the jurors were asking only for testimony relating to events immediately preceding the killing. "They want to get into the nitty-gritty," he optimistically commented. But he was equally suspicious that the jury verdict was taking too long.

In a small room on the sixteenth floor reserved for the defense, Jack Litman encouraged the somber group of Herrin's family and friends. The longer the jury is out, he told them, the better it is. Meanwhile, he kept up his omnipresent coverage of every strategic opening beneficial to his client.

As soon as he heard about Paul Garland's outburst, Litman rounded up eyewitnesses, reconstructed the scene, and walked into the judge's chambers. In the presence of the prosecutor, Litman asked that Garland be barred from the courtroom. He told Daronco of Garland's "inappropriate and veiled threatening comments" and suggested that he might be dangerous.

"At the time he was making these comments, Your Honor," the defense attorney exclaimed, "he took his hand—I believe his right hand—and in a threatening manner, as if to simulate a gun, pointed it very repeatedly at several people. . . . I'm concerned not only about the reaction it could conceivably have upon the jury, were he to do anything at all in their presence, but I'm also concerned for the safety and welfare of my client and the other people who have a right to be sitting in that courtroom."

Listening to Litman, Bill Fredreck considered his complaint little more than a defense ploy to clear the courtroom of anyone not sympathetic to Herrin. He knew that where there was no antipathy, there would be sympathy. "Mr. Garland," Fredreck now explained matter-of-factly to Daronco, "upon hearing the testimony of Drs. Train and Rubenstein read back, was very upset insofar as it was the first time he heard the actual details of what the defendant did to his daughter." The prosecutor paused. "I think, and I submit to the Court, that the man, under the circumstances, showed remarkable restraint."

Fredreck also had his own complaints about what he believed were inappropriate influences on the jury. Throughout the trial he had been especially annoyed by the behavior of Herrin's religious friends. He didn't like the idea of their wearing clerical garb in the courtroom or their unembarrassed public manifestations of sympathy for Herrin, a scene he once described as "lovey-dovey up there with the clergy and the priests all over the courtroom having prayer meetings." Fredreck was himself a Catholic and his uncle was a priest, but the prosecutor felt that the Church-State barrier had been broken in this case. "Sister Ramona. My friend Sister Ramona," he later said incredulously. "She would sit in the second row in front of the courtroom and pray. Pray! With her rosary beads and her eyes closed!"

Now that Jack Litman was trying to evict Paul Garland from the courtroom trial of his daughter's killer, Fredreck couldn't help but remind Judge Daronco, as diplomatically as possible, of what had been going on on the other side of the aisle. "Given the conduct of the people who have been sitting in the courtroom with the defendant—to wit, specifically Sister Ramona—and their influence on this jury throughout the five-week period, I don't think this Court has any power or authority to ask Mr. Garland not to be in the courtroom."

Daronco needed little convincing. He quickly denied Litman's application.

But the defense attorney would not relent. Litman came back with an alternative suggestion. "Is there any possibility of ordering a search of Mr. Garland in view of his gestures?" he pushed.

Daronco again denied the request.

"Judge," Litman responded, "can we have a security officer in the courtroom itself? Usually they are near where the jury is. Would it be possible to have one near where the spectators are?"

With the proviso that it be done inconspicuously, Judge Daronco finally acceded to the Litman request, diluted though it was.

AS THESE TACTICAL maneuvers continued in the judge's chambers, the twelve jurors wrestled with Richard Herrin's fate and their own claustrophobia. They had missed Paul Garland's confrontation with Herrin. They had spent all of Friday night at loggerheads over the psychiatrists' testimony. "There was never any silence," recalled the soft-spoken Patricia Policriti. "Everyone had a hangup about the case. Everyone had an opinion."

The jurors took their jobs seriously. As Jack Litman suspected, this worked in Richard Herrin's favor. On rehearing Rubenstein's and Train's testimony, any doubts in the jurors' minds that Bonnie Garland was the immediate cause of Richard Herrin's stress had been removed. But how severe, and how reasonable, the stress was could not be agreed on. As if playing a game of musical chairs, the men and women frequently shifted their seating positions to talk, as one juror remarked, "to the people who needed help."

As the night advanced, they also had to contend with their quarters. The deliberation room seemed purposefully designed to expedite a verdict. It was difficult enough to be locked up with near strangers for hours on end; it was more unbearable that it was summer. "It was like a tiny schoolroom," one juror remembered of the ordeal. "The walls were all bare. There were no pictures or anything. Just functional. One table with just enough space for twelve people. Nobody could pace around. There was no window. It was hot."

By ten o'clock of the second day of deliberations, jury complaints were increasing. A note was sent out: "Dear Judge Daronco: The jury has decided to recess for tonight and ask that we wait to hear Dr. Schwartz's testimony in the morning. Thank you. Some jurors are extremely tired. Patricia Policriti."

The next day, the jurors were allowed to move to larger quarters on the fourteenth floor of the courtroom. The new jury room had a bank of windows that opened on an expansive view of the suburb's low, tree-covered hills. A large fan was rolled in. They had room to pace and many availed themselves of that luxury during what proved to be a grueling day.

When Fredreck heard the jury's request to hear Dr. Schwartz's testimony, he took it as a good omen. The prosecution's psychiatrist had found Herrin perfectly capable of distinguishing right from wrong as well as of appreciating what he was doing the morning of July 7. Schwartz had also said that he had found nothing in the psychological reports on Herrin to indicate that he was "the type of person that would break down more readily than others when under stress.'' The prosecutor hoped that his testimony would move the jury toward a verdict of guilty of murder.

The psychiatrist's testimony had exactly the opposite effect. On Litman's cross-examination, Schwartz had admitted that Herrin was suffering from a ''transient situational reaction.''

For those jurors who felt that Herrin was not insane and yet not quite the premeditated murderer described by Fredreck, Schwartz offered an avenue of compromise. Frank McDermott told his colleagues that he had changed his mind again. He would vote for manslaughter instead of murder. ''Herrin was not the kind of guy I'd have a beer with or go to a ballgame with,'' he later explained. ''He wasn't my kind of guy. But I tried to put myself in his shoes. Could he do it under an extreme emotional disturbance? . . . Can a person get in those kinds of circumstances and act impulsively? Yes. Was it possible that he didn't have a choice at the time? Yes.''

''He is sane and is guilty of a murder,'' another juror said later. ''But he is not really a criminal. . . . He was under a lot of pressure and stress at the time.''

Dr. Schwartz had become an expert prop for the jurors. But it was Litman's tightly woven tale of youthful love and passion that had become the emotional center of their deliberations. ''From Fredreck you could feel a subtle pressure, a suspicion about our capabilities as jurors,'' a juror later remembered. ''But Litman was telling us a story, and you could follow it from the beginning to the end.'' According to Judge Daronco, the law of extreme emotional disturbance required that the jurors see the situation from Herrin's point of view, and Litman had provided them with an engrossing personal vista. ''We all tried to recall the times when we had been hurt by a relationship,'' recalled one juror, ''so we could know what Herrin felt like.''

As the third day wore on, most of the jurors had come to believe that Herrin, as one put it, ''loved Bonnie so much that he flipped out.'' They gradually pulled those who had leaned toward ''guilty of murder'' into their fold. By late afternoon the tally was ten to two against murder.

"Because of Herrin's personality," remembered Patricia Policriti, "people believed that *for him* this was a stressful situation, this was the extreme emotional disturbance. Somebody else could certainly handle the fact that a girlfriend wanted to break up with him. . . . People break up and the normal thing is not to go out and commit murder. Most people could handle it better and not fall apart and not lose control, not lose contact with reality. And everybody believed that he did. He loved Bonnie so much, this was so stressful for him, this was the extreme emotional disturbance. . . . No one ever doubted that he was deeply in love. It was really so sad."

But despite the opinion of their peers, two jurors, Richard Pfeifer and Daniel Cardinale, still would not believe that Herrin could have been under such stress from the break-up of a relationship. They felt it was not a reasonable excuse for murder. For hours the two holdouts frustrated all attempts to persuade them to make the decision unanimous, as required by law. After another twelve-hour day, when the panel finally gave up for the night, some had come to believe that this would be a hung jury.

THE LONG DELIBERATION was taking its toll. In another small room down the hall the four alternate jurors, as isolated as the regular jurors but with absolutely nothing to do, felt completely imprisoned. That morning alternate juror Sebastian Sora had complained to Judge Daronco. "The alternates are really beginning to feel abused," he wrote, "and though this has no bearing on the overall situation, feelings of uselessness, ineffectiveness, and frustration are not good."

Alternate Helen Washenko had already asked to be excused. She had to go to her father's home in Connecticut, she explained to Daronco. "My father is a semi-invalid, and we're having a gathering up at his house, and I'm to do the cooking."

"What is the occasion?" asked the judge. However oppressive the alternate system, Daronco knew that should a regular juror have to leave, if there were no sufficiently screened replacement, it would probably result in an entirely new trial for Herrin.

"Well," replied Mrs. Washenko, "Father's Day, his birthday, and my sister's birthday. And he is a widower. I have to clean his house first and all that." After discussing it with Litman and Fredreck, the judge allowed Mrs. Washenko to go.

On June 18, the jurors made still another trip from their hotel, The Tarrytown Holiday Inn, to the Westchester Courthouse. On this quiet Father's Day morning, sleep had hardly relieved their fatigue. They had drained themselves of argument, and were frustrated by their inability to break their deadlock.

Soon after they arrived at the jury room on the fourteenth floor, Pfeifer and Cardinale announced that they would still vote "guilty" of murder. They seemed unreachable, as determined as they had always been.

On the streets below the courthouse hundreds of people had gathered to run in a Father's Day marathon. Everyone in the jury room crowded around the window to watch. "It was great," recalled one juror. "At that point we were just about losing our minds." Lorraine Kwasnica, Frank McDermott, Pat Policriti, Anneliese von Gruenberg, and Jennie DeMilto decided to ask Daronco for permission to attend Mass. "We were grasping at straws by this point," Policriti remembered. "A bunch of us thought we'd go to church for inspiration."

The argument continued in the jury room. Those jurors firmly committed to "not guilty" of murder took turns appealing to Pfeifer and Cardinale that Herrin deserved a break. But the dissenters would not budge. "They just couldn't believe that anyone could become so distraught over losing a girlfriend," recalled one juror. The emotional level of the argument rose as jurors reached into their own lives for examples to prove that indeed it could happen.

A little before noon, seventy-two-year-old Domenic

Sarno rose to talk. The white-haired man had become a pivotal force in the jury room, assuming exactly the role that Jack Litman had projected for him when the defense attorney first questioned him three weeks before. The septuagenarian pleaded with Pfeifer and Cardinale to use their common sense. He traced the story of Richard Herrin once more, arguing passionately that Herrin's obsessive love for Bonnie Garland was a tragedy, that it had overwhelmed him, that it could happen to almost anyone. Herrin was weak, Sarno implored, but he wasn't really a murderer.

The jurors were in tears as the old man spoke. When he finished, Pfeifer quietly nodded his assent. He had joined the others. He, too, would vote "not guilty" on the murder charge. Soon after, Cardinale also yielded. At noon, after thirty-six hours of deliberations, Pat Policriti wrote a final note to Judge Daronco. The jury had reached a verdict.

"In the end," one juror summed up, "it came down to whether you followed your heart. If you went with your instincts or your heart—that's what made people go for manslaughter instead of murder."

THE WORD that a verdict had been reached by the jury was quickly passed throughout the courthouse where journalists, lawyers, friends, family, and spectators had been waiting for four arduous days. By 12:45 P.M. they had all gathered in the courtroom. Herrin's friends and supporters filled five rows on the same left side of the room.

On the other side of the room the parents of the victim, Paul and Joan Garland, with just one other friend in attendance, seemed strangely outnumbered.

"Madam Forelady, please stand," the court clerk ordered.

Pat Policriti slowly rose from her seat at the far end of the jury box. In her hand she held the verdict sheet. She was nervous, but she appeared composed to the audience.

"Madam Forelady, and members of the jury," said

the clerk, "how do you find Richard J. Herrin under the first count, murder in the second degree? Guilty, or not guilty, or not guilty by reason of mental disease or defect?"

"Not guilty, Your Honor."

"Now, as to the lesser, included charge, manslaughter in the first degree," Daronco asked Policriti, "how do you find?"

"Guilty, Your Honor."

Seated at the defendant's table on the left side of the room, Richard Herrin was staring straight at the judge's bench. His eyes welled with tears. But he didn't cry. "It's over," he thought. "The verdict is back; now they'll send me to jail."

In one of the spectator rows, Linda Ugarte listened dejectedly as Sister Ramona broke down in tears, shattered at the thought that this Christian brother would have to go to jail at all.

Across the aisle, Joan Garland was also weeping. But for her, the few years that Richard Herrin would have to spend behind bars was inadequate, a polite slap rather than true retribution. The man who had confessed to brutally killing her daughter had just been declared innocent of murder.

THE VERDICT was in. Herrin would go to prison and everyone else would go home. Before the jurors were excused, Judge Daronco turned to the panel and commended them for their long, careful deliberations. "Today is Father's Day," he said. "You all have other things to do, I'm sure. You have families who have been waiting for your return."

"As I indicated to you at the outset of this trial," the judge reminded them, "only you, as the jury, can decide what really happened, and the verdict remains your decision alone. Justice is served by whatever verdict is justified by the evidence."

No sooner had the jury left the courtroom than argument resumed between the two attorneys. Prosecutor Fredreck rose and asked that Herrin's bail be revoked;

that he be sent to prison to await sentencing. Jack Litman objected as strenuously as he had during the trial, but this time his plea did not persuade the judge.

"At the time that the bail application was made," Daronco said firmly, "the defendant stood in the eyes of the law and before the court innocent of any crimes. He now stands before the court a convicted felon, convicted of a killing, a very serious crime. . . . Bail is hereby revoked. The defendant is remanded to the custody of the sheriffs for transportation to the County Jail."

Jack Litman was on his feet. "Can we have about a half an hour, so we can collect his belongings, sir, before you do that?"

"I oppose that, Your Honor," Fredreck exclaimed.

With the verdict in, Daronco had lost some of his amiability. "You certainly may collect his belongings, but he's now convicted," he told the defense attorney, "and in my opinion, we have given all the opportunities afforded under the law. But now it is a different situation."

"Could he have, kindly, a courtroom visit with his mother before, sir?" asked Litman. "For a minute or two?"

"Don't pull on my heartstrings," Daronco replied.

"Judge, I'm asking if he can say goodbye to his mother." Litman seemed as frustrated as Daronco. "Is that possible?"

"He can turn around and say goodbye to his mother, and she can visit him at the jail. Don't put me on trial."

"Am I, sir?"

"Yes, I think you're trying to."

The angry exchange ended the trial of Richard Herrin at one P.M. on June 18, 1978. A sheriff put handcuffs on Herrin's wrists behind his back. Turning to face the row of spectators, Herrin smiled dimly at his mother and was led out of the courtroom.

RICHARD HERRIN'S murder acquittal was a model decision under the law, for the confessed killer was found to be both sane and suffering from extreme emotional disturbance. His sentencing became as significant as his trial. Now out of the jury's hands, it was completely up to Judge Daronco, whose leeway was enormous. He could sentence Herrin to as little as one to three years or he could order the maximum term of eight-and-one-third to twenty-five years.

Immediately after the verdict was handed down by the jury, Herrin was taken to the County Jail and placed in the psychiatric unit, where he remained while the judge considered his sentence.

After ten months of freedom it was a shock for Herrin to be imprisoned again. He realized how much more vulnerable he was as a convicted felon. When word leaked out that he was housed in the air-conditioned forensic unit, there was public outrage. This time it made a difference. Angry phone calls to the warden decrying the special treatment resulted in Herrin's being moved to cell-block 1-G in the regular prison.

On July 27, 1978, a little more than a month after the verdict was handed down, Herrin was taken to the Westchester County Courthouse for his sentencing. As it had been during the trial, the courtroom was packed with spectators, friends, and relatives. Joan and Paul Garland were seated on the right side of the center aisle; Linda Ugarte and Sister Ramona took their seats on the left. Herrin sat impassively at the defense table, barely acknowledging his friends except for a wave to his mother. His mouth was dry as he awaited the chance to make his first public statement since the killing of Bonnie Garland.

Bill Fredreck first addressed the judge, asking for the maximum sentence for the crime of manslaughter. Richard Herrin then rose to speak. "Your Honor, Bonnie Garland meant everything to me," he began. He spoke so quietly that the court stenographer had to tell him to speak up. "She was my whole life. I don't think I was able to adequately describe the intensity of depth of the relationship on the witness stand and I don't think I would be able to do it here either, but she was my whole life. I was living for her."

Herrin took long pauses between sentences. He had no notes but he had given his statement considerable thought while in jail. "When I saw the priest in the County Jail the day after I was arrested," he continued, "he told me that God would forgive me and through God Bonnie would forgive me. He said the hardest part would be for me to forgive myself and he has been correct. I know that I need to be punished for what happened. I feel I have already been punished severely. The burden of guilt knowing what I did, knowing how much the Garlands have suffered, Your Honor, because of what I did, the vivid recollection of what happened, which I will always carry with me—these are some of the punishments which I have already borne.

"I am truly sorry for the suffering and grief that the Garlands had to go through," Herrin continued. "I am praying for their comfort and healing. I feel that someday I can resume my life. I don't know what direction it will be in, but I will try to work just as hard now to be twice as productive, to contribute twice as much as I normally would have. I know part of my new direction will be some kind of psychiatric help, some sort of psychotherapy which I gladly accept. I wish to dedicate my life to serving others in Bonnie's memory, to perpetuate her name, her loveliness, the riches and joys that her short but precious life brought to me and to others. Thank you, Your Honor."

After Herrin sat down, his attorney, Jack Litman, rose to address the bench. In an impassioned plea, Litman read letters from people who had met Herrin while he was out on bail and reports from psychiatrists who had seen Herrin since the verdict, all of them urging Judge Daronco to impose the minimum sentence. If granted, it could mean that Herrin would be out of jail in as little as one year.

Judge Daronco listened as the three men spoke, then addressed the court, explaining that sentencing was a balance between retribution and rehabilitation. It was a difficult balance to maintain, but Daronco quickly hinted which way he was leaning.

"Bonnie Joan Garland had a right to live out her

life," he said. "Because, as a young woman, she became infatuated with and fell in love with a young man, and later, upon reflection, wished to see other men before deciding upon a mate, can under no stretch of logic, reason, or imagination justify the brutality of the assaultive acts committed against her. To hammer her to death while she lay asleep in bed was a needless, heartless, cruel, and brutal act."

As for mercy for Herrin, Daronco seemed to have decided that the jury had already granted it in its "not guilty of murder" verdict. Daronco concluded that "the act of killing another person, even under extreme emotional disturbance is inexcusable. . . . The Court has given careful consideration to the arguments of counsel, the most awful and painful facts presented, and the conscience of the community, and has come to the inescapable conclusion that the only just and fair and equitable sentence under all the facts and circumstances would be the maximum sentence allowable under the present law of the State of New York."

Herrin was sentenced to eight and a third to twenty-five years, making him eligible for parole in 1986. Daronco adjourned the court and Herrin was led away. Sister Ramona took Linda Ugarte by the hand and escorted her out of the courtroom. The proud nun refused to answer questions from the crowd of reporters. Walking away, she said, "The family wants to have a day of reverence."

———

CHAPTER TEN

A Visit With Richard Herrin

ON JULY 28, 1978, Yale graduate Richard Herrin was put in leg shackles and handcuffs and driven a dozen miles from the Westchester County Jail to the Ossining penitentiary known as Sing Sing. There he was strip-searched and officially received into the New York State community of convicts as number 78A2518.

Three days later, he was put on a prison bus with other new arrivals, manacled to his seatmate, and driven 250 miles due north almost to the Canadian border. At the check-in at the maximum security prison in Danne-mora, Herrin told the guard that he was contemplating suicide. For the next four days he lay in a semi-conscious state on a small foam mattress in a 'strip-cell' by himself, naked, heavily sedated, "bugged out," as his prisonmates later explained.

In early September he was moved again, this time to the Great Meadow prison at Comstock, near Lake George on the Vermont border. After two weeks at Comstock, another bus took him almost two hundred miles west, past Syracuse, to the maximum security prison at Auburn, his home for the next nineteen months. During this time, his attorney was working on an appeal of his conviction and his sentence. On February 20, 1979, Herrin received a summons from the Supreme Court of Westchester County advising him that he was being sued by Paul Griffith Garland, as Administrator of the Estate of Bonnie Joan Garland, deceased, and Paul Griffith Garland and Joan B. Garland, individually, for wrongful death damages in excess of three million dollars.

In April of 1980, at his request, Herrin was transferred to the medium security prison at Napanoch, a tiny village in the foothills of the Catskill Mountains. On June 22, 1981, the Appellate Division of the State Supreme Court, in a 4–0 decision, dismissed Herrin's appeal without comment. Later that month, he consented to be interviewed by this author.

"I'm not bitter about the fact that I didn't win my appeal and I'm not bitter about the fact that the Garlands have continued their persecution, which I feel they have a right to do," Herrin said. "I wish they could see my point of view, but they don't have all the information at hand, the sum total of everything I know about myself: my past, my potential, who I am now."

What had Richard Herrin learned about himself? Who was he *now*? Convicted of a crime of bizarre brutality, what could his point of view be? Where had he placed the guilt of having killed a twenty-year-old girl?

FROM A DISTANCE, the Eastern Correctional Facility at Napanoch resembles a chateau on the Loire as it looked over the forests. Driving north on Route 209 toward the Catskills, one catches glimpses of the greenish copper cupola atop great white stone walls. The midsummer day air was heavy and the castle seemed as frozen in time as Chambord. But it was a mirage.

At the end of a long asphalt drive was a rookery of prisoners, over eight hundred of them, as alive as bars and walls would allow. I arrived at the visitors' entrance on July 8, 1981, four years and a day after Bonnie Garland's death. The entry routine would be the same for each visit. I emptied my pockets, opened my briefcase to inspection, filled out a form, signed in on inmate number 78A2518's visitor's register, and recited a blessing for not being one of the incarcerated.

Taking off my metal arched shoes, I passed through the metal detector, refilled my pockets, and regathered my belongings. A prison guard waited until I arrived at a wire-mesh and steel door, then buzzed me into a small glass-enclosed room. When the door had slammed convincingly shut, another door on the opposite wall opened.

The spacious visitors' hall in front of me was already filled with scores of people. The cement floors were polished, the high walls were clean white, the long fluorescent tubes on the ceiling bright. Hand-painted signs hung on some of the orange pillars: "Keep your feet off the furniture." And on the wall were other signs: "Please use garbage cans and ashtrays."

There was noisy chatter, children crying, even laughter. All the black, orange, and green molded-plastic chairs, arranged so that one row faced another, were occupied by kids and mothers, brothers, sisters, cousins and lovers. The lovers kissed gently, quietly gazed at one another, or talked or argued. Some simply sat close and held hands.

It was a ritual unlike any other in America. These were lock-and-key families, the only ones to conduct all of their domestic business in public during visiting hours, nine to three-thirty on weekdays and nine to three on weekends. It was the price one paid for robbery or rape or murder.

To one side of the hall were two small, semi-private rooms reserved for lawyering and interviewing. Herrin and I would meet in the "click-click room," so called for the polaroid pictures which could be taken in front of the bright blue palm tree painted on one of its walls. For a buck or two an inmate could send an inappropriate South Pacific mug shot home.

Richard Herrin moved quietly into the room. He was

wearing baggy olive-green prison-issue pants, a beige short-sleeved shirt, and yellow-striped blue tennis shoes. His handshake was soft and he seemed shorter than six feet tall. Politely he asked, "Have you been waiting long?" He explained that he had been at a meeting of *Latinos Unidos*, helping plan a special meal the group was preparing. Had his pants been khaki-colored instead of green, had he thrown a cowl-neck sweater over his shoulders and worn grubby deck shoes instead of new sneakers, Herrin could have easily passed for the ivy-leaguer he once was.

He looked healthy and relaxed; his face had slimmed and was now richly tanned. His weight was down to a trim 190 pounds, almost fifty fewer than when he was a senior in high school. He had grown a new mustache, which he kept neatly groomed. There was no more beard and his black hair was cut stylishly to a length just above his collar.

He looked as distant as one could be from the stereotype that one nineteenth-century criminologist had devised for men convicted of homicide: "murderers had bloodshot eyes, aquiline noses, curly black hair, strong jaws, big ears, thin lips, and menacing grins." If times had changed, so had Richard Herrin.

Three years of shackles and handcuffs, cell-blocks, high walls, armed guards, and a rigidly enforced discipline have had a dramatic impact on Herrin. In a way, the incarceration has freed him by teaching him the ways of assertiveness and responsibility. During seven days of conversation, thirty hours in all, Herrin spoke candidly of his life, reflected calmly on his mistakes, defended himself as "a good person" and described what he called "the forces that were in control" when he killed Bonnie Garland.

He has been undergoing a three-year prison metamorphosis, attempting to purge himself of the "forces" and to replace them with his own will power. He has tried to divorce himself from his past. Since those first days after the killing, when friends described him as a man wallowing in self-hate, he has turned 180 degrees and believes now that he has suffered enough.

"I used to let what other people thought of me dominate my life," he said. "I had to do or say certain things because that's what was expected of me. I don't think that way anymore. . . . I don't feel that I'm under any control from that upbringing any more. I don't think that I'm an immoral person or a bad person who disregards people or disrespects people, but I can make up my own mind now. . . . I'm trying to free myself from my past so that I don't use it as a crutch or a scapegoat. I'm trying to wipe the slate clean and build a whole new character. In the future only I will be responsible for my decisions. Everything will be entirely my choice."

The newly assertive Richard Herrin began to emerge shortly after the trial as he began to feel the sterner, more obvious pinch of institutional domination. He was upset when kicked out of the county jail's psychiatric unit while awaiting his sentencing. "The social worker asked me if a nine o'clock move would be all right," Herrin recalled. "And I said, 'no, that's not all right,' and proceeded to tell her that I didn't want to move out."

He now sought to rebel against the little injustices he once would have let simmer inside him. The slights were often innocuous and his reactions often childish, but he was only now learning what it was to take a risk. When a guard who was transferring Herrin to Sing Sing made a joke about the box of books that Herrin had accumulated, the young convict, like the old Richard Herrin, was angered and hurt, but silent. "He turned to the other officer and said, 'What is this? The Bonnie Garland memorial library?' I didn't say anything but I was seething inside. Not only was he trying to insult me but he was really disrespecting Bonnie. I thought of him as less than a human being for having said that and having laughed about it. It's something that's always stayed with me."

Three years later Herrin remembered. And now he wanted to voice his displeasure. "I want Officer Eberle—that's E-B-E-R-L-E—I want him to know that I've never forgotten what he said."

Under his circumstances of confinement, the remark may not have been the best example of *realpolitik*. But however infantile the "seething," or impractical the retort, Herrin had decided that it was better than risking an explosion.

PRISON LIFE has seemed to benefit Herrin. After the initial week in the Clinton strip-cell, he said his adjustment had gone well. "There were certain things I had to learn about how to conduct myself as an inmate," he explained. "I tried to keep my eyes and ears open to know how other people behaved. I tried to keep a low profile and not draw attention to myself."

As he had survived amidst the violence of the barrio, Herrin had adjusted to the ghetto of the prison. "I stay out of other people's business and I don't get involved in the kinds of things that lead to trouble." Instead he has thrown himself into penitentiary service and activity. He became the chairman of the Jaycees Grievance Committee, the secretary of Latinos Unidos, conducted a weekly math tutoring class for inmates preparing for their high school equivalency test, and led another class on Native American Culture.

One radical change occurred early in Herrin's prison tenure. When he first got to Auburn in late 1978 he had instinctively sought out the organization that had been the apparent backbone of his life up to then: the Church. He went to the prison chaplain and volunteered his services as guitarist at Sunday morning Mass. But after a few months, he suddenly had a religious experience, in reverse.

"I woke up one Sunday morning and said to myself, 'There's something wrong. I can't go to church this morning. Something's not right. I've got to ask these questions that I've been suppressing for so long.' . . . That's when I embarked on my dialogue with myself, saying, 'All right, let's get it out. What do you *really* believe? Don't worry about what people are going to think.' I never went back to the services again. I retired from religion as of then."

The "retirement" represents a major renunciation of the past. The Church, along with his mother, had been the stable rock of his survival in the barrio of East Los Angeles. When all else failed him at Yale, the More House Catholic Chapel had sustained him, spiritually and socially. When he killed Bonnie Garland, the Catholic community at Yale had rallied to him. They had prodded the court to grant him bail, raised a defense fund, put up property as bail, found him a Christian retreat in which to live, secured the services of an expert defense attorney, and displayed a bond of loving support at his trial. It was all done for a fellow "Christian brother." Now the Church had been forgotten in the creation of a new personality. As Herrin now describes himself, he is an "atheist."

"My decisions will not be made based on whether or not an action is a 'sin,' " he said. "If it's a violation of people or something that's alive, maybe I'll have to consider it. But not because it is a sin as taught by the Catholic faith. I won't be guided by that. I won't be under that influence."

There would be no more confession, no praying to God for forgiveness. For Herrin there is no more God to sin against. "There is no one up there to answer prayers. I feel that if there is something in my life that I need to change, I'll do it myself. . . . It doesn't take a belief in any God to be a good person. And I consider myself to be basically a good person: I'm fair, I treat others with respect. I wouldn't put myself any lower than anyone who has religious beliefs."

Herrin began to see a prison psychologist every week to help him with a self-housecleaning. The process would affect everything from his attitude toward his ancestral roots to his views on the justice of his imprisonment. He desperately wanted a new character, to shed the old and bloodied skin and begin anew. His single act of brutality had stained every aspect of his life that had preceded July 7, 1977. Now his reconstruction was guided by what he believed had caused him to kill Bonnie Garland.

Herrin accepts the blame for what he did, but with

reservations that prevent him from acknowledging complete responsibility. "I'm not going to blame anyone else," Herrin said. "But there were a lot of factors which prevented me from seeking the help I really needed. I don't know where to point the finger of blame about not seeking the help which would have prevented the act that resulted in Bonnie's death. . . . The full entity of Richard Herrin was not in control. I know it was me but it wasn't the part of me that controlled my life for the first twenty-three years. The control was gone. It was removed. There were different internal forces at work—not devils or spirits—*internal* forces that took over. . . . You have to understand the psychological profile. The forces that prevented me from expressing anger were important factors: the fear of abandonment, the feeling of needing to be wanted and loved and accepted. They are very important. You can't look at what happened without looking at those causes that are traced all the way back to childhood."

But aren't there many people who have those same problems and don't commit murder, I asked.

"Right. The causes that can be traced back to childhood are important. But ultimately at that moment there is no one else to blame. I committed the act. That was me who walked down the stairs. That was me who did it. But there were different forces in control at the time. Forces that had never been in control before."

And what were those forces?

"The forces that would allow me to express anger, rage, and hurt; to express things that were part of me but had been shoved deep inside," Herrin answered. "The forces that had been dominant didn't allow the expression of anger, rage, or violence. They weren't a part of me; I was a very controlled person. . . . It may be hard to believe that a person could totally deny having any problems when he was obviously beset by problems; but that's how I was. I bottled everything up. And I'm not going to be like that anymore. I've seen what it did. It killed Bonnie."

The "it" that helped acquit him in the court of psychiatry was now protecting him from overwhelming guilt. Just as the mitigating circumstance of "extreme emotional disturbance" served to reduce the charges against him from murder to manslaughter, the psychological explanations helped diminish his spiritual scars.

How can he see himself again as a "good person"?

"There's no denying that the act of killing Bonnie—of hitting Bonnie and her dying as a result—there's no doubt that I did it," Herrin explained. "But afterwards, in prison, after a lot of the hurt and the shock and the terror had gone away—not all of it, but a lot of it—after the remorse and guilt over what happened had eased so I could deal with it, after it had eased up somewhat, I took stock of what kind of person I am now. I can't change the past, but I can put it behind me and try and decide how I am going to live the rest of my life. . . . Outside of admitting that I believe in God, what more can people ask of me now? How would they want me to change my life so that I could be a better person. I don't see how they can ask anything more of me."

Herrin's metamorphosis has given him a personal reconciliation with his guilt. He would now like the public to use the same criteria when viewing his prison sentence, one which he thinks is unnecessarily long. "In my own view I think I've served enough time to compensate," he explained. "But I also understand society —represented by a small body of the judicial system of New York State—and their view that three years and two months is not enough to compensate for the taking of a life, regardless of the circumstances.

"I feel that the rehabilitation that I needed was to recognize that I had been a shallow person before, was not in touch with my feelings, was not in touch with myself on a deep level. And for me the rehabilitation that was required was to break through and take that deep look, and come to terms with who I really was. . . . I am willing to admit that I have problems and seek help for them. That's the breakthrough, the rehabilitation that I needed."

But isn't the prison sentence also meant to reflect society's need and desire to punish those who have violated its laws, regardless of rehabilitation? I asked.

"Well, again what I think is that for me three years and two months is enough. Again, taking all things into consideration."

Is that enough for the taking of a life?

"I'm not saying for any taking of any life. I'm very sorry for what happened. . . . But in my case, the self-punishment, the horror of reliving the scene over and over—no one can appreciate that but me. I lived it for the first six months after the incident. I didn't take any medication. I faced every second of terror that came to me. I faced it. So really the punishment occurred before the trial. If you want to be punished, just try to imagine yourself doing what I did and then reliving it over and over every night for six months. After a week you'll see what I mean.

"I'm not going to continue to punish myself for what happened," he explained. "I'm not going to live my life to repay all of society for Bonnie's loss. I've suffered enough because of it, and I felt the loss perhaps more than anyone else."

Herrin admits that it is perhaps an unrealistic ideal, but he doesn't believe that retribution and punishment should be a part of the judicial system. By the same token, he didn't expect to be exonerated and freed as a result of the trial. Surprisingly, he now says that he would not have been satisfied had the jury freed him by declaring him not guilty by reason of mental disease or defect. Why?

"Because I disagree with a system that doesn't provide for a guilty-but-mentally-diseased verdict. They have provisions for not guilty and I think that's the reverse of what it should be. There should be a guilty verdict and at the sentencing take into account the person's state of mind. I *totally* disagree with the choices that the jury had. I never considered myself not guilty. I knew I had committed the act. There was no denying that. And being a reasonable person I knew that some punishment was to be had. If I didn't want to face it, I had ten months to leave the country. I had access to a car every day, a credit card for getting gas. I could have driven to Canada or anywhere I wanted to. But I was preparing myself for the trial and the possibility of a prison term.''

At one point in the conversation, Herrin seemed particularly pensive. "If there were any way I could go back in time and change what happened," he said, "I would. I would, so that Bonnie could still be alive. . . . If I would have recognized that things were piling up and would have sought help, I might have had a breakdown and spent some time in a hospital getting my life together, but Bonnie would not have died. I might have suffered more, but she would still be alive today.''

But in the process of building a whole new character, Herrin has screened out everything from the past over which he believes he had no control, everything about his life that he now considers dishonest. "I had a good relationship with my mother," he explained. "But I wasn't open. I never looked too deep into myself. And these deep things were never shared with anyone, not even myself.''

It was one of the failings Paul Garland had seen in Richard Herrin. "It's a facade," Bonnie's father once commented about Herrin's personality. "From what I've been told he's been able to go through life operating behind a mask. Say nothing controversial. Say nothing at all. Never contend what others say or do. Be universally amiable. All his relationships were essentially superficial. People did not know him—they don't like to admit that now.''

Herrin now admits it, and the revelation has turned upside-down his view of the most important relationship of his life, his love affair with Bonnie. "I always lied. I always said I'm open, I have an open relationship with Bonnie and I know myself. That was all lies. I couldn't tell her my fears. I played them off as something else. . . . There were certain things that I didn't want to reveal, that were too dangerous to reveal—my real intentions or thoughts—for the sake of holding things together or keeping her love or not having her think badly of me.''

In the stifling summer heat of the "click-click" room, Herrin squeezed a red bandana in his hand and mopped his forehead. He was polite and candid but rarely animated. He spoke dispassionately about his problems, even about the killing. Only once during our many hours of conversation did he seem nervous or edgy: When we spoke about the first year with Bonnie. I asked what kind of person she was, her likes and dislikes. Herrin began to withdraw into brief "yes" and "no" responses and became testy. Finally, he motioned for the tape recorder to be turned off. "I'm going to have to take a rest for a while," he said. "I'm kind of a little bit worked up. I'm not even thinking."

He leaned back in the plastic chair and looked out the wire-mesh window into the visitors' hall. The room was crowded with weekday families. The muffled noise filtered under the door of the "click-click" room where Herrin and I sweated in hundred-degree heat. The perspiration glistened on his forehead as he brushed at it again with the bandana.

For the first time he seemed flustered. He said he had a knot in his stomach. The day before, he explained, he met with the prison psychologist for what was to be his final session. But the counselor said they would have to postpone their parting. The psychologist wasn't feeling well and wouldn't be able to write a good evaluation report under those circumstances. Herrin said he was upset by it.

We took a break, walked into the visitors' room, and to the bank of coin-operated food machines. Herrin selected a can of ice tea and we walked outside, to a large grassy yard about a fourth the size of Yale's Old Campus. After we returned to the interview room, Herrin began to relax again as he spoke about another personal discovery. At the same time that he threw over his Catholic background, he began to search out his American Indian ancestry, the Papago roots given him by his grandmother. The Mexican-American culture of his youth, he has decided, is "contaminated with a lot of different ideas." He now seeks a new race for himself as well as a new character.

"The native part of me had lain dormant, unrecognized, and unexpressed for so long," Herrin continued. "And when I started to get into it, I thought this is really something that I could adopt, believe in and work for." Herrin has begun to read voraciously the literature of the American Indian Movement. As he spoke about his plans to work with the Indians to get their lands back, build energy consortiums, and set up self-sufficient solar energy communities, Herrin showed an enthusiasm he rarely manifested during the seven days of interviews.

There was little about the past that prompted such excitement, except for a few moments when he felt he had experienced mastery over his destiny. He spoke excitedly about his geology field trips to Mexico, where he spoke the language, had relatives, and was able to act as a guide for his geology colleagues. He remembered with a smile Bladderball Days at Yale. He drew diagrams of the Saybrook strategy to steal the ball, even went into intricate detail about the ropes and pulleys strung between dorms. "It was a release, a time to have fun and quit being a grind, quit being an ivy league student. I felt relaxed and animated."

And one Bladderball Day was the best day of his life. It was November 2, 1974, when he met Bonnie Garland. As he described his dash from the roof of Saybrook to confront two Branford College saboteurs, Herrin's eyes danced and his voice rose as if he could feel the adrenalin that was pumping that morning. "The whole time I was thinking, 'That looked pretty good, didn't it?' Bonnie was up there in the tower. She watched my heroics. I did it for her. She loved me for it." Herrin smiled with the same relaxed pride he felt that morning seven years before. It was a day in his life when he felt he had everything, when there was no humiliation.

A prison guard knocked on the door. "It's three o'clock," he said. All the other visitors had left. "Time's up."

Richard Herrin rose to return to his cell-block. He has tried to turn his back on the past, but he would never forget Bonnie Garland.

CHAPTER ELEVEN

Epilogue:
Was Justice Served?

RICHARD HERRIN is in jail serving a minimum of eight and one third years and the Garlands have lost their eldest daughter. But the final argument in the Bonnie Garland killing—and in similar crimes—is not yet over.

During the trial, the question posed most frequently had been why Richard Herrin had killed Bonnie Garland. After the trial, people asked why the judicial system did what it did. Could it be, as Paul Garland bitterly concluded, "Richard Herrin successfully got away with murder"?

"People kept asking me how we could have done such a thing," remembered jury forelady Pat Policriti. "How could we let a murderer get off?" Daniel Cardinale, one of the last to cast his vote for "not guilty," felt his hands had been tied by "the injustices of the system: Herrin got off easy." For juror Milton Nelson, "it's a part of my life that I would just as soon forget." The jurors were on the defensive, trying to explain their action to a disbelieving public. "I tried to tell people that they just didn't understand," remembered one juror. "They weren't there."

After the trial, letters streamed into the District Attorney's office, Judge Daronco's chambers, and the Garland home. They had come from all over the country, more than a thousand to Daronco alone. The vast majority complained of the verdict, which they considered too lenient. "To say that I share your distress would be understating my feelings," a psychiatrist wrote to Fredreck. An outraged Manhattan secretary told the *New York Post*, "They should put him away forever. I have gotten mad enough at my boyfriend to kill him, but I haven't, and Herrin should be responsible for what he did. Killing is killing."

Joan Garland told a reporter a few days after the trial that her phone had not stopped ringing. "Three of the people who contacted me today," she said, "had a child or a close family member murdered. And in all the cases, either the murderer got away without any penalty, or received a light sentence."

The pendulum of sympathy had swung back to the victim and her survivors. The trial had changed the balance. To the outraged, the verdict struck an emotional chord that even Bonnie Garland's death had not touched. The criminal justice system seemed to be falling apart; criminals were not only having their day in court, but also having the run of the courtroom. A kind of judicial anarchy was turning the country over to butchers and brigands, some believed. There was in Bonnie's death and Richard's trial a glaring image of *déjà vu*. It seemed too easy to find killers engendering more sympathy than their victims.

In the neighboring state of Connecticut, a month after Bonnie Garland was killed, a sixteen-year-old girl lost her life to a shotgun blast. Ten days after Richard Herrin was convicted of manslaughter a young man was sentenced to prison for the girl's murder. The girl's father, Gregory Vickers, had never heard of Paul Garland; he was too busy learning his own lessons about twentieth-century empathies. But when he told his story

in a letter to the *Hartford Courant*, it seemed as if
Vickers and Garland could have been the same person.

"On August 25, 1977," Vickers wrote, "my daughter, Valerie Jean Vickers, was murdered by Gary Stankowski in Moodus while attending a small gathering of
young people. A few days later, Valerie was buried.
Near the end of the funeral service at St. Stephen's
Episcopal Church in East Haddam, the priest, Father
Earle Fox, asked that a special collection be taken. Half
of the proceeds would be given to the Vickers family to
defray funeral expenses, and the other half would go to
the Stankowski family to help pay for legal expenses. I
wanted to get up and stop the service but I kept quiet in
respect to my daughter and relatives and friends. . . .
My family and I were very upset at the time and this
matter only made it worse.

"In April of this year [1978] Gary Stankowski was
convicted of murdering my daughter in the first degree.

"On June 23, Gary Stankowski was sentenced to
prison for twelve and a half years to life. He will be
eligible for parole in eight years.

"What has happened to us in this country? Our
judicial system, with its liberal ideas, has elevated murderers, cutthroats, and thieves higher than the good
people it is supposed to protect."

The Garlands knew they were not alone in their
feeling of being victimized by a criminal, then ignored
by the judicial system. In the spring of 1981 they took
action by forming the Crime Victims Assistance Agency
to help all victims. "We've been thinking for a long time
about what to do," said Paul Garland at the time. "We
both felt if we had enough left after this holocaust, we
ought to do what we could to try to make life better for
others."

THE PUBLIC REACTS instinctively to such cases, but
often it is not aware of the revolution that has taken
place in the courtroom, one that has given extraordinary
power to psychiatrists and to concepts that seem ephe-

meral, at best, to much of the community.

Ten years before the trial of Richard Herrin, the well-known psychiatrist Karl Menninger wrote an indictment of the traditional criminal justice system in his book *The Crime of Punishment*. One of Menninger's major complaints was that the law took no account of the reasons individuals commit crimes. "The law is concerned only with the fact that its stipulations were *broken*, and the one who breached them—provided he can be convicted —must pay the penalty," Menninger wrote. "On the other hand, science, represented by psychiatry, looks at all such instances of lawbreaking as pieces in a total pattern of behavior. It asks, Why? What was behind the discovered act which brought the matter to our attention? What pain would drive a man to such a reaction, such a desperate outbreak, and such a deliberate gamble?"

If Menninger was a spokesman for a revolution already under way, by 1978 Richard Herrin was its beneficiary and the Garlands may have been one of its victims.

"If you have a $30,000 defense fund, a Yale connection, and a clergy connection," a tearful Joan Garland told reporters after the verdict, "You're entitled to one free hammer murder."

Prosecutor Fredreck was equally frustrated by the verdict. "I've prosecuted people who had less intent to kill than Richard Herrin had, and have convicted them of murder. And they are now serving life sentences. . . . In my opinion, under our law the guy committed murder. Did Herrin get a break because he is Herrin? Did he get a break because he's able to afford a high-priced attorney and a $30,000 defense fund? Is that fair? . . . I am upset by the fact that the people of the community that I represented in my opinion did not call a spade a spade because of who the defendant was."

Critics of the verdict spoke of the "miscarriage of justice" and the "special treatment" afforded Herrin. They did not realize that equal treatment was the opposite of what the new laws demanded. If Joan Garland left the courtroom thinking that "everything is absolutely upside-down," she was right. It was not because the verdict was necessarily unjust or inequitable. It was because it was a contradiction in terms to expect equity from what such modern trials have become: complex clemency hearings. In this new type of trial, the jury still decides but it mainly bases its decision on the "expert" opinion of psychiatrists.

Defenses based on "insanity" or "extreme emotional disturbance" have increased in number and have stimulated an enormous debate within both law and psychiatry, creating strongly felt opposing views on whether the new emphasis is humane or nonsensical.

"The insanity defense is a legal fiction," argues Dr. Abraham Halpern, a prosecution psychiatrist in the Herrin trial.

Halpern believes that the only reason the insanity defense was accepted in the courtroom was to give the jury a chance to avoid sending someone with whom they sympathized to the executioner's block. "With the virtual abolition of capital punishment in this country," he says, "the use of the insanity defense is an anachronism. Many judges and prosecutors see it as a mechanism to trigger indeterminate detention; many defense attorneys see it as an alternative to a mandatory lengthy period of imprisonment holding out a possibility of earlier release from confinement. In either case, misuse of psychiatry is an inevitable consequence. It does violence to the integrity of both the criminal justice system and the psychiatric profession."

Halpern has become a crusader for the abolition of the insanity defense in New York State. Gradually, he has made converts. "I find even the most ardent defender of the insanity plea will yield when one can tear away the emotional and religious fervor and explain how it is implemented," he commented.

Those who support the insanity defense believe that it is necessary to maintain the moral bedrock of criminal law. Alan Dershowitz, a Harvard law professor, argues that "We need the insanity defense to tell us why those who commit crimes should be held responsible. It's a very important moral line. To abolish it would be a disaster."

Proponents also cite the legal concept of *mens rea*— the guilty mind or purpose. Culpability, they argue, is essential to the judicial process. It was what Judge David Bazelon had in mind in 1954 when he wrote that "our collective conscience does not allow punishment when it cannot impose blame."

But critics claim that neither of these arguments addresses the question. "I think the idea of guilty intent as a way of determining blameworthiness is irrelevant," says Steven Brill, editor-in-chief of *The American Lawyer.* Like an increasing number of other legal and psychiatric professionals, Brill believes that the trial and the sentencing are two different arenas. He proposes that psychiatrists should be excluded from the courtroom in the determining of guilt or innocence and only be called on later to help in the sentencing.

"Society's determination about guilt or innocence— about holding people responsible for their acts—should deal with the bottom line: did defendant Jones commit this crime?" says Brill. "Then, if a judge, upon getting expert testimony, decides Jones . . . needs treatment rather than hard labor, he should sentence the convicted defendant accordingly."

Meanwhile, the psyche has become paramount in the modern court. Jack Litman took advantage of two powerful urges in the contemporary American ethos: the Christian one to forgive, and the Freudian one to treat emotions in the "unconscious" as the main determinants of human actions, including those of the criminal. In Richard Herrin, Litman had the perfect modern defendant. He was the child of the ghetto, a model son, member of an American minority, a good Christian with good Christian friends, a financial and emotional indigent.

Although Herrin's trial, and others of this type, seem to focus on the inner mind of the killer, some critics believe it is actually a ruse to acquit defendants for whom the jury is sympathetic. "Most of the time," comments Manhattan criminal attorney Edward Rappaport, "juries either like or dislike a defendant and reach their decision on that basis and not because of the merits of the case. If you can get them to like your guy, then insanity gives them the pretext to acquit."

The vagueness of terms used in such defenses often gives a jury little else to go on. "The effort to devise a standard for criminal nonresponsibility based on the effects of mental illness," Dr. Halpern wrote in 1980, "has continued for almost 140 years, and juggling with legally undefinable terms such as 'lack of substantial capacity,' 'appreciate criminality,' 'mental disease or defect,' and 'conform conduct' goes on apace. . . . Yet the fiction persists. . . ."

Laws vary from state to state, but in most courts a law breaker can be acquitted if it is shown that he "lacks substantial capacity to know or appreciate either the nature and consequence of such conduct or that such conduct was wrong."

"On that basis," comments Steven Brill, "a psychotic who escapes from an asylum and is found running naked in a school yard and is arrested for indecent exposure might be acquitted. Most of us might think that would be fine. But by the same reasoning Adolf Hitler, if he had been arrested for war crimes and genocide, could have and should have been acquitted if he sincerely believed what he was doing was lawful and in the world's best interest."

Ronald Crumpley, a former New York City transit policeman who killed two men and wounded six others and whose defense psychiatrist claimed that Crumpley thought "demons in the guise of homosexuals" were stalking him, was found "not guilty by reason of mental disease or defect." Brill concludes that the insanity defense is intellectually dishonest. "Almost all crimes, by definition, involve transgressions of societal norms that could be called insane. The contract murderer, one of the most unsympathetic criminal types, is obviously so devoid of conscience as to be a monster, while the wealthy white-collar thief . . . is often so self-destructive as to be certifiable."

The lack of a true standard has created the courtroom spectacle called "the battle of the experts." One psychiatrist, or two or three, will testify with a "reasonable degree of medical certainty" that a defendant did not know or appreciate what he was doing. Another psychiatrist, again perhaps two or three, will testify with the same degree of medical certainty that the defendant did know and appreciate.

The jury is left confused, and the psychiatric profession is subject to ridicule. In his closing argument to the jury of the Sirhan Sirhan trial, the prosecutor declared, "I have heard that Charles Dickens wrote in a book that 'the law is an ass.' I think the law became an ass when it let the psychiatrist get his hands on it. It would be a frightening thing for justice to decide a case of this magnitude on whether [Sirhan] saw clowns playing pattycake or kicking each other in an ink blot test."

THE LEGAL PRECEDENTS for the insanity plea date back centuries, but the key formulation stems from a case in England in 1843. Daniel M'Naghten, who had killed the private secretary to Prime Minister Robert Peel, pleaded at his murder trial that he suffered from "morbid delusions" at the time of his crime. The court declared M'Naghten not guilty by reasons of insanity, stating that he did not know right from wrong at the time.

This "right-from-wrong" criterion became the rule for judging culpability in American courts until 1954, when Judge Bazelon of the U.S. Court of Appeals applied a new test for criminal responsibility. The case was "The People vs. Durham," in which Monte Durham was appealing his conviction for housebreaking on the basis of insanity. Hoping to take advantage of what he believed were phenomenal conceptual advances in psychiatry, Bazelon amended the M'Naghten rule of right-from-wrong and extended the theorem of criminal innocence. He said that an accused man was not criminally responsible "if his unlawful act was the product of either a mental disease or a mental defect."

By 1974 Bazelon had somewhat changed his mind about the door he had helped open to psychiatry in the courtroom. "Psychiatry, I suppose, is the ultimate wizardry," he wrote. "My experience has shown that in no case is it more difficult to elicit productive and reliable expert testimony than in cases that call on the knowledge and practice of psychiatry."

Psychiatrist Seymour Halleck, author of *Psychiatry and the Dilemmas of Crime*, agrees. "When the psychiatrist confines himself to simply trying to understand and treat the disturbed individual, he uncovers dynamic patterns and uses techniques which are relatively consistent. In the courtroom, however, it often appears that psychiatrists are a group of inconsistent, disagreeable, and even ludicrous amateur philosophers."

But many people have argued that the psychiatrist is just another dupe of the law. Like the priest of another day, he is endowed with the privilege, even the duty, to explain a person's behavior. But his fundamentally deterministic approach to human behavior may be at odds with a legal system that believes that people operate with free will, that a criminal *decides* to break the law. Dr. Alan Stone, professor of law and psychiatry at Harvard Law School, asks, "How can a psychiatrist whose discipline cannot give a convincing account of free will be expected to tell the law which defendant lacks that capacity?"

THE INSANITY DEFENSE is coming under increasing attack. Some ask why only the insane should be singled out for such special benefits in the courtroom. "Why not a defense of 'dwelling in a Negro ghetto'?" asks Norval Morris, professor of law and criminology at the University of Chicago. "Such an adverse social and subcultural background is statistically more criminogenic than is psychosis."

A similar defense has been made possible by the relatively new laws involving "extreme emotional disturbance," which became the crux of Jack Litman's case. Though it can only be used to help those charged with murder, extreme emotional disturbance can be interpreted to include, in a manner of speaking, a multitude of sins.

Jack Henry Abbott, the convict-author befriended by Norman Mailer, came as close as anyone to pleading a defense of "dwelling in a ghetto." In the summer of 1981 Abbott stabbed a young man to death outside a Manhattan restaurant. At the time he had been free from prison only six weeks. Abbott immediately fled the scene and eluded police for several months before being captured in Louisiana. When brought to trial, the lifetime convict asserted that the killing was a "tragic misunderstanding" caused by the paranoia he had acquired during twenty-four years in prison.

Making reference to the book Abbott had written which earned him the acclaim of critics, *In The Belly of the Beast*, his attorney told the jury that "he went from the belly of his mother to the belly of the beast." Because Abbott had been in jail since he was twelve, the attorney argued, his perceptions had been shaped by a lifetime in prison. "His sense of everything came from inside. That's all his world has always been."

The judge instructed the jurors that they were allowed to consider Abbott's prison experience in deciding his state of mind when he killed, and after a day and a half of deliberations, they acquitted him of murder. Like Richard Herrin, Abbott was instead convicted of manslaughter because of extreme emotional disturbance. "I guess the jury felt they made scrambled eggs out of his soul in prison," his attorney concluded. "That was the operative force behind their decision."

Like the insanity law, the statute involving extreme emotional disturbance has eluded all attempts at precise definition. "You can read tons of cases that go on *ad infinitum* explaining extreme emotional disturbance," concluded Westchester County District Attorney Carl Vergari, "but my feeling is that when juries come in with that finding, it's more a gut reaction than an intellectually arrived at decision."

As in insanity, the courts and legislatures have called on the language of psychiatry to explain this new defense. The language is different but it draws on the old "heat of passion" defense, expanded and psychologically sanitized. "An action taken under the heat of passion," explained the New York State Court of Appeals in an important 1976 ruling, "means that the defendant had been provoked to the point that his 'hot blood' prevented him from reflecting upon his action . . . . Furthermore, the action had to be immediate, for if there was time for 'cooling off,' there could be no heat of passion."

The medieval metaphor was replaced by a twentieth-century psychological one. As the Court of Appeals continued, "An action influenced by an extreme emotional disturbance is not one that is necessarily so spontaneously undertaken [as heat of passion]. Rather, it may be that a significant mental trauma has affected a defendant's mind for a substantial period of time, simmering in the unknowing subconscious and then inexplicably coming to the fore."

Whatever the public at large believes, courts now recognize emotional disturbance as an excuse for murder. Is this reasonable?

"Retrospectively psychiatrists can find reasons for anything," explained Dr. Laurence Loeb, a Westchester County psychiatrist and professor of law who followed the Richard Herrin trial closely. "Given the dynamic approach, we can find motivation for any irrational act . . . . We don't know what makes one person act violently and another not. The question is what approach does society take to any kind of criminal action. Why not the sociological one instead of the psychological one? There are any number of valid explanations why a person does what he does. But what it comes down to is: Did he do it? It's been said before, but the point must be that 'by the fruits you shall know them.' The Herrin case is a perfect example of what's wrong with the extreme emotional disturbance statute.''

As Dr. Loeb points out, placing psychiatric analysis on top of legal issues inevitably produces a kind of circular reasoning that befuddles most juries. How does one know that Richard Herrin was extremely emotionally disturbed? Jack Litman asked his psychiatrists. We know, they responded, because of the vehemence of the attack. The assumption that Herrin was not commiting ''murder'' was both the end product and the basis of Litman's psychiatric defense.

District Attorney Vergari makes the chilling point that *all* killers may be disturbed. Is there, therefore, no crime of murder? ''You might say that anybody who commits a murder has to be emotionally disturbed because it's a most unnatural thing to do, is it not?'' reasons Vergari. ''To take the life of a fellow human being? You can say that anyone who kills is emotionally disturbed by the very fact of killing.''

The courts may present a confident front, but many have come to doubt the expert opinion that sustains the emotional defense. ''What is at issue is the continuing unwillingness on the part of our courts to recognize that an opinion does not become a fact merely because it is held by a doctor,'' argues Daniel Robinson, a professor of psychology at Georgetown University. He believes ''that there can be no expert testimony where there is no settled body of knowledge.''

The use of psychiatry in the courtroom awaits radical reform. In the meantime, apparently sane killers such as Richard Herrin are being acquitted of murder.

Has justice really been served?